D0766517

The Goals of Social Policy

The Goals of Social Policy

Edited by

MARTIN BULMER

JANE LEWIS

DAVID PIACHAUD

LONDON
UNWIN HYMAN
BOSTON   SYDNEY   WELLINGTON

Published by the Academic Division of
Unwin Hyman Ltd
15/17 Broadwick Street, London W1V 1FP, UK

Unwin Hyman Inc.,
8 Winchester Place, Winchester, Mass. 01890, USA

Allen & Unwin (Australia) Ltd,
8 Napier Street, North Sydney, NSW 2060, Australia

Allen & Unwin (New Zealand) Ltd in association with the
Port Nicholson Press Ltd,
Compusales Building, 75 Ghuznee Street, Wellington, New Zealand

First published in 1989

British Library Cataloguing in Publication Data

The Goals of social policy.
1. Great Britain. Social policies
I. Bulmer, Martin II. Lewis, Jane, *1950–*
III. Piachaud, David
361.6′1′0941
ISBN 0–04–445131–8
ISBN 0–04–445132–6 pbk

Library of Congress Cataloguing-in-Publication Data

The Goals of social policy / edited by Martin Bulmer, Jane Lewis, and David Piachaud.
p. cm.
Includes bibliographies and index.
ISBN 0–04–445131–8
ISBN 0–04–445132–6 (pbk).
1. Social policy. I. Bulmer, Martin, II. Lewis, Jane (Jane E.)
III. Piachaud, David.
HN17.5.G63 1989   361.6′1–dc19   88–35552   CIP

Typeset in 10 on 12 point Bembo by
Computape (Pickering) Ltd, North Yorkshire
and printed in Great Britain by
Billing and Sons, London and Worcester

Contents

Tables and Figures

Contributors

Brian Abel-Smith *London School of Economics and Political Science*
Martin Bulmer *London School of Economics and Political Science*
David Donnison *University of Glasgow*
David Downes *London School of Economics and Political Science*
Zuszsa Ferge *Hungarian Academy of Sciences, Budapest*
Janet Finch *University of Lancaster*
Howard Glennerster *London School of Economics and Political Science*
A. H. Halsey *Nuffield College, Oxford*
José Harris *St Catherine's College, Oxford*
Walter Korpi *Swedish Institute for Social Research, University of Stockholm*
Hilary Land *Royal Holloway and Bedford New College, University of London*
Jane Lewis *London School of Economics and Political Science*
S. M. Miller *Boston University*
Ramesh Mishra *Atkinson College, York University*
Caroline Moser *London School of Economics and Political Science*
David Piachaud *London School of Economics and Political Science*
Robert Pinker *London School of Economics and Political Science*
Frances Stewart *Queen Elizabeth House, University of Oxford*
Kari Wærness *University of Bergen*
Albert Weale *University of East Anglia*

Preface

The Department of Social Science at the London School of Economics (LSE) was established in December 1912. To mark its seventy-fifth anniversary, a two-day conference was held on 17–18 December 1987 to examine the past and future of the subject of social policy. Some 140 scholars, practitioners and students from Britain and around the world participated in the Conference; this book is based upon the contributions to the Conference and discussion in its sessions.

The title 'The Goals of Social Policy' refers to the academic study of social policy and to how it is conceived. The late 1980s is an exciting time to be addressing this set of questions, since more radical changes have been made in social policy in Britain and the United States in the last decade than in the preceding quarter of a century. The scope and nature of government intervention has been changing, particularly in the direction of cutting back on expenditure and services. The voluntary and not-for-profit sectors have expanded. The private market is playing an increasing role, particularly in relation to health, pensions and the care of the elderly. There is increasing debate about the role of the family and varieties of informal care. What are the foundations on which one can build the study of such phenomena, their organization and the principles which guide provision?

The term 'social policy' is a comparatively recent one in British academic life, and is still not reflected in the title of the LSE Department. The department originally began in 1912 with the dual purpose of carrying out investigations of social conditions and training social workers. Both were integrally connected to the social and political theory of the day, a connection which has continued. For the first thirty years of the department's existence the teaching of social work predominated. Then under the leadership first for five years after the end of the Second World War of T. H. Marshall, and subsequently for nearly a quarter of a century of Richard Titmuss, teaching and research in social policy and administration became its central concern, while the training of social workers continued. It is still difficult to gain the necessary distance to assess fully the contributions of Marshall and Titmuss, particularly since the latter was a dominant figure whose influence may perhaps be compared to that of Keynes in economics or Popper in social philosophy.

Whether or not the LSE department completely dominated the field, it was one of the most important influences in establishing social policy and administration as a field of study in British universities and polytechnics, particularly in the quarter of a century between 1945 and 1970. A major aim of the conference was to reach a fuller understanding of the intellectual history of the subject in its LSE setting, and to dispel some of the myths which exist about the department. One is that it was set up, and continues primarily, to train social workers. Historically this is effectively disposed of in José Harris's chapter, but the misapprehension persists. Some years ago a distinguished LSE professor from another field referred to the department in an article in the _Times Higher Education Supplement_ as the Distressed Affluent Folks Aid Society, and clearly thought that it was a department that only taught social workers. In fact, as Ramesh Mishra shows, since 1945 social policy and administration have formed its intellectual core, while Robert Pinker provides a reminder that social work teachers and students, still a significant group in the department, have interests which are now closely integrated into the study of social policy while remaining in certain respects distinct.

The closeness of social policy and administration to social and political theories of welfare has given rise to another misapprehension, the prevalence of a belief that the department stood for particular forms of collectivist welfare provision, embodied in nicknames like the 'Department of Applied Virtue'. A variant of this view holds that the study of social policy is a normatively loaded pursuit in which prescription takes precedence over evidence and analysis. Not only is this a caricature of the range of views and styles of work represented in the department, as Howard Glennerster shows, but it is refuted by the range of courses presently offered, which include social policy and planning in developing countries, health planning and financing, the management of voluntary organizations and housing administration, in addition to core courses in UK social policy.

If one aim of the conference was to look backwards, reflect, and correct certain misconceptions, the second was to look forward critically and explore future possibilities for the study of social policy. With what sorts of issues would the study of social policy be likely to be concerned in the 1990s and into the early years of the twenty-first century? By choosing the themes of social policy and the family, social policy and the community and social policy and the economy it was hoped to provide a fresh perspective and to reflect some of the radical changes which have taken place in the study of the subject in the last decade. There is thus more focus upon developments outside Britain, on welfare detached from the concept of the welfare state, and on the growing interdisciplinary character of the subject. The re-emergence of uncertainty as a crucial variable in the lives of late twentieth-century individuals finds reflection here too, a source at the same time of stimulation and of strain. *The Goals of Social Policy* seeks to raise such questions as much as to provide definitive answers to them, but asked they must be if the study of social policy is to develop and keep abreast of changes in society and social provision.

The book consists of seven papers which were pre-circulated, delivered and discussed at the conference, the comments of nine discussants on the substantive papers about family, community and economy in social policy, and two concluding overviews of the conference, one from within and one from outside the department. Some discussants addressed themselves primarily to the paper as delivered, others ranged more widely in their comments. Notes and references follow each chapter, rather than being combined at the end of the book. The editors have written a general introduction to the collection as a whole, and provide commentary on family, community and economy in social policy which takes account of the tenor of discussion in the conference sessions.

It remains to thank those who made possible the conference on which this book is based. Our principal thanks go to the dual financial sponsors of the event, the Joseph Rowntree Memorial Trust and its director, Robin Guthrie, and the LSE Suntory–Toyota Centre for Economics and Related Disciplines (ST–ICERD) and its chairman Tony Atkinson, which jointly provided support to bring together the speakers and discussants who appear as authors of this book. Howard Glennerster, Convenor of the Department of Social Science and Administration, supported the original idea of the conference and provided helpful advice at various stages in its planning, as well as himself contributing. To the paper-givers and discussants we are greatly indebted for providing the substance of this consideration of the past and future of social policy. And to those who participated in the conference we hope that this volume will both recall the event and provide the impetus to reflect further about the directions which the study of social policy may take in the future.

London School of Economics, August 1988   *Martin Bulmer*
                                                                         Jane Lewis
                                                               David Piachaud

PART I

Introduction

1 Social policy: subject or object?

MARTIN BULMER, JANE LEWIS and
DAVID PIACHAUD

The study of social policy in separate academic departments of universities in Western Europe and North America is largely a phenomenon of the second half of the twentieth century. At the London School of Economics and Political Science the Department of Social Science and Administration is, however, considerably older, dating back to 1912. When the Department marked its fiftieth anniversary in 1962, the speeches (one by Earl Attlee) celebrated in unquestioning fashion the traditions of the department, the range and number of new courses and the expansion in the numbers of staff.[1] On the occasion of the Department's seventy-fifth anniversary, we chose to undertake a more searching examination of the nature and distinguishing characteristics of our academic clothes. In this endeavour we looked both at the past – reflected in the papers on social policy in retrospect and prospect – and towards the future.

What direction has the study of social policy taken in the past, and where will it go in the future? From both the formal presentations and the discussion at the conference two clear themes emerge. The first is the need to remap the content of the subject, a project which the foci of the papers in the latter part of the book indicate is well under way. The second is to consider how the boundaries of social policy as a field of inquiry are drawn.

The first group of papers on social policy in retrospect and prospect raises broad questions about the origins of this field of academic study and practice. Three are historical. José Harris examines the historical circumstances and setting in Britain in 1912 when the Department was first established. Ramesh Mishra provides an assessment of the post-war period of influence under Richard Titmuss, while Robert Pinker reflects on the relationship between social policy and social work through the twentieth century. The last paper in this section, by Howard Glennerster, bridging past and future, considers the prospects for social policy in the last decade of the twentieth century.

In sections three to five of the book certain substantive themes central to the subject of social policy in the coming years are identified. These are social policy and the family, social policy and the community and social policy and the economy.

The papers on social policy and the family are focused on the theme of dependency, and all take gender as the primary variable for analysis. Given the government's commitment to creating greater independence of the state, Hilary Land examines the meaning of the policies designed to achieve this for women who might be caring for children or elderly or disabled dependants, or who might themselves be part of the growing population of elderly and struggling to maintain an independent existence. She signals the narrowness of the current definitions of independence and the danger that many current policies, for example in public transportation, may have the perverse effect of increasing dependency. Janet Finch examines how far government can expect, now and in the 1990s, successfully to manipulate either social and economic relationships or values in the family. Kari Wærness pursues the theme of tangled dependent and independent statuses in the family in the Scandanavian context, while Caroline Moser draws attention to the very different configuration of those statuses in the developing world, where the role of state welfare is small and a correspondingly greater burden of provision is thrown on the informal sector.

The papers on social policy and the community begin with David Donnison's chapter on the community-based approach to social policy. He examines means of empowering local communities and community action by the deprived and dispossessed sections of British society, disproportionately located in inner cities. He suggests the need to develop new forms of collective consumption, new patterns of authority and new patterns of relationship between citizen and state. S. M. Miller takes up this theme in discussing contemporary community development, and links it to the debate about the 'underclass'. A. H. Halsey, too, points to the growing social polarization of British society, and the threat which this poses to social policies based on notions of equity and universal welfare. David Downes reviews evidence of the location and causation of crime in the community, and offers some pertinent comments on the concept of the 'underclass'.

The section on social policy and the economy begins with a review of how studies of social policy and of economics have been related, or unrelated, in the past and how this has changed. Zsuzsa Ferge from Budapest examines the role of social policy at different stages of economic development in both capitalist and socialist economies; she draws on the experience of Hungary to indicate areas of conflict and harmony between economic and social policies. Frances Stewart examines the experience of developing countries with particular regard to policies affecting the primary and secondary distribution of income. Walter Korpi examines how provision for unemployed people has changed over time in different countries and tackles the broader question of how welfare provision affects efficiency.

The three sections on social policy and the family, the community and the economy discuss aspects of social policy which have importance for future developments. The book ends with an internal and an external review of some of the important themes.

Social policy in Britain

The Department of Social Science and Administration at the London School of Economics is closely identified with the study of social policy in Britain and internationally. First established in 1912, since 1945 it has been in the forefront of the academic development of the subject. Under T.H. Marshall's guidance from 1944 to 1950 and led by Richard Titmuss from 1950 until his death in 1973, an original approach to the study of social policy and social welfare was carved out, which was pioneered in Britain and which is still internationally distinctive.[2] There are few departments of social policy, for example, at American universities and only recently has the subject developed a separate identity at German universities. Scholars studying social policy in these countries are typically found in other departments such as sociology or in professional schools in fields such as public health, social work and education. On the continent, this may not be unconnected with the fact that the French and German languages make no clear distinction between the words 'policy' and 'politics' – both are rendered by one word, 'politique' in French and 'politik' in German.[3]

Britain has been different. Drawing upon the constituent social science disciplines of economics, politics, sociology and psychology, as well as upon social history, philosophy and statistics, the study of social policy in Britain has developed in separate departments with a distinctive focus. Though this is not easy to define exactly, the analysis of the principles and practice of welfare provision in the fields of health, housing, income maintenance and education has been central. Other topics such as the family, criminology and law, race relations, unemployment, and development in the Third World have also been encompassed. The field's distinctiveness, exemplified par excellence in the work of Richard Titmuss, lies in its blending of historical and institutional analysis with philosophical reflection and a sharp policy focus.

The changing academic field of social policy

The study of social policy has evolved hand in hand with state social provision. There has been a particularly close link to the postwar 'welfare state'. In the mid-1970s, however, the word 'crisis' began to enter the titles of books on social policy and about welfare states. Much energy since has been devoted to analysing the nature of the crisis, particularly the relationship between economic performance and public expenditure, and issues about the legitimacy of state involvement in particular areas of individual and social life became much more salient. Sharp questions were raised from various standpoints about the relevance of the paradigmatic basis of the subject as it had been developed by Titmuss, grounded in a commitment to redistribute the surplus and closely linked to the idea of a welfare state. (One critic has characterized the approach as 'a mixture of down-to-earth investigative pragmatism and evangelical moral uplift'.[4]) Students of the subject were plunged into uncertainty about the basis of the field of study, and its claims to distinctiveness were subjected to close scrutiny.

The terminology has been at issue – are '*social* state' or '*welfare society*', for example, more appropriate terms to characterize contemporary social policy provision? One major focus of recent academic debate has been on whether it is still possible to speak of a 'welfare state' at all, or whether it is more fruitful to examine social policy issues from the point of view of the mixed economy of welfare. Several recent volumes have usefully addressed these issues.[5] While a crisis mentality continues to infect debate over social policy and the welfare state, it has become apparent that prescriptions for, and fears of the termination of, the welfare state have not been realized. The literature today talks more frequently of 'restructuring'. There remains substantial disagreement as to how fundamental this has been and will prove to be.

This changed climate within which social policy issues are publicly discussed poses a considerable challenge to the field of study. The political sea-change in Britain and the United States in the last ten years – particularly the injection of market forces and the reassertion of individualistic values in relation to welfare provision – calls for a rethink about the future direction of social policy analysis. This is one purpose of the present volume.

The state of the subject of social policy within the academic community is not easy to summarize. Certainly the optimistic Whiggish history favoured by so many social administrators, charting the growth of government toward the nirvana of post–war Beveridgean/Keynesian consensus, contributed to the ill-preparedness of many for the recent transformation in the focus of social policy debates.[6] Paradoxically, social policy has become much more central to political debate in the last decade than it was in the previous quarter of a century, but the premises from which right-wing governments started were so different from those of the Titmussian orthodoxy that it has taken time to comprehend the change.

Nevertheless the world – and the subject – had been changing quite independently of these political changes. Intellectually the subject had never been as unified as its critics had maintained. Even in the heyday of welfare-statism, the Institute of Economic Affairs provided a dissenting form of analysis to which most students of the subject were exposed. The end of post–war expansionism and the economic crisis in the 1970s focused much more attention to the hard choices between competing ends which have to be made in social policy. Increasing use was made of the vocabulary of efficiency and cost-effectiveness, and the skills of economists in particular were apparent in programme-budgeting and studies of health care delivery and the organization of social services.[7]

This broadening of approach was a sign that the subject was becoming more interdisciplinary, with important contributions also from political scientists, social historians and philosophers, contributions often made, moreover, from a firm base in their own disciplines with which they primarily identified. The distinction between the *topic* of social policy, common to all working in the area, and the *discipline* within which an individual worked, which varied, became an accepted one.[8] Friendly argument occurred about which disciplines had most to contribute, but there has been an observable tendency in the last decade and half for the close historical association between social policy and sociology to be succeeded by much more varied interdisciplinary relationships. Since 1950 the LSE department had in any case had members drawn from a variety of constituent disciplines. Within social policy departments, much more lively debate occurred about different theoretical approaches to the subject, aside from the Titmussian orthodoxy, producing a much greater diversity and sharper intellectual engagement of opposing positions.[9]

The interdisciplinary and theoretical flowering of the field, however, led to corresponding perplexity on the part of students trying to identify the common features of social policy as an academic pursuit. To be sure, there was a fairly readily identifiable subject-matter in terms of the core areas of social provision. Beyond that, however, it was increasingly difficult to provide a satisfactory unified definition of what academic social policy was concerned with. It was easier to say what it was not.

It was not merely the welfare state, since that term conventionally meant the key social services and did not embrace the social policy aspects of other areas of government and social activity. It was not simply social administration or the management of social services, since that would be to ignore what they do, why they do it and the consequences – rather like an economist studying automatic cash dispensers. It was not merely Titmuss's social division of welfare, for challenging and important as that was as a classification – even if extended to include family and community – it was still only a classification. It was not political economy, since that role (à la Gough) was to interpret welfare's role in unfolding capitalism but essentially as a retrospective, analytic, task. It was not solely about public goods and externalities – try as they may, most people involved with social policy do not get very interested in, for example, the environment. It was not about all public policy, since social policy is only peripherally concerned with public policy on defence or agriculture, for example, and in some areas social policy is concerned with non-public matters such as community care. It was not solely about the treatment of 'dependent' groups, since poverty is known to be relative and the problems of the weak are frequently caused by the strong. It was not about a discipline in the conventional sense with its own set of academic tools, since the crew of the ship 'social policy' is a motley one from diverse backgrounds. It was not about a field, since a field needs hedges, and these have been rooted up. It was not merely description and analysis, since 'policy' is still there in 'social policy' and calls for more than social analysis.

In rejecting each of these conceptions as inadequate – although each overlap with and form part of the subject of social policy – the question remains: what precisely *is* social policy? This is a difficult matter. The issue is not so much one of interdisciplinary territoriality as coming to agreement regarding the establishment of some coherence on the way in which boundaries are expanded or contracted, a project that must involve greater attention to developing a range of interdisciplinary conceptual tools. Taking 'the world' as our province is perfectly legitimate – early twentieth-century students of the subject had no qualms about doing this – as long as we are not merely responding to outside events, but rather have a clearly developed rationale for approaching particular problems.

The past – narrowing the universe of social policy

The papers in the second section of this book examine the development of the subject. The early history of the study of social policy is usually linked to the LSE and often described as being synonymous with the pragmatic study of British social administration inspired by a desire for moral improvement and greater national efficency. This is misleading. The intellectual heritage of the subject is rich and complex; idealism and even religious conviction (in the shape of the Bosanquets, pillars of the Charity Organisation Society, and Urwick, the LSE Department's first head from 1912 to 1921) played a greater part in its early twentieth-century history than either utilitarianism or positivism.

At two crucial points in its history, it is possible to see the LSE department reflecting broader intellectual shifts in the nature of social science education as well as influencing contemporary diagnosis of social problems and their solution. The Bosanquets and the Webbs, leaders of the Fabian Society and founders of the LSE, were poles apart in terms of their political philosophies and yet, as José Harris (Chapter 2) shows, it was a merger of the Charity Organisation Society's School of Sociology with LSE that was central to the formation of the Department in 1912. Such an apparently paradoxical development should alert us to the dangers inherent in recourse to simple and seemingly irreconcilable dichotomies such as 'individualism' and 'collectivism'. When Bernard Bosanquet spoke to the Fabian Society in 1890, he cheerfully declared that while he would be taking issue with their approach on that occasion, he took pleasure in speaking to the outside world in the language of the Fabian Essays. In other words, while their visions of the society of the future were radically different, especially in respect of the eventual role of a centralized state bureaucracy, the Bosanquets and the Webbs shared a commitment to social investigation and to social action.[10] In particular, they were committed to the training of social workers. To the Bosanquets, social workers were but a means to a greater end whereby, raised to independence and self-sufficiency, each individual would be able to maintain him or herself without state support. To the Webbs the training of professionals was an important step toward a more efficient state apparatus.

The presence of the other element in the department at its outset, the commitment to social investigation represented by the Ratan Tata involvement and R. H. Tawney's presence, was congruent with these interests – Beatrice Webb in her youth had after all been an assistant to Charles Booth – but it went beyond them. Social policy was seen to be grounded in a firm empirical base. Knowledge of social conditions was essential for the framing of effective policies to deal with those conditions. If the initial place for social investigation was not sustained after a few years due to withdrawal of Tata support, it nevertheless planted the seed which florished much more significantly after 1945.

A number of issues of continuing importance to the subject are raised by a close examination of the specific conjunction giving rise to the appearance of social policy within the university. One is the relationship between social fact and social theory, another the relationship between social intervention (in the form of social work) and social theory. One of the fundamental sources of difference between the Bosanquets and Urwick on one side and the Webbs on the other lay in the belief of the former that theory should precede the collection of the 'facts' and the equally firm conviction of the latter that only empirical investigation would reveal first patterns and then theoretical frameworks. However, all were committed to seeing social policy and administration as part of a much broader framework of political and social ideas. People like the Bosanquets had a powerful command of political and economic theory and a clear view of the proper relationship between the individual, the family and the state. Indeed, it is José Harris's considered opinion that the Edwardian years represent the only period when discussion of social policy was central to intellectual life.

In comparison, to turn to the later period covered by Ramesh Mishra in Chapter 3 in this volume, the post–war boundaries of social policy appear much more tightly drawn, irrespective of the originality of the mapping of the content of the subject during the 1950s and 1960s. Mishra would go further and charge post–war social policy and admistration with failure to develop strong theoretical frameworks and a tendency to immerse itself instead in fact-gathering.

One of the corollaries of this narrowing process, irrespective of how it is perceived, was that the place of social work within the academic universe of social science and administration was no longer clear. Social work was no longer integrated in a broad-based social and political theory that informed the debates about Edwardian social issues. In Chapter 4 Robert Pinker charts the separation of the social work and social policy strands, emphasizing the part played by a psychoanalytic frame of reference in distancing the two fields. But it may be argued that the revitalized and yet slimmed down social policy and administration of the Titmuss years also regarded social work as a separate endeavour. (This is certainly suggested by the course of the crisis over social work teaching at the School in the 1950s.[11]) One of the ironies for social work would seem to be that, in its current more isolated and residual position, it may indeed be inappropriate, as Pinker argues, for social workers to act as agents of social change, yet within their grander conception of the universe of social policy this is precisely the role that the Bosanquets and the Webbs intended for them.

The future: where and how to draw boundaries

All this raises the issue as to how departments of social policy and administration, once established, derived their focus of study. Mishra contends that given the objective of bringing about change within a broadly consensual framework, an obsessive concern with fact-gathering was inevitable; the underpinning framework of ideas was assumed to be shared. Many would dispute this construction and its suggestion that there is continuity between the 'facts before theory' orientation of the Webbs and the Titmussian approach to the subject; as José Harris's chapter shows, world views other than the Webbs were stronger when it came to establishing social administration as an academic subject.

This argument over interpretation only begs the further question of how Titmuss derived his extraordinarily influential approach to the subject and in particular his mapping of the 'social division of welfare' to comprise three main categories: occupational, fiscal and state welfare. On this, Mishra's contention that Titmussian social administration set out to be critical but within an already established consensual framework is important. During the 1950s and 1960s social administration succeeded in seizing the initiative. During a period favourable to the promotion of state collectivism, it helped to set the policy-making agenda, which was conceived within the Beveridgean and Keynesian commitment to the institutions of the welfare state.[12] In his own commitment to welfare, Titmuss contrived to look beyond the state, but the desirability of a welfare state was nevertheless a crucial assumption. To this extent, Titmussian social administration depended too strongly on a particular social, political and economic conjuncture to become a free-standing subject.

The field has also had to contend with related handicaps. The academic study of the development of social policy has been particularly prone to Whiggishness, the assumption that the history of the subject shows a long-term general unilinear trend from less adequate to more adequate and superior provision, so that the present is both better than the past and the transition from one to the other was in some sense inevitable. In this view the history of social policy has been one of long-term improvement. In the study of contemporary policy, this has been associated with what has been called the 'social conscience' thesis, that social policy manifests, through the state, the love that people have for each other.[13] It is benevolent, and social policy is provided for the benefit of the recipients and for the community as a whole. Changes in social policy result from a widening and deepening sense of social obligation and increasing knowledge of need. As one sympathetic outsider, economist A. J. Culyer, has put it:

> The articulation of an ideological commitment to welfare, to altruism, to the idea of service to the community, to universality, to the importance of understanding 'what it is like' to be poor, discriminated against, and so on, helped to provide an intellectual focus that was otherwise lacking.[14]

It is certainly arguable that without its distinctive moral commitment, social policy would never have developed as a distinct subject in British universities as it did.

Though at times critical of 'the placid conventional romance of the rise of the welfare state', Titmuss implicitly endorsed particular value assumptions in his work, most obviously in *The Gift Relationship*.[15] Social policy retains a moral aura in part due to his influence. Such a stance still finds favour. David Donnison, for example, has recently argued for a proper place for moral prescriptions in the academic study of social science. The cleansing of academic disciplines of passion and values, he argues, has led to the subdivision of fields of study into ever-narrower specialisms. This makes difficult the prescription of action in the real world, since effective action requires a multidisciplinary approach. By bringing back together analytical, empirical and moral discourses, it will be possible to formulate prescriptions for action which can be more effectively debated, and bring moral theory back into the academy.[16]

On the other hand, this moral stance has been increasingly criticized in the last two decades. The place of values in academic social policy remains problematical because values alone are an inadequate basis for scholarly analysis. Robert Pinker argued in the early 1970s that

> in [British] social policy and administration we begin with fact-finding and end in moral rhetoric, still lacking those explanatory theories which might show the process as a whole and reveal the relations of the separate problems to one another.[17]

The postulation of 'needs' which should be met through state welfare provision has come under attack, particularly from economists, who argue that the concept of 'demand' is a more reliable guide to the allocation of scarce resources between competing ends. Della Nevitt incisively attacked what she called 'needology', purporting to discover new requirements on the part of any and every disadvantaged group, without adequate criteria for comparing different groups or justifying the allocation of resources to those particular ends.[18] More generally it may be that the strength of the 'social conscience' approach to the study of social policy, with its emphasis on unlinear improvement in Britain, inhibited the development of *comparative* social policy research and explains the ethnocentrism which was in the past characteristic of the field.

Just as policy has often been considerably influenced by learning from experience overseas,[19] academic social policy is increasingly finding through comparative research some defence against the tendency to prescription (or at least the making of prescriptive assumptions) which has been so strong for so long.[20] Moreover, as Albert Weale points out in the final chapter of this book, moral theory is undergoing a renaissance in political philosophy, a development with implications for the study of social policy. It may be also that the empirical study of social problems is now less value-laden than formerly. A former Director of the LSE, Ralf Dahrendorf, for example, has observed that '(m)y own impression is that there's been quite a significant change in the past few years from prescriptive social policy research, which either by obvious implication or by deliberate intent was supposed to resolve problems, to the analysis of the effect of social policy, and I see much more of that than one did in the past'.[21]

These are signs, among others, that the field is changing. No one has ever questioned the originality of Titmuss's mapping of the field in the post–war decades, and yet as discussion at the conference showed, there is now both a desire to re-map its territory, emphasizing different categories for analysis and a concern about whether or where to hedge the field. Inevitably new categories and re-mapping pushes back particular boundaries. In Titmuss's 'social division of welfare', informal care – both voluntary and family – was conspicuous by its absence. As the disciplinary backgrounds of the contributors to the panel on the family and social policy showed, recent exploration in this area has drawn heavily on sociological concepts and methods. Similarly, Titmuss's categorization did not leave adequate room for consideration of local communities as producers, as well as administrators and consumers, of welfare. It may be suggested that these two categories – family and community – are not mutually exclusive, for family care may be considered under the umbrella of the community. This does not impede their usefulness. Titmuss's original classification was important because of the questions it prompted about the distribution of welfare between social classes. Inserting the variables of gender, race and age, lengthening the list of welfare providers to include the family and the voluntary sector as well as employers and the state, and putting more emphasis on the means of producing, as well as of distributing and delivering, welfare, prompt similar and wide-ranging questions.

As well as the increasingly interdisciplinary character of social policy, the field is becoming an increasingly specialized one. More and more, advanced expertise is concentrated in specialist departments, agencies and institutes. Some are academic research centres separate from teaching departments, like those in social policy at the University of York, and in personal social services research at the University of Kent. Some are outside the academic world altogether, like the Policy Studies Institute and the Family Policy Studies Centre. Some research is concentrated within operating agencies, like research carried out within the Home Office and the Equal Opportunities Commission.

Two results of such concentration are apparent. One is the tendency for expertise to be channelled into areas of substantive specialism, whether this is income maintenance, or health policy, or criminology, or whatever. Expertise is expertise in that area rather than in the field of social policy as a whole. The other is the tendency for the approach to become a more specialized one, easily accessible only to those familiar with the assumptions and discourse of a particular discipline. Such contributions are made to social policy analysis from a variety of disciplines, either through individual research by, for example, economic historians or lawyers, or in university research centres – such as that in health economics at York, for example. It may be argued that this is in fact more fruitful than the interdisciplinary blunderbuss (tackling a topic from the standpoint of several disciplines simultaneously), but the effect is the same – a considerable narrowing of focus. It is correspondingly more difficult to achieve a broad overview of social policy as a whole.

The implications of interdisciplinarity in particular for analysis and explanation have not fully been faced. Those who urge greater infusions of theory into social policy often have in mind either a particular discipline (such as sociology) or a particular body of theory (such as a version of neo-marxism) as providing the magic elixir. The questions of what different disciplines are to contribute, and how their various contributions are to be reconciled analytically, are sidestepped or ignored.

In practice one of three different outcomes is likely. According to the first, what the different disciplines have in common are the rigour of their methods. This is the lowest common denominator which they all share, so effective collaboration is ensured by using these rigorous methods to attack a policy problem. There are distinguished examples of such an approach succeeding – for example, in the statistical work underpinning the Robbins Report on Higher Education in 1963, directed by Claus Moser[22] – but it tends towards the kind of atheoretical empiricism for which social administration has traditionally been criticized.[23]

A second, more common, approach is what may be termed disciplinary imperialism, whereby the theoretical framework of the dominant discipline is used to tackle the problem, and other factors are incorporated in that framework. An example would be the use of cost-benefit analysis to assess alternative courses of action, in which non-economic factors (social costs and benefits) are given a notional monetary value in order to incorporate them in the analysis. In the sociology of housing, Rex and Moore's theory of housing classes is an instance of one discipline putting forward a theory to explain much of the observed variation between the situation of different sorts of tenants.[24] The limitations of such imperialism are obvious, and reinforce the difference between interdisciplinary and multidisciplinary work.

Truly multidisciplinary work is the third possibility, when two or more disciplines come together in genuine exchange and collaboration and together provide a more convincing analysis of the problem than any one discipline would provide on its own. Though such a mix of disciplines is not easy to achieve, there are a number of examples of success. In the field of health, exchanges between proponents of 'need' and 'demand' have advanced the study of the delivery of health care and led to better understanding of the measurement of states of health. In the study of distributive justice, political philosophers and economists have made important contributions to a common enterprise, drawing on a shared ancestry in utilitarianism. Questions such as the social desirability of equality have formed part of this, an issue on which economists such as Amartya Sen have made notable contributions to social policy.

Interdisciplinary advances can also be made by new analyses of old problems from a different disciplinary perspective. Political science provides three instances. Douglas Ashford's comparative historical study of the emergence of welfare states sets developments in Britain alongside those in France, Germany, Sweden and the United States, emphasizing the political and institutional constraints of the time, many of which had no bearing on social welfare.[25] Stein Ringen's analysis of the fit between the expectations and the outcomes of welfare policies draws on insights from politics, philosophy and economics to produce new insights, for example, about poverty.[26] Daniel Fox's analysis of the American and British health systems is set within a framework of comparative public administration somewhat different from that conventionally used in the study of the health service.[27] All three cases are instances of a fresh perspective being brought to bear from a different standpoint.

If today's map of the contents of the field of social policy and administration is becoming a more complicated matrix, this is the not inconsiderable product of some radical rethinking. But there is a sense in which it may be argued that such initiatives are reactive rather than proactive. The conjuncture has changed; there is no consensus about the idea of a welfare state, no matter that (paradoxically) public expenditure in certain areas of it has indeed increased under successive Thatcher governments. The abandonment of the post-war commitment to full employment and the encouragement given to a greater role for the informal sector as well as the market demands academic analysis of family care and the distribution of paid and unpaid work. The fact remains that without careful attention to developing the conceptual underpinnings of the subject, the sort of legitimate reaction represented by radical rethinking stands in danger of assuming the character of 'commando raids' attributed to it by Mishra.

As well as remapping the content of the subject, there has to be a firmer conceptual base. The neo-Marxist critique of the subject, which began in earnest a decade ago, urged a new theoretical perspective and a focus on the relations of production rather than on the politics of redistribution. The hackles of social administrators still tend to rise when the virtue of theory is expounded, usually and unfortunately in opposition to empirical work. The field still has relatively few examples of the fertile combination of rigorous theory with empirical evidence, perhaps the most impressive being within economics, although constrained by the limiting assumptions of microeconomic theory. Certainly there is a good case for arguing that, rather than employing more sophisticated theory, the need is as great for the subject to be more innovative in terms of the methods it employs in empirical investigation, drawing on advances made in neighbouring fields such as sociology and psychology.

There remains, however, an uneasiness about boundaries. What justification does social policy and administration have for studying what it does in the way that it does other than the need of the moment stimulated by the appearance of particular issues on political agendas? Without greater conceptual clarity the boundaries of the subject will always be a matter of concern.

The challenge regarding the development of conceptual tools to provide a sense of direction in the future is essentially an interdisciplinary one. There can be little point in adopting a purely economic approach to the issues of choice and constraints; for example 'a woman's right to choose' in the matter of abortion must immediately raise political and moral questions as to individual and social rights. Similarly, in the case of one of the most fundamental conceptual dichotomies employed by students of the subject, individualism and collectivism (tackled by Howard Glennerster in Chapter 5), all too often a simplistic opposition is assumed to exist betweeen the two. Worse still, a simple identification is made of individualism with the concerns of the political right and collectivism with those of the political left, thereby offering one of the best examples of the need for greater conceptual understanding.

In the end, re-mapping amounts to little more than categorization. Without conceptual clarity research and teaching initiatives become fragmented responses to particular social concerns of the day, and the subject stands to be taken by surprise and thrown into confusion when the rules of the policy-making game change suddenly. In these respects, Bosanquet's grasp of the subject at the beginning of the century may well have been firmer than that of Titmuss, grounded as it was in political and moral philosophy;

Titmuss's paradigm provided little by way of a guide to the changing nature of political culture and institutions. The issue is not as simple a one as 'lack of theory'; there are probably more and richer theoretical frameworks available to students of the subject today than there were to the Edwardian founders. What, however, distinguished the efforts of the Bosanquets, in particular, was the breadth of their ideas and their integrative approach to social fact and social theory, and to social action and social theory. The strength of the whole seems to have provided them with a clear sense of direction.

Which direction for social policy?

Social policy as a field of study ultimately derives its justification from the intellectual significance of its attack on substantive problems. Theoretical and methodological clarification is a necessary, but not a sufficient, condition for its health and welfare. So what can be said of the substantive concerns of social policy at the end of the twentieth and the beginning of the twenty-first century? With what degree of confidence can one identify the substantive issues which are likely to be of major significance? Looking into the future is no easy task, yet some attempt to anticipate future trends is surely appropriate. Despite its difficulty, some brave souls will attempt such a prognostication.

The very week of the conference, there appeared one scenario for Britain a quarter of a century hence, in the year 2013, by geographer Peter Hall, at the time chairman-designate of the Economic and Social Research Council (ESRC).[28] He foresaw a society looking like an exaggerated version of the 1980s: a small upper class, a vast middle class, already prosperous and striving ever upward, and a residual underclass of the one-third of the population who were unemployed, living in the middle-city housing estates of the 1920s and 1930s which had become urban wastelands, ringed by a brooding police presence.

This underclass would have progressively segregated itself into self-protected and inward-looking racial and cultural ghettos. (He was also on recent record criticizing academic social policy in Britain for living too much in the past and being unwilling to engage with long-term inner city deterioration.) Even if Hall's exercise seemed more of a commentary on *contemporary* Britain than a genuine exercise in futurology, it had a few ancestors, such as Michael Young's *The Rise of the Meritocracy*.[29] Someone gazing into a crystal ball is on shaky ground in presuming to foretell the concerns of social policy as far into the future as the year 2012. What one can do is to look back in the history of the subject and ask whether one could have anticipated future developments at certain points in the past.

If a time traveller were transported back in time to 1937 or 1962 for the twenty-fifth or fiftieth anniversaries of the Department of Social Science and Administration, what might they have foretold in those years about the future development of the academic subject? In 1937, Clement Attlee, the first new appointment to the department as lecturer in social work in 1912, had long left for national politics. The department in the 1930s was mainly concerned with the training of social workers under C. M. Lloyd (head of department from 1922 to 1944), and there was little sign of the transformation which war was to effect in social policy in general and social insurance, through the Beveridge Report, in particular. Nor was there much inkling of the future post–1945 social welfare legislation under Attlee's premiership, nor of the development of social policy under Marshall and particularly Titmuss, who was then still working in the insurance industry, though becoming known through his writings. Our time traveller might have been expected to extrapolate a future of continued contributions to social welfare training by the department, with perhaps some greater research activity looking at social conditions. But in 1937 there were no signs of the changes which were to transform the subject within fifteen years.

Consider, for example, the future-oriented language of the Beveridge Report in 1942. The specific proposals were presented in the framework of the author's vision of the new society which was to emerge in Britain after the war. 'Now, when the war is abolishing landmarks of every kind', he wrote, 'is the opportunity for using experience in a clear field . . . A revolutionary moment in the world's history is time for revolutions, not for patching.' Striking imagery was used to identify the five giants on the road of reconstruction, Want, Ignorance, Squalor, Idleness and Disease.

One of the most striking features of the evidence submitted to the Beveridge Committee was the very widespread expectation among witnesses that the inquiry was going to lead to radical, even 'Utopian', social change. Quite where this expectation came from is not entirely clear, but it may well have derived from Beveridge himself and from his frequent references in articles and broadcasts to the abolition of poverty and to post-war social reform. A second striking feature was the very widespread support among witnesses for the kind of reform that Beveridge already had in mind – a measure of the extent to which Beveridge himself was interpreting rather than creating the spirit of the times.[30]

When the Beveridge Report was published, it caught the public imagination. Within a month, over 100,000 copies were sold and a cheap edition was printed for circulation to the armed forces. Who would have foreseen this in 1937?

By the fiftieth anniversary in 1962 the subject of social policy had been created and taken something resembling its modern form. The outlook was more optimistic, not to say ebullient, in so far as one can ever be so in the contemplation of social deprivation and disadvantage. Members of the department were making important contributions to the study of housing, the condition of the elderly and the provision of health services. There was a growing literature to which students could be directed assessing the condition of the post-war welfare state. Social work education continued, but the intellectual high ground was now held by social policy and administration. What would our time traveller have made of this, asked to speculate about likely future developments in the next two decades?[31] Again, extrapolation from the existing trends is the most likely response, foreseeing seeing a widening and deepening of the academic coverage of the field, and a maturation of the subject (as indeed Titmuss himself anticipated in the passage quoted by Ramesh Mishra on page 79). An increase in the political influence of the subject could also have been foreseen, given the Fabian links of its leading figures and the likely imminence of a Labour government. In the short term this latter prediction would be fulfilled, as Keith Banting has since eloquently described,[32] but in the longer term this political influence was dramatically reduced, due to the political sea change of the late 1970s. Intellectually, social policy was caught short by the shift to market-oriented approaches in the early 1980s, and took some time to recover. As the argument over the concept of 'underclass' suggests, there is still strong resistance to this changed intellectual climate and to confronting issues of 'welfare dependency' in particular. But how could our time traveller in 1962 have been expected to anticipate these later developments, given the broad consensus between both political parties over many social policy issues in the 1950s? The time traveller voyaging forth from the present to the hundredth anniversary of the department in 2012 may encounter a world which we do not at present anticipate. What is clear is that there is no certainty about social policy. Some may see change and a lack of consensus as a source of confusion, alarm and even despair. Others, including ourselves, see diversity as a source of development and see the subject of social policy in the years ahead as dynamic and exciting.

Notes

1 See the pamphlet *Link: LSE Department of Social Science and Administration – 1912 Jubilee 1962* (London: London School of Economics, privately printed, 1962; copy in the Department of Manuscripts and Special Collections, British Library of Political and Economic Science).

2 For brief discussions of the history of the department, see Richard M. Titmuss, 'Social administration in a changing society' (inaugural lecture delivered at the LSE on 10 May 1951) in *Essays on the Welfare State* (London: Allen & Unwin, 1958), pp. 13–33; R. M. Titmuss, 'Time remembered' in *Commitment to Welfare* (London: Allen & Unwin, 1968), pp. 48–55; Kit Russell, Sheila Benson, Christine Farrell, Howard Glennerster, David Piachaud and Garth Plowman, *Changing Course: a follow-up study of students taking the Certificate and Diploma in Social Administration at the LSE, 1949–1973* (London: London School of Economics, 1981), Chapter 2; and José Harris's chapter in this book.

3 A. Heidenheimer. 'Politics, policy and policy as concepts in English and continental languages: an attempt to explain divergences', *Review of Politics* 48 (1), winter 1986, pp. 3–30.

4 R. Klein, 'The study of social policy', *The Political Quarterly*, January–March 1988, pp. 97–101.

5 R. Klein and M. O'Higgins (eds), *The Future of Welfare* (Oxford: Blackwell, 1985); R. Berthoud (ed.), *Challenges to Social Policy* (Aldershot: Gower, 1985); J. Le Grand and R. Robinson (eds), *Privatisation and the Welfare State* (London: Allen & Unwin, 1984); M. Rein, G. Esping-Andersen and L. Rainwater (eds), *Stagnation and Renewal in Social Policy: the rise and fall of policy régimes* (Armonk: NY: M. E. Sharpe, 1987). For responses more in line with traditional social policy,

see P. Bean, J. Ferris and D. Whynes (eds), *In Defence of Welfare* (London: Tavistock, 1985); P. Wilding (ed.), *In Defence of the Welfare State* (Manchester: Manchester University Press, 1986); and M. Wicks, *A Future for All: do we need the Welfare State?* (Harmondsworth: Penguin, 1987).

6   Cf. D. Cannadine, 'British history: past, present – and future?', *Past and Present*, 116, August 1987, pp. 169–91.

7   Cf. A. Williams and R. Anderson, *Efficiency in the Social Services* (Oxford: Basil Blackwell, 1975; A. J. Culyer, *The Political Economy of Social Policy* (Oxford: Martin Robertson, 1983); Bleddyn Davies and David Challis, *Matching Resources and Needs in Community Care: an evaluated demonstration of a long-term care model* (Aldershot: Gower, 1986).

8   A. J. Culyer, 'Economics, social policy and social administration: the interplay between topics and disciplines', *Journal of Social Policy* 10 (3), 1981, pp. 311–29.

9   Cf. R. Pinker, *Social Theory and Social Policy* (London: Heinemann, 1971); I. Gough, *The Political Economy of the Welfare State* (London: Macmillan, 1979); V. George and P. Wilding, *Ideology and Social Welfare* (London: Routledge & Kegan Paul, revised edition 1985); P. Taylor-Gooby and J. Dale, *Social Theory and Social Welfare* (London: Edward Arnold, 1981).

10 Cf. A. M. McBriar, *An Edwardian Mixed Doubles: the Bosanquets versus the Webbs: a study in British social policy 1890–1929* (Oxford: Clarendon Press, 1987).

11 See D. Donnison, V. Chapman, M. Meacher, A. Sears and K. Unwin, *Social Policy and Administration Revisited*, Chapter 11 'Taking Decisions in a University' (London: Allen & Unwin, 1975), pp. 253–85; K. Jones, *Eileen Younghusband* (London: Bedford Square Press, 1984), pp. 25–71.

12 K. Banting, *Poverty, Politics and Policy* (London: Macmillan, 1979).

13 J. Baker, 'Social conscience and social policy', *Journal of Social Policy*, 8 (2) 1979, pp. 177–206, analyses the emphases in elementary textbooks in social administration in use in British universities and polytechnics in 1976. On the distinction between social *administration* and *social policy* see H. Glennerster, 'A Requiem for the Social Administration Association', *Journal of Social Policy* 17 (1), 1988, pp. 83–4, and G. Smith, 'A Paean for the Social Policy Association: a response to Glennerster', *Journal of Social Policy* 17 (3), 1988, pp. 375–79.

14 A. J. Culyer, 'Economics, social policy and social administration', op. cit. pp. 322–3.

15 R. Titmuss, *The Gift Relationship: from human blood to social policy* (London: Allen & Unwin, 1970).

16 D. Donnison, 'Reasonable passion', *Times Higher Education Supplement*, 8 April, 1988, p. 14.

17 R. Pinker, *Social Theory and Social Policy*, p. 12.

18 D. A. Nevitt, 'Needs and outputs', in H. H. Heisler (ed.), *The Foundations of Social Administration* (London: Macmillan, 1977), pp. 113–28.

19 E. P. Hennock, *British Social Reform and German Precedents: The Case of Social Insurance 1880– 1914* (Oxford: Clarendon Press, 1987).

20 J. Higgins, *States of Welfare: comparative analysis in social policy* (Oxford: Basil Blackwell and Martin Robertson, 1981).

21 Interview with Ralf Dahrendorf recorded in Bob Mullan, *Sociologists on Sociology* (London: Croom Helm, 1983), p. 42.

22 Committee on Higher Education, *Higher Education* (The Robbins Report), Appendix 1, 'The demand for places in higher education', Cmnd. 2154–1 (London: HMSO, 1983), especially Part III, 'The pool of ability, and Part IV, 'Past trends and future estimates'.

23 H. Glennerster and E. Hoyle, 'Educational research and educational policy', *Journal of Social Policy*, 1, 1972, pp. 193–212.

24 J. Rex and R. Moore, *Race, Community and Conflict* (London: Oxford University Press, 1967); J. Rex, 'The sociology of a zone of transition' in R. E. Pahl (ed.) *Readings in Urban Sociology* (Oxford: Pergamon, 1968), pp. 211–31; and for a stimulating recent critique, M. J. Daunton, *A Property-Owning Democracy? Housing in Britain* (London: Faber & Faber, 1987), Chapter IV, 'How Valid is Housing Class?'

25 D. E. Ashford, *The Emergence of Welfare States* (Oxford: Blackwell, 1986).

26 S. Ringen, *The Possiblity of Politics* (Oxford: Clarendon Press, 1987).

27 D. M. Fox, *Health Policies, Health Politics: The British and American Experience, 1911–1965* (Princeton, NJ: Princeton University Press, 1986).

28 P. Hall, 'Britain 2013', *New Society*, 18 December, 1987, pp. 39–41.

29 M. Young, *The Rise of the Meritocracy* (London: Thames & Hudson, 1958).

30 J. Harris, *William Beveridge: A Biography* (Oxford: Clarendon Press, 1977), pp. 414–15.

31 Cf. M. Bulmer 'Where will society go? Looking into the future of social welfare', *Futures*, Vol. 20 (5), October 1988, pp. 549–56.

32 K. Banting, *Poverty, Politics and Policy* (London: Macmillan, 1979).

PART II

Social Policy: Retrospect and Prospect

2   The Webbs, The Charity Organisation Society and the Ratan Tata Foundation: Social policy from the perspective of 1912

JOSÉ HARRIS

I

The period between the 1890s and the outbreak of the First World War was a classic age of social policy debate in Britain. It was a period in which 'social problems' were given unusual prominence in the wider study of ethics, economics, science and political thought – and yet before the treatment of those problems had become technical, specialized and hived off into discrete areas of expert, professional concern. A reader who surveys the Edwardian literature on social questions cannot but be struck by the degree to which such questions caught the attention, not just of professional administrators or of persons temperamentally inclined to good works, but of historians, scientists, economists, moral and political philosophers. For perhaps the only time in its history social policy was central rather than marginal to the most powerful currents of British intellectual life. Debate ranged from the strictly practical to the highly theoretical, often involving an ambitious and speculative synthesis of the two. Discussion of public provision of school meals, for example, nearly always involved not merely measurement of need and administrative practicalities, but reflections upon the anthropology of the family, the role of mothers, the maintenance of incentives, and the whole ethical and political relationship between the citizen and the state. Discussions of poverty were closely bound up with wider discussions about optimal patterns of distribution, the continuing validity of free trade and the efficiency of the Empire. Many Edwardian reformers were uneasily conscious of a potential clash between the needs of the individual, the needs of society and the needs of the 'race'; were the interests of all three coterminous? (as early Victorian social theory would have assumed) or was there a sense in which the rights of individuals, the ethical imperatives of social life and the biological requirements of the race were in conflict with each other? Thinking about social policy was also closely bound up with thinking about constitutional issues; with conferring upon the community and upon state power an element of legitimacy which in earlier times had been derived from defence of property and maintenance of public order. Social welfare policies were not necessarily a product of crude majority democracy, but they were closely intermeshed with the political and social culture of a 'democratic' age. Even the vocabulary of social policy was changing, as both conservative and progressive theorists sought to purge social concepts of the stigmatic and deterrent connotations of past usage. Thus, the 'destitute' became the 'necessitious', 'mental defectives', 'persons suffering from brain trouble', and a Royal Commission on the Feeble-Minded recommended 'the disuse of all terms to which objection is felt in the public mind, as, for instance, "Lunatics", or "Idiots", "Lunatic Asylums", "Workhouses" etc. Such names tend to deter people from allowing their friends to obtain proper care.'[1]

It was against this intellectual background that the LSE's department of Social Science and Administration was founded in the autumn of 1912. The department was the fruit of a marriage between the Charity Organisation Society's (COS) School of Sociology and a poverty research unit financed by an Indian millionaire, Mr (later Sir) Ratan Tata. The bare fact of this institutional union has been recounted many times, yet the seemingly bizarre nature of this wildly improbable union has rarely been commented on and never fully explained.

Numerous histories of early twentieth-century thought have portrayed the dichotomy between COS-style voluntarism and Fabian collectivism as a key political leitmotif of the period. How then did it come about that the Charity Organisation Society, reputedly the heartland of freemarket values and ethical individualism, came to throw in its hand with an institution such as the LSE, founded and dominated by those arch-prophets of collectivism, Sidney and Beatrice Webb? More specifically, how could such an event have occurred in 1912, when both popular and expert opinion on social policy was still heaving in the wake of the great national controversy generated by the Royal Commission on the Poor Laws, a controversy in which the Webbs and the COS were (or perceived themselves to be) the leading antagonists? And where does the Indian philanthropist Ratan Tata fit into the picture? Why did this scion of India's greatest industrial and commercial dynasty choose to put his money into studies of the under-feeding of English schoolchildren rather than into the immeasurably greater problems of poverty and malnutrition in India? What was the relationship between the LSE and the Ratan Tata foundation, and what impact did the foundation make on the development of social science and social policy? How did the infant department of Social Sciences and Administration survive and take shape in face of the ideological mésalliance of its parents? This paper will attempt to answer some of these questions, and to set them in the context of the varying cross-currents of early twentieth-century social and intellectual history. The setting up of the department of Social Science and Administration will emerge as more than just an experiment in social work training, rather as a microcosm of many of the shifting social forces of its age.

II

The oddity of the marriage of 1912 is most clearly hinted at in two of the three major institutional histories of the Charity Organisation Society. Charles Loch Mowat recorded that amalgamation with the LSE had been considered initially in 1903, when the COS first set up its School of Sociology for the training of social workers. At that time the COS had 'rejected co-operation with the School because of the absence of a "social and ethical" side to its teaching and because of its conspicuous association with one school of thought'. When the union did take place nine years later, it was stipulated that there should be no change in staff or syllabus for at least two years. But, commented Mowat, the COS contingent found that the London School of Economics was 'strongly coloured by the socialist views of its founders, the Webbs. Its approach to training for social work was much more theoretical than that of the School of Sociology and the COS, and this inevitably influenced the work of the new Department; and there was also some lack of sympathy with voluntary, charitable work.' The fate of the School of Sociology was 'from the viewpoint of the COS something of a tragedy'.[2] Madeleine Rooff similarly remarked that 'there were some misgivings in the Society about the influence of the Webbs and of socialist theories on the School's teaching and on the attitude of its students'. Rooff concluded that the COS was never 'completely satisfied' with the training courses provided by the new department, and that by the end of the First World War 'it was looking to Bedford College as the more sympathetic institution to provide courses of lectures in Social Economics and Social Ethics.'[3]

Such comments merely deepen the mystery of why the COS ever agreed to the amalgamation of its training school with the LSE in the first place – or indeed why the LSE wished to absorb within itself so potentially hostile an agency as a body of workers and teachers committed to the principles of the COS. And the mystery is not solved by the rather different account given by one of the major participants in the social controversies of the period: Helen Bosanquet. Mrs Bosanquet, writing the history of the COS much closer to the events that took place than either Mowat or Rooff, portrayed the amalgamation of 1912 as merely a logical expression of the fact that social work education had outgrown its pioneering phase and now needed more substantial academic establishment: 'it was thought well to place it on a firmer basis by incorporating it with the London School of Economics, which was in possession of large grants from the Government.' There was no hint in Mrs Bosanquet's account of ideological tensions; contrary to the story as told by Mowat, she was at pains to stress the 'theoretical' contribution made to social work training by the COS educational tradition (which she defined as 'a definite attempt to induce people "to think" and not to shrink from applying theory to practical work').[4] Mrs Bosanquet's emphasis on the painless continuity of COS principles under the aegis of the LSE is given some credence by the fact that Professor E. J. Urwick, who had been director of the School of Sociology since 1903, continued to be head of the Department of

Social Administration until 1919. Moreover, as will be demonstrated in more detail below, Urwick's approach to the teaching of
social policy and to the study of social problems generally was
nothing if not 'theoretical'. On the other hand, Mrs Bosanquet's
account glossed over the undeniable fact that many within the COS
did perceive the Webbs, if not the LSE, as the arch-enemy. Mrs
Bosanquet's own husband, Bernard Bosanquet, had written some
years earlier that the Fabians were 'frightfully anti-COS . . . I could
never work with them or with any of them in any practical effort,
we should be at daggers drawn on every detail'.[5] Mrs Bosanquet's
account also obscured the fact that, far from being in a position to
bail out an ailing voluntary society, the LSE in the late 1900s was
itself in dire financial straits, desperately seeking both governmental
support and aid from private institutions.

What then lay behind the apparently paradoxical transformation
of an individualist and voluntarist School of Sociology into a
reputedly collectivist department of Social Administration? The
answer must be sought not merely in the immediate circumstances
of 1912 but in the long-term development of social science education
after the 1890s. As mentioned above, the two decades before the
founding of the Social Administration department had seen an
enormous explosion of public interest in questions of social theory
and social policy. Major changes had occurred in the administration
of the poor law, in provision of new social services, and in the scope
and variety of voluntary institutions. The advance of 'organic'
perceptions of society on all points of the political spectrum meant
that poverty, malnutrition, infant mortality, bad housing, etc.,
were increasingly seen as diseases of the body politic and not just as
misfortunes for the individual. Knowledge about 'society' erupted
in all directions, challenging the abstract and self-regulating model
of classical political economy, and stimulating the growth of
sociology, psychology, anthropology, social medicine and public
administration. The foundation of the LSE itself in 1896 was an
important symptom of these new currents of thought, and of
optimistic hopes about their relevance to practical problems. The
research of private investigators headed by Booth and Rowntree,
and of a long series of departmental committees and royal commis-
sions, generated an immense amount of data about the ways in
which English people lived (nearly one-third of them in some
degree of poverty). Instinctive benevolence and abstract theory

seemed increasingly inadequate as the tools of the would-be social reformer; hence the increasing interest in the 1890s in methods of training voluntary workers and in the more systematic application of new knowledge to concrete issues of policy.

Members of the Charity Organisation Society were to the forefront of this new interest in both theoretical and applied social sciences (as indeed – in spite of their reputation for reactionary conservatism – they had been in many of the social and institutional innovations of the late nineteenth century). The wider history of the COS cannot be recited in detail here, but it had been founded in the 1860s as a response to the mid-Victorian upsurge of private philanthropy – which in turn had been a reaction against the crude and undiscriminating harshness of the 1834 Poor Law. The goals of its founders were defined, and to some extent caricatured, in the Society's full title: the Society for Organising Charitable Relief and Repressing Mendicity. Headed by a group of classically trained Oxford graduates – Charles and Bernard Bosanquet, C. S. Loch, Thomas Mackay and others – it was at its core a highly intellectual movement, influenced by and expressing ideas derived from Malthusianism, Benthamism, Ruskinian hierarchic mediaevalism, and the political philosophies of Aristotle, Plato, Kant and Hegel. The COS theory of social work was part of a wider political philosophy that was consciously Aristotelian: the family was a microcosm of the polis, and the task of the social worker was to transmit the natural functions of mutual assistance from the one sphere to the other.[6] The philosophic coterie that headed the COS was also closely associated with the London Ethical Society, located at Essex Hall in the Strand, which in the 1880s and 1890s organized popular lectures on philosophical and sociological questions, and became a major centre of the University extension movement.[7] At a more practical level, local committees of the COS had worked away for many years, not primarily at giving charitable relief, but at influencing and 'organizing' the work of other charities and encouraging co-operation with, rather than replication of, the work of the Poor Law guardians. Central to the practical philosophy of the COS was a cluster of beliefs that formed the nucleus of the subsequent development of social casework: the belief that it was possible to distinguish needy persons who were 'helpable' from those who were not; that such persons should be helped by sympathetic advice from a charitable visitor rather than, or in addition to, material relief; that thorough and adequate assistance to a selected few was a more efficacious mode of social improvement than inadequate doles to the many; and that the family rather than the individual was the natural unit of wider society. Central also was the belief that all human beings, however destitute, were fundamentally rational, that the circumstances of each individual were unique, and that policies which ignored these facts were destructive and self-defeating. Contrary to what has often been claimed, the COS was not uniformly opposed to structural, collectivist and environmental social reforms, but it *was* opposed to the administration of such reforms by an impersonal centralized bureaucratic state.[8] Neither was the organization inherently 'paternalist' or 'oligarchic', though it is not difficult to see why many contemporaries perceived it as such.[9] Some older COS members, like Thomas Mackay, Sir William Chance and C. S. Loch himself, were militant free marketeers, but the ultimate ideal of the Society's 'progressive wing' – headed by Bernard and Helen Bosanquet – was one of 'social collectivism', in which friendly societies, co-operatives, trade unions, savings clubs and so on would be financed and managed by their beneficiaries. Like many Victorian rationalists, however, such people believed that an ideal like this could only come about incrementally and historically. In the interim, the latent rationality of the many needed to be guided and catalyzed by the wise leadership of the already rational few; hence the central emphasis on the medium of social casework. It should be stressed, however, that in the period down to the First World War, the COS did not see its own task as being the practice of casework; rather it was the guidance and co-ordination of the casework of others, and the inculcation of a philosophically based civic culture within which the practice of face-to-face charity should take place.

COS members were always a tiny minority among Victorian philanthropists, but from the 1860s to the 1880s they played a dynamic role in the development of social policy and in shifting the emphasis of social thought away from the mechanistic individualism of the Benthamite era. During this early period their great rivals were not collectivists and state interventionists but the large-scale mid-Victorian revivalist charities[10] – Barnardo's, the City Missions, the Salvation Army and so on – whom the philosophers of the COS saw as wholly lacking in coherent social, political and economic principles. From the 1880s through to the First World War, however, their position as the leading intellectuals of English social policy came increasingly under attack. The depression and distress of the 1880s and the piecemeal advance of democracy led to widespread disenchantment with COS theory and practice. Trade unionists, some at least of whom had initially been receptive to the idea of discriminating between the 'respectable' and 'professional' poor, turned against the COS ideal, and in Walworth, Bermondsey and other poor suburbs charitable visitors were regularly mobbed by gangs of children shouting 'There goes Old Organisation!'[11]

In the late 1880s the Fabian Society began its sustained campaign to re-educate the public mind on the nature of the 'social problem' and the explosion of knowledge mentioned above generated a whole new range of systemic rather than personal explanations of poverty and social failure. At the same time Canon Barnett's famous renunciation of COS principles cut at the heart of the process of personal investigation through which those principles were sup-posed to be practically expressed.[12]

It was against this background that COS sources began to call for more systematic training of charitable workers in the theoretical implications of their calling. 'Let there be students and teachers of charity, poor law and social economy' to counteract 'blundering good will and confused endeavour', proclaimed the Society's Annual Report for 1888–9.[13] In the following year Octavia Hill, a leading exemplar of COS ideas, set up a special training scheme to educate her housing managers, and the COS itself set aside a special fund to provide lectures on social economics through the university extension movement. Much of the work of conceptualizing and systematizing an intellectual basis for social work education was initially done by women. In 1894 Mrs Rose Dunn Gardener set out a classic blueprint for 'The training of volunteers' and a few years later Mrs Bosanquet argued that such training must be set within a context of rigorous and coherent social theory. Margaret Sewell, the warden of the Women's University Settlement in Blackfriars, was a discreet but powerful influence in pressing for academic open-mindedness rather than doctrinaire adherence to the established tenets of the COS.[14] The first paid lecturer, a Miss Sharpley, was appointed in 1896, and by the end of the century a joint 'Social Education Committee', set up by the COS, the Women's University Settlement and the National Council of Women Workers was promoting evening courses on social administration in many parts of the country.[15] In 1897 an attempt by Bernard Bosanquet to found a London School of Ethics and Social Philosophy modelled on, and complementary to, the newly founded LSE was a short-lived financial failure,[16] but in 1902 a national conference of charitable and academic bodies called for the absorption of training for social work into higher education. Directly following from this conference, lecture courses on social work and social problems were set up in the Universities of Birmingham, Liverpool, Manchester, Bristol and Edinburgh, and in London the Social Education Committee was transformed into a School of Sociology and Social Economics which began to admit full-time and part-time students in Michaelmas 1903. A densely packed audience gathered at the United Services Institution to hear the inaugural lecture of the new director, E. J. Urwick, who told it that social work was 'still in the rule of thumb stage, like the barber surgeons of old', and set out a programme of teaching which included 'social growth and evolution', social philosophy, social economics and social psychology.[17]

Various interesting points emerge from COS records of the period about the work of the School of Sociology and its various informal antecedents.[18] One is the very high level of popular demand for its teaching, both among social workers and the public at large; most lectures were open to non-members of the School, and throughout its life-span lecturers on a wide variety of subjects regularly addressed audiences of several hundred. Another point is the quite dramatic change that occurred over a very short space of time in the character of the students who formally enrolled on its courses. The lectures of the late 1890s were largely geared to the needs of clergymen, parish visitors, and members of COS district committees; whereas by 1910 the school was providing research training and one- and two-year academic courses for would-be 'professional' social workers, some at least of whom had little or no prior COS affiliation. A third point is that, although the School strongly emphasized the interplay of theory with practical experience, the practical side of its courses was in no sense designed to provide training in 'casework'; rather it was meant to offer experience and opportunity for observation in COS local offices, labour bureaux, Poor Law reception centres and other social and civic institutions of the modern state. The purpose of the practical work was imaginative expansion of citizenship rather than vocational training. A fourth point is that although the School of Sociology

was founded, housed and partially financed by the COS, formal
control over its activities by the COS Council appears to have been
minimal. From the start the School was constituted as a legally
independent body, and its sponsors appear to have believed (like
Sidney Webb in his dealings with the LSE) that social truth was best
served by a free exchange and clash of academic opinion.[19] The
liberality of the COS on this issue was evident in the appointment of
Urwick as director, since though Urwick shared the Society's
ethical idealism and was a member of several COS district committees, he was also a strong advocate of fiscal redistribution and a
warm (if qualified) admirer of J. A. Hobson's theory of underconsumption.[20]

A further very striking point is that throughout its short history
the character of the courses provided by the School was highly
ambitious and theoretical. If, as some histories of social thought
have suggested, there has been a long-standing gulf in British
sociology between a philosophic and speculative tradition on the
one hand and an empirical and descriptive tradition directed towards
social 'amelioration' on the other,[21] then this was certainly not
eivdent in the early social work training inspired by the COS. On
the contrary, courses were quite deliberately geared to a synthesis of
praxis and grand theory, with, if anything, an intellectual bias
towards the latter. The academic courses contained powerful echoes
of the courses of lectures given at the School of Ethics some years
earlier; and although there was no formal connection between the
two institutions there was clearly much continuity of ideas and
personnel.[22] Moreover, though social work might popularly be
referred to as 'slumming', there was nothing slum-like about the
School's regular and occasional lecturers, who included some of the
major sociological stars of the Edwardian era – Patrick Geddes,
Bernard Bosanquet, William Beveridge, Leonard Hobhouse,
Leonard Darwin, Karl Pearson. Problems discussed by speakers
ranged far beyond the boundaries of practical social work, taking in
such questions as the tension between ethics and biological efficiency and the epistemological limits of social knowledge. Indeed,
one is tempted to wonder what an audience of trainee social workers
would have made of a lecture such as that given by Bernard
Bosanquet in November 1911 on 'A Question of Method' – when
Bosanquet discoursed at length about the prevailing crisis in French
higher education, the onslaught of Agathon upon the disciples of

Emile Durkheim, and the implications of this conflict for philosophy, French culture and the development of sociological
method.[23]

III

Very soon after its establishment, therefore, the School of Sociology
was an academic success, both in terms of the quality of its lecturers
and of the popular demand generated for its product. During the
later years of the Edwardian era the School was buzzing with plans
for expansion,[24] and Helen Bosanquet was clearly right to suggest
that establishment within the university was a logical development –
particularly in ·view of similar developments in social science
education taking place in other British universities and in the United
States. Records of the Hutchinson trust suggest that, in spite of
earlier reservations about the LSE's ideological perspective, discussions between the LSE and the School of Sociology were under way
and 'proposals agreed upon' as early as 1905, and it is clear that the
two institutions were regularly exchanging guest lecturers and
speakers well before 1912.[25] What is perhaps surprising is that the
School of Sociology did not seek incorporation within London
University as a school of social work in its own right (comparable
with other vocational research and teaching schools such as the
London hospitals). According to Urwick, this had been the original
intention of the School's founders, but it was not sought immediately because COS leaders were well aware that the University
would not incorporate institutions of higher learning, however
academically strong, without an assured endowment.[26] And, before
the question of university status had been formally mooted, an event
occurred which changed the whole political and intellectual context
of social policy in Britain. This was the publication of the Majority
and Minority Reports of the Royal Commission on the Poor Laws
in 1909. As already indicated, the Royal Commission antipodized
public opinion on social issues, between supporters of the Majority
Report – largely embodying the views of the COS Council – and
supporters of the Minority Report – drafted by Sidney and Beatrice
Webb. To this day, the historiography of the Poor Law Commission is still heavily influenced by the manichean struggle between
collectivism and individualism, progress and reaction so dramati-

cally portrayed in the diaries of Mrs Webb.[27] A sober reading of the actual text of the commission's reports suggests that the stark conflict of principle existed largely in Mrs Webb's imagination, and that the two reports shared a great deal of common ground in their analysis of poverty, sickness, unemployment and many other social problems. There were, however, some key differences between them in terms of practical social administration. Both reports proposed that Poor Law guardians should be abolished and their duties transferred to county and county borough councils. The Webbs, however, proposed that different types of social problem (sickness, unemployment, child welfare, and so on) should henceforth be dealt with by specialist committees employing social workers, whilst the Majority Report favoured the continuance of an all-round 'destitution authority' focusing on multi-dimensional family casework and largely staffed by charitable organizations.

(One point that should be made clear is that the differences between the Majority and Minority reports did not necessarily entail the difference between paid, trained 'professionals' and unpaid 'volunteers'. When the COS defended the 'voluntary' principle they envisaged, no less than the Webbs, that the social services of the future would involve fully trained professional social workers – but employed by voluntary, not statutory, organizations. The COS were certainly more sympathetic than the Webbs to the continued use of unpaid philanthropic assistance, but it would be quite wrong to suppose that, in the context of 1909, voluntary meant the same thing as unprofessional.)

These differences of emphasis may seem now to be of little more than technical interest: but it is a measure of the intensity of popular involvement in social questions during the Edwardian period that for several years the rivalry between the two reports became one of the burning public issues of the day. Moreover, technical details of social administration were widely perceived as symbolic of much profounder issues; critics of the Majority accused it of trying to subvert democracy by buttressing an out-of-date philanthropic oligarchy,[28] while critics of the Minority prophesied that 'the new helotry in the servile state run by the archivists of the London School of Economics means a race of paupers in a grovelling community ruled by uniformed prigs'.[29] Rival publicity organizations were set up by the two sides to canvas popular and governmental opinion in favour of one or other of the two reports. In this contest the Webbs largely failed to convince the politicians, but they enjoyed considerably more success than the COS in winning over the hearts and minds of the socially conscious sector of the public. This loss of the propaganda battle had serious consequences for the COS at a number of different levels. Never a wealthy organization, it suffered a drastic fall in income between 1909 and 1911 and incurred a large working deficit; even more seriously, its links were severed with the Association of Subscribers, a body of wealthy City philanthropists under the chairmanship of Lord Lichfield the members of which had previously allowed themselves to be guided by COS principles.[30] Historians who portray the COS as a bastion of capitalism have so far singularly failed to explain its conspicuous lack of success in attracting capitalist financial support for its policies;[31] a lack of success that strikingly contrasts with the capitalist philanthropy so effectively wooed by Sidney and Beatrice Webb. And, within the ranks of the COS itself, the Royal Commission precipitated a major crisis of loyalty and identity. Several prominent figures within the COS (such as Alexander Paterson of the Finsbury COS and Thomas Hancock Nunn and his associates in the Hampstead Council of Social Service) were publicly critical of many of its policies, and at COS conferences, convened to endorse the Majority Report, speakers frequently complained that the Society should also be prepared to learn from the Minority. Among COS district committees there was much restless dissatisfaction with the autocratic leadership of the COS Central Council – culminating in 1911 with some major structural reforms and a modification of the Society's name ('repressing mendicity' being replaced by the more emollient phrase 'helping the poor'). Moreover, while the Fabian Society enjoyed a boom in membership, the COS found it increasingly difficult to recruit young members – even those sympathetic to its principles preferring to join Violet Markham's Personal Service Association, which had been founded specifically to promote a more systematic, informed and classless approach to problems of neighbourhood visiting.[32]

All these factors meant that it was increasingly difficult for the COS to continue to support the School of Sociology as an independent institution, let alone to seek its incorporation as a school of London University. Reports of COS committees between 1910 and 1912 increasingly emphasized the need to reduce expenditure, to define priorities and to concentrate resources on areas of special

need. Papers written by C. S. Loch during these years suggest that
the COS council was mainly concerned with publishing non-
socialist analyses of social questions and to maintain a strong COS
presence on the growing number of municipal welfare schemes – a
goal which increasingly absorbed the Society's manpower and
financial resources. In these circumstances even the limited financial
help which the COS had previously given to the School of Sociology was an unwelcome liability.[33]

Just as the support of social work training became increasingly
burdensome to the COS, however, the possibility of establishing
such training became increasingly attractive to some of the leading
figures at the LSE.[34] One of the major practical criticisms levied at
the Webbs' minority report had been that it was predicated upon the
services of a large body of trained, professional social workers and
social administrators who simply did not exist in 1909, and it was a
nice irony of history that the only people who were supplying that
gap were the Webbs' chief rivals and critics. Like the COS,
however, the London School of Economics was itself going
through a period of acute financial crisis in the late 1900s. Its assured
annual income was only £7,000, its income from charitable donors
was whittled down by the depression of the late Edwardian
stockmarket, and during the labour unrest of 1910 its subsidy from
railway companies was only saved in the nick of time by Sidney
Webb's resignation from the chairmanship of the governors.[35] Even
more seriously the London County Council, originally a generous
supporter of the LSE, was now in the hands of a Moderate majority,
committed both to reducing public expenditure and to combatting
progressive and socialist economics.[36] The School's third director,
William Pember Reeves, had been appointed in 1908 specifically to
raise funds and to arouse confidence among City business men, but
the public appeal launched in 1910 was a conspicuous failure.[37]
Absorption of the School of Sociology – supposedly a bastion of
orthodox social and economic thought – offered two quite separate
advantages: it reaffirmed the LSE's academic catholicity in the eyes
of would-be benefactors, and it offered the prospect of advancing
and controlling the kind of professional expertise and training that
the Webbs' vision of the future of society imperatively required.

The exact circumstances of the takeover are not fully spelt out in
either the COS or the LSE archives, but it is clear that the initial
overtures came from the London School of Economics and were

regarded by COS members as veiled financial blackmail. 'We have no money and the school of Econ., wh. is rich, comes along and says "we are going to compete, or will you 'Cooperate'?" Of course they could undersell us to any extent.'[38] Details were negotiated between E. J. Urwick and the LSE's Professor of Sociology, Leonard Hobhouse, and were announced by Pember Reeves to the Court of Governors in the summer of 1912.[39] Under the terms of the agreement the School of Sociology was absorbed into the newly created Department of Social Science and Administration, under the general direction of a very broad-based Advisory committee (which included representatives both of the Fabian Society and of the 'old guard' of the COS).[40] E. J. Urwick, R. C. Davison and Miss Rosalie Bosanquet[41] were taken on to the staff of the LSE, and a guarantee was given that no change would be made in the old School of Sociology syllabus for at least two years. In the COS official archives there is no definite record at this time of the apprehension and sense of tragedy mentioned by Mowat and Rooff. The COS Council minutes merely recorded the fact of the takeover and the arguments in its favour put forward by Bernard Bosanquet; namely, that the COS had neither the funds nor the premises to carry on the School of Sociology, and that its unique combination of practical and intellectual training 'would be continued on the same lines by the London School of Economics'. The annual report of the COS council remarked that the work of the LSE was 'akin to the work of the School of Sociology and this made the transfer of it to the former body a comparatively easy matter.'[42] But the conspicuous silence on the subject in the pages of the *Charity Organisation Review* (which normally commented on social work education in great detail) is evidence that something was felt to be amiss, and this is confirmed by the private comments of the Bosanquets. 'That confounded School of Economics has mopped up our little School of Sociology in London', wrote Bernard Bosanquet to a nephew, '. . . we have made the best terms we could and are putting up the shutters with heavy hearts. They retain our man Urwick director for two years interim, and take over our best members . . . But it will be – I fear – like absorbing a small bank in a big one; a director is put on the board for a year or two and then drops off.'[43] Even Bosanquet admitted, however, that the LSE's offer was a very fair one, and there was a widespread feeling in COS circles that necessity must be made into a virtue. If state social services were going to expand in

any event, then it would be much better to have them managed by
trained, professional workers and administrators than by senti-
mental enthusiasts or by demagogues courting the popular vote. As
Helen Bosanquet herself had succinctly put it some years earlier, the
best antidote to weak policies and false ideologies was 'experience of
good case-work on a background of economic history'.[44]

IV

The marriage between the LSE and the School of Sociology was
therefore one of mutual financial and administrative convenience. It
was facilitated by the fact that – in spite of the apparent ideological
gulf between their founders – the two institutions were the product
of the same intellectual climate and shared in many respects very
similar academic ideals and goals. From the start, however, the new
partnership was not just a marriage but a *maison à trois*, and so far I
have made only cursory mention of the third partner in the
enterprise, Mr Ratan Tata. Who was Ratan Tata, and how did he
come to be involved in the setting up of a department of Social
Administration at the LSE?

Ratanji Tata was the second son of Sir Jamsetji Nussewangi Tata,
a Bombay Parsee 'of an unbroken priestly line', and the greatest of
India's commercial and industrial millionaires.[45] The dynastic
history of the Tatas curiously mirrored many wider aspects of
nineteenth- and twentieth-century economic and social history.
They lost a fortune in the American Civil War, restored it by
contracting supplies to Disraeli's Abyssinian expedition, and laid
the foundation of India's modern textile industry by importing new
technology such as ring-spinning while Lancashire was still wedded
to the old-fashioned mule. Symbolically the great Tata cotton mills
at Nagpur, which were to spell the doom of Lancashire's textile
hegemony, were opened on the very day that Queen Victoria was
declared Empress of India.[46] By the end of the nineteenth century
Tata interests had spread to iron and steel, hydroelectricity, building
and construction. Tata funds rebuilt large parts of Bombay, and a
Tata Institution for Technological Research was established at
Bangalore. Tata firms were pioneers of industrial social welfare; an
employees' pension fund was founded in 1886 and an accident
compensation scheme in 1895.[47] Sir Jamsetji Tata died in 1904, but

three years later his two sons founded the Tata Iron and Steel Company, which built a giant steel works and model industrial city at Jamshedpur.[48] Both the Tata sons were childless, and both were to become major international philanthropists. The elder son, Sir Dorabji Tata, was primarily interested in the endowment of education and science; he founded the largest of the great permanent Tata trusts in 1932 (a body that in size and range of functions rivalled the giant philanthropic foundations in the United States).[49] The younger son, Ratanji Tata, was a semi-invalid who took little active part in the management of Tata industries and spent much of his life living in seclusion in Twickenham. He was 'a sensitive and artistic personality', interested in painting and sculpture, who eventually left a large collection of modern European art to the Bombay museum. He was also interested in social questions, and gave substantial funds to the Swadeshi movement, to Ghandi's campaign in South Africa, to Gopal Krishna Gokhale's Servants of India Society and to various movements for the advancement of women. In his will he bequeathed the residue of his estate 'for the relief of human suffering or for other works of public utility . . . such work is not [to be] undertaken from a stereotyped point of view but from the point of view of fresh light that is thrown, from day to day by the advance of science and philosophy on problems of human well being.[50]

Such a benefactor clearly had much to offer the adolescent social sciences, particularly those with a practical and ameliorative bent. Initially, however, Ratan Tata's plan was to set up an institute for the study of social sciences in his native India. Early in 1912 he and his brother offered to endow a social and economic research foundation in Bangalore, as a complement to their father's Institute of Science and Technology. This proposal was, however, 'rejected by the Institute, lock, stock and barrel; and the money refused'. According to Beatrice Webb, the 'ground of refusal was that any economic research was bound to be, or seem, "political", and likely to bring down on the Technological Institute government displeasure. The refusal seems to have been accompanied by contemptuous references by the science men at Bangalore to the futilities of any investigation into economic matters.'[51] At this moment in time the Webbs were fortuitously travelling in India, where they spent some time as guests of the Servants of India Society (whom they appear to have viewed as the Fabian nucleus of a future Indian state).

It was probably through this connection that they first came into contact with Ratan Tata. They were introduced to the Tatas by a B. J. Padshah, 'a benevolent, enlightened, somewhat pretentious Parsee', who had been the ward and protégé of Sir Jamsetji and was the Tatas' chief advisor on all their philanthropic projects from 1896 until 1931.[52] Beatrice's diary recorded her highly favourable impressions of Bombay's cultivated and enlightened Parsee merchant autocracy; and her admiration seems to have been reciprocated.[53] Ratan Tata thereafter transferred his offer to London University, and proposed the setting up of a research institute within the London School of Economics. A draft scheme was drawn up by Hobhouse and Urwick, and the deal was clinched by Sidney Webb during the Webbs' visit to Bombay in the spring of 1912.

Under this arrangement a research unit known as the Ratan Tata foundation was established in London University for an initial period of five years. It was to be housed at the LSE and administered by a trust headed by Urwick as honorary secretary and Hobhouse as honorary director. Surviving records do not discuss the question of why it was decided to link the trust with the new department of Social Administration. But the reason seems a fairly obvious one: absorption of the School of Sociology into the LSE had not *per se* cured the financial problems of either body, and the Tata foundation offered an obvious source of income for lecturers who could be employed both in the conduct of research and in the teaching of students. The trust was to receive an income of £1,400 p.a. (a substantial sum by the standards of the time, equivalent to one-fifth of LSE's whole annual budget). The stated purpose of the foundation was 'to promote the study and further the knowledge of the principles and methods of preventing and relieving poverty and destitution'.[54] The social emphasis of the foundation differed markedly from the policy of 'constructive philanthropy' (that is, 'help to the best and most gifted') favoured by Ratan Tata's father and brother,[55] and it seems probable that the concern with poverty and destitution reflected the personal interests and sympathies of Ratan Tata himself. The same may also have been true of the foundation's preference for inductive and statistically based research methods, since such an approach certainly did not reflect the characteristic outlook of the three men mainly responsible for administering it – namely Urwick, Hobhouse and, from 1913, R. H. Tawney.[56] Whatever the reason, the foundation produced over the next five years a series of highly empirical research studies, whose common theme and focus were measurement and evaluation of the consequences of the social legislation introduced by the Liberal government since 1906. These included Tawney's studies of minimum wage legislation in low-paid industries affected by the Trade Boards Act; Mildred Bulkley's study of the state feeding of schoolchildren; Arthur Greenwood's account of school medical inspection; Felix Kolthammer's analyses of the impact of direct and indirect taxation; and Bowley and Burnett-Hurst's study of poverty in five industrial towns. All these studies were based on very thorough collection and analysis of data and – in the case of those by Greenwood, Bowley and Burnett-Hurst – the use of very advanced and imaginative statistical techniques. One study stood rather apart from the rest: V. de Vesselitsky's study of 'homework', which (though almost wholly ignored by historians) still reads as a minor classic of modern industrial, urban, female life, and of the 'subjective' impact of social administration from the recipient's point of view.[57]

Why and how did the lucrative and academically fertile connection between the department of Social Administration and the Ratan Tata foundation come to an end? A recent study pinpoints 'the conflicting demands of practical and academic work', the tensions between social workers and academic researchers, and the fact that 'the Ratan Tata Trustees were interested in research, not teaching'. Therefore funds dwindled, staff were reduced to half-time posts, and there proved to be 'an irreconcilable conflict of aims in a small department financed to undertake research but also providing training courses'.[58] Archival evidence suggests, however, that this interpretation is wholly incorrect. Hobhouse, Urwick and Tawney – the principal Tata trustees – were all deeply committed both to the teaching of social science students and to the promotion of academic research. Moreover, far from growing apart from each other, minutes of the Court of Governors in 1914, 1915 and 1916 report continuing convergence and interchange of personnel and ideas between the department of Social Administration and the Ratan Tata trustees, including provision by the latter of research supervision for suitable social science students. 'The Ratan Tata Foundation has developed on lines which have steadily brought its work nearer to that of the School in the Department of Social Administration,' recorded a minute of 6 July 1916. 'Mr Heath has been appointed Director of the Foundation, in place of Mr Tawney, who

enlisted last year, and part of his work has definitely been arranged
for him in the Department . . . in which it has been agreed that his
position shall be honorary vice-head.'[59] Similarly, far from with-
drawing its funds, the Tata foundation in 1916 increased its benefaction to take over the financing of the whole of the department,
including the training of social work students – a commitment that
amounted to an additional £800 p.a.[60] It was at this point that, for
reasons which surviving records do not make fully clear, the whole
department was renamed the Ratan Tata department and transferred
to the direct control of London University – continuing to be
housed in, though no longer technically part of, the LSE. 'I admit it
is with some regret', reported Pember Reeves in 1917, 'that I see a
department which we have, without question, made very successful, transferred to the University. Still, the needs of the department
were growing at a greater rate than funds at the School's disposal for
its benefit, and the benefaction of Sir Ratan Tata will make possible
developments which I think will result in the establishment of
courses of training for social work better than any to be obtained
elsewhere in the UK.'[61]

All this suggests that, far from being a small department rent by
academic and financial difficulties the Ratan Tata department at the
end of the First World War was a major financial and academic
success. The original endowment was renewed in 1917 and this,
together with a rapidly expanding fee income, made it potentially
one of the largest and richest of London University's departments.[62]
The war and its aftermath generated an immense growth of demand
for trained personnel both in social work and in applied social
research, and in December 1918 the Court of Governors in a letter to
the Board of Education cited the 'extraordinary success' of the Ratan
Tata department as a principal argument for government funding to
expand the LSE's premises.[63] It was also coming to be regarded as
the country's leading authority on welfare work by government
departments, other universities and private agencies.[64] In 1919 the
Tatas themselves sought advice from the foundation and invited a
committee which included Urwick, Hobhouse and the Webbs to
carry out an inquiry into welfare facilities at the Tata steel capital of
Jamshedpur. This committee reported in rather critical terms and
cast some doubt upon the Tatas' reputation as model paternalist
employers;[65] there is no evidence, however, to suggest that the
report was in any way resented by the Tata family. On the contrary,

the report is mentioned favourably – even proudly – in the various Tata in-house histories, and a study by Burnett-Hurst published in the mid–1920s suggested that the Tatas were making great efforts to put Fabian-style social welfare schemes into effect.[66] Sir Ratan Tata himself died in 1918 and did not specifically mention the Social Administration department in his will, but the LSE was assured that his executors had every intention of honouring his pledges, and there was 'ground for hope that the endowment might be made permanent'.[67] Tata Industries was in the midst of a great post–war expansion programme, and had founded India's first modern investment bank; it seemed not improbable, therefore, that the Social Administration department might become the beneficiary of an endowment comparable with that recently set up by the trustees of Sir Ernest Cassel for the study of business and economics. Such hopes were torpedoed, however, by the collapse of the Tata bank and by the international slump in steel prices that began in 1921 and crippled Tata enterprises for the next two decades. At the same time the Tata steel and textile factories were hit by a wave of strikes and bad labour relations. In 1922 the profits of Tata Steel fell to 4 per cent and in 1923–4 it paid no dividend for the first time in its history.[68] In December 1921 the Ratan Tata trustees informed the School's director, now Sir William Beveridge, that the existing level of benefaction could no longer be maintained, but that the Tatas would continue to support research funding if the School would take over responsibility for the more general work of the department.[69] The Social Administration department was consequently reabsorbed into the LSE in 1922. It was not therefore internal conflict but the misfortunes of the international economy and of capitalist philanthropy that turned a dynamic, powerful and independent department into an academic poor relation of the expanding Faculty of Commerce.[70]

V

How far did the early days of the Social Administration department reflect its diverse intellectual antecedents? And how did the new department respond to and articulate the pressing social problems of the day? The supposed tension between teaching and research had little basis in fact (except in so far as such tensions are the daily bread-and-butter of all university departments). On the face of it, however, there *were* potential sources of conflict between those members of the department who came from the COS tradition with its emphasis on character and personal responses to individual problems, and those who sought to analyse social problems in more impersonal terms. The very fact that right from the start of its history nearly two-thirds of the departmental budget was earmarked for non-social work purposes meant that the department was never *just* a school of social work; it aspired from the beginning to be a department of 'social philosophy' or 'social policy' in the broadest sense of those terms. At some stage in its history 'social policy' seems to have replaced 'social philosophy' as the term by which the department described its core intellectual activity. The change was clearly a significant one in a number of ways; but I have not had time to pursue it here. Some suggestive comments and problems of interpreting the historic language of social work are made by Asa Briggs, 'Social welfare, past and present', in A. H. Halsey (ed.) *Traditions of Social Policy Essays in Honour of Violet Butler* (Basil Blackwell, 1976), especially pp. 7–8 and 12–14.

Moreover, Tawney's inaugural lecture as director of the Ratan Tata foundation contained some scathing and distinctly uncharitable references to charity,[71] and the COS itself was critical of the department for allowing social science students to spend too little time on practical work and too much on research.[72] When some years later the COS began to sponsor social work training at Bedford College it was careful to retain much greater control over staffing and syllabus than had been possible at the LSE.[73] COS comment on the publications of the Ratan Tata foundation ranged from cautious approval to frank hostility, and nicely illuminated some of the differences of principle between the two groups. Credit was given for the thoroughness of data collection, and *Livelihood and Poverty* in particular was praised by no less stringent a COS theorist than Sir Edward Brabook for its ingenious research methods. But the (not unreasonable) complaint was made that none of the studies was in a position to predict the long-term impact of legislation on economic and social structure. Tawney's study of the chainmakers of Cradley Heath was approved as a piece of meticulous economic history, but its value for social policy was judged to be limited by the fact that British chainmaking enjoyed a world monopoly and therefore gave no clue as to the likely impact of minimum wages under normal conditions of competition. A review of Miss Bulk-ley's *Minimum Wages in the Box-Making Industry* remarked that her data clearly showed that minimum wages did lead to unemployment, and the reviewer sarcastically proposed that where state welfare legislation led to loss of livelihood further legislation should invest the aggrieved party with a claim for statutory compensation.[74]

Nevertheless, it is possible to exaggerate the polarity between a socialistically inclined school of social policy and the social work tradition of the COS. When in 1914 an anonymous benefactor gave a sum of money for the provision of C. S. Loch scholarships, the gift was made conditional upon the continuing association between the department and COS ideals;[75] these scholarships were still being awarded out of the same fund three-quarters of a century later. There were many areas of contemporary thought in which the two traditions overlapped. Both sides emphasized professionalization and the functional adaptation of social institutions to changing conditions; both agreed on many substantive areas of contemporary social policy – such as the need for some degree of eugenic improvement and the provision of institutional treatment for many different kinds of social distress. Both sides claimed to support the integrity of the family – and both were prepared to tolerate a high degree of public interference in family life in cases where the normal functioning of the family was deemed to have broken down.

Despite differences of theoretical emphasis, both sides laid emphasis on the need for careful measurement and factual observation. Moreover, there was no 'orthodox' position in the Social Administration department's academic teaching; social history was taught to social science students not just by Tawney, but by the high Tory, Mrs Lilian Knowles. Leonard Hobhouse, whose lectures and classes were shared by Sociology and Social Science students, was equally critical both of socialist class analysis and of the paternalism of the COS, yet he shared with socialists a strong commitment to state intervention in industry, and with the COS a belief in personal moral responsibility and in the Kantian principle that 'rational good is obligatory and binding'.[76] In the sphere of social work it is true that in 1916 the COS began once again to promote its own training course, but a major impetus behind this scheme was not so much ideological dissatisfaction with the LSE (though this undeniably existed), as the imperative need to provide concentrated short-term courses to meet the demands of wartime.[77] An even more important factor was that the character of the COS itself was changing. Even among the 'old guard' there was increasing awareness of the practical limitations of social work and the need to reinforce it with more broadly based social policies aimed at 'prevention of destitution' rather than relief of individual cases of distress.[78] And by 1914 it was by no means the aggressive and coherent ideological force that it had been only a decade earlier. The crisis of 1909 and its traumatic impact on the Society's esprit de corps has already been noted. *The Charity Organisation Review* after 1912 contained little of the mixture of sustained polemic and academic philosophizing that had characterized it a few years before, and it became increasingly a mere house journal for professional social workers, particularly young women living away from home. Moreover, a new generation of social administrators was emerging, the members of which who had often worked an apprenticeship on COS committees and shared the COS tradition of ethical idealism, but who differed profoundly from the COS in their view of social structure and class relationships. Clement Attlee, who joined the department in 1914 as a tutor in social work, was a case in point.[79] Those who did remain within the orbit of the COS were increasingly, not ideologues and political theorists, but practitioners of a new kind of highly specialist casework, rooted not in social philosophy but in theories of personal and family psychology.[80]

The most important medium of continuity between the older and newer tradition was, however, almost certainly the character and philosophy of the department's first head, Professor E. J. Urwick. Urwick is a neglected figure in Edwardian intellectual history, who deserves more than the cursory mention that he has so far received from historians of social thought. The son of a Congregational minister, Urwick had graduated from Oxford with a first in Greats, and from 1897 to 1903 had preceded William Beveridge as Canon Barnett's assistant at Toynbee Hall, where he frequently defended an 'individualist' stance against the rising tide of social welfare 'collectivism'. A founder member and vice-president of the Sociological Society, Urwick had played an inconspicuous but important part during its early days in trying to build bridges between the speculative studies of Bosanquet and Hobhouse and the more empirical disciples of Booth and Rowntree. His academic career strikingly embodied the fluid and still unspecialized character of the social sciences in the early twentieth century, since he had combined the directorship of the COS School of Sociology with the Tooke professorship of Economic and Statistical Science at King's College (a post which he continued to hold for some years after the merger with the LSE). In 1914, while continuing to head the department of Social Administration, he was appointed to the London University Chair of Social Philosophy, and later in life he became head of the departments, first of economics and later of social work, at the University of Toronto. He was an inspired and much-loved teacher, who combined 'humility approaching that of sainthood' with a caustic sense of humour and a great deal of old-fashioned charm. 'We were especially impressed by his courtly manners,' recalled one former pupil. 'I have never known anyone who could tip his hat like Professor Urwick – in what I imagine was the cavalier fashion of the seventeenth century it seemed to go down to his waist.'[81]

Urwick's published works ranged widely over such topics as welfare economics, ethics, social work practice, and the political philosophy of Plato. Like much turn-of-the-century 'idealist' writing, his books were written in a style that tends to strike the modern reader (or at least the author of this paper) as convoluted and opaque. Certainly they fall short of conveying the powerful intellectual and moral impact that Urwick undoubtedly made upon many contemporaries. Yet Urwick's opacity and eclecticism masked a very consistent and distinctive approach to social phenomena and social problems, since – remarkably in one who headed so many social science departments – he was convinced that 'social science' in the strict sense of the term did not really exist. He wholly rejected the positivistic vein in English economics and sociology which sought to replicate the logic and precise methodology of the natural sciences. This was not to say that the social sciences should take no account of facts or experience, but that the ordering of social data involved a process of intuition, vision, moral and intellectual leaps in the dark. In the last resort, social understanding was akin to an act of religious faith; the epistemological basis for more concrete and verifiable knowledge was lacking, and those who thought otherwise were, in Urwick's view, in error.

This approach was central to all Urwick's mature works. In *Luxury and Waste of Life* he set out the economic arguments for a pattern of income distribution in which no one received more than £200 a year (that is, four times the existing average per capita income). He invoked the attacks of the early classical economists on luxury expenditure, and the more recent attacks of Hobson on underconsumption, and concluded that both 'moderate altruism' and 'simple considerations of social morality' pointed towards some equalization of wealth. Such material reforms were not, however, to be confused with ultimate justice; indeed, in the highest morality, distribution of resources was strictly irrelevant,since 'detachment' rather than 'satisfaction' was the goal to be sought and was the 'root of social progress'.[82] Similarly in *The Philosophy of Social Progress* (the published version of his lectures to the School of Sociology) Urwick explicitly rejected what many people would have seen as the core of sociology as a systematic discipline: namely the premise that human behaviour was susceptible of generalized social explanation. Social data could be marshalled to illuminate certain problems, Urwick argued, and it was good that such data should be recorded more rather than less accurately and classified scientifically. But facts alone could never add up to more than the sum of their parts; meaning and significance were derived from the 'supra-social' character of human beings. 'Our ideals are drawn from a non-social source, inspired, if you will, by something beyond this world.'[83] This perspective was most fully developed in *The Message of Plato*, the book on which Urwick was working throughout his period as head of the Social Administration department. In this he attacked Jowett, Bosanquet, Green and other late nineteenth-century authorities for portraying Plato as a precursor of Hegel and the modern 'absolute state'. On the contrary, he claimed, Plato was a quintessential individualist who believed that total understanding of social reality could only be grasped by the human mind through communion with a transcendental vision. The key to Plato's message lay not in Western rationalism but in Plato's debt to the mystic doctrines of the Indian Vedas (which Urwick claimed had permeated the intellectual life of fifth-century Athens). Plato's *Republic* was not a Webbian blueprint for a well-administered élitist state, but an attempt to convey by metaphor, myth and allegory a truth that went beyond the reach of language and rationality. This truth in Urwick's view was a religious truth, but it was far from being other-worldly; quite the opposite, it was integrally embodied in all aspects of day-to-day human relationships.[84] Neither, by contrast with much turn-of-the-century idealism, did it find its expression in some kind of 'group mind' or 'organic whole'. 'You and I – and God: that is the final analysis of all that is real in human society ... when I say that society is progressing I mean that relations between us three are better than they were; just that and nothing else. When I say that all is not well with society, I mean that there is disharmony in the relations between us three – that and nothing else.'[85]

Urwick's philosphy – derived not just from Plato but from modernist Christianity and Vedantic Buddhism[86] – may seem to late twentieth-century readers a surprising one for a man who presided over such mundane activities as the training of social workers and the measurement of poverty. But it accurately represents a powerful underlying theme in Edwardian social science; a theme, moreover, that transcended more obvious operational divisions between collectivists and individualists, empiricists and intuitionists, statisticians and philosophers, or devotees of Majority or Minority reports. Urwick very explicitly applied his philosophy to education for social work, which he thought should 'send out first-class *persons* of character and responsibility rather than people merely trained in techniques'. Social workers should 'let their minds dwell on the idea of the good life rather than concentrate on mechanical techniques and methods'.[87] Such a belief helps to explain why Urwick's approach was congenial to the idealist philosophers who reigned over the COS – even when Urwick went far beyond COS orthodoxy by dabbling with such dangerous ideas as redistribution of wealth or allowing clients of social work agencies a share in the planning of policy. On the face of it, his approach was less immediately relevant to the empirical researches of the Ratan Tata foundation; such an impression is, however, in fact misleading.

Urwick was actively involved in administering the Ratan Tata trust from its beginnings, and from 1917 to 1923 was director of its research. It was he who commissioned the trust's earliest inquiries into the health and feeding of schoolchildren, and almost certainly it was Urwick who recruited R. H. Tawney and J. St. John Heath, his former colleagues at Toynbee Hall, as the trust's first and second working directors. As noted above, the methodology of the Tata studies was strongly empirical, however, with the partial exception of *Livelihood and Poverty*, the studies all contained a strong normative dimension in which empirical data was used not merely to reach conclusions but to demonstrate certain preconceived committed beliefs (such as Miss Bulkley's strongly held view that parental and state responsibility were not antagonistic but mutually supportive). Moreover, Tawney's *Commonplace Book* (covering the years 1912–14) makes it clear that he wholly shared both Urwick's objections to the logic of positivism and his theocentric vision of ultimate social reality. Tawney's social ethics and mode of understanding society echoed that of Urwick at nearly every point. 'Scientific' economics and 'detailed research into social conditions' were 'twaddle' unless they threw some light upon the proper ethical relationship between man and man; a world 'where there is no rivalry but only service is the supreme human good'. Perception of social reality ultimately stemmed not from the social sciences but from the percipient's belief in a transcendent God; the aim of historical research was not to support but to refute the absurd and pretentious claims of positivistic social theory.[88]

VI

Urwick and Tawney were the two key figures who both reflected and determined the character of the Social Administration department until the advent of Richard Titmuss nearly forty years later (and even then it may be argued that the mental outlook of Titmuss was cast in a very similar mould). Their writings clearly indicate that, in spite of its emphasis on professional training and empirical research, the department was wedded from its earliest days to a philosophy of the social sciences that was broad, speculative, intuitive and humane – and even in certain respects 'mystical'.[89] They indicate also – in spite of folklore to the contrary – how relatively little the early work of the department owed to the theoretical perspective usually ascribed to Sidney and Beatrice Webb. The department was a product of the intellectual and political climate induced by the Poor Law Minority report, and it was a major beneficiary of the Webbs' talent for tapping capitalist philanthropy. Yet the underlying philosophy of its early members was in many ways very remote from the atomistic sociology and mechanistic social engineering that characterized many of the Webbs' writings on questions of social policy (only Miss Bulkley fitted squarely into the classic 'Fabian' mould).

The Webbs themselves however seem to me much more 'idealist' in perspective than is often supposed. This was particularly true of

Beatrice's private diaries, which were full of half-formulated hankerings for a social philosophy of the kind articulated by Urwick. Urwick himself, however, was never mentioned in Beatrice's text. Conversely the debt to the Charity Organisation Society was greater than is usually supposed, not merely in the obvious sphere of practical social work training but in the inheritance of a style of social thought that was idealist and normative rather than utilitarian and positivistic.

Both Urwick and Tawney served an apprenticeship with the COS and both of them moved away from a strict COS perspective – Urwick gradually merging this perspective with progressive liberalism, Tawney making a more dramatic break by becoming a socialist. Yet both of these men retained certain beliefs which, though not confined to theorists of the COS, had nevertheless been strongly articulated by them in the 1880s and 1890s: a belief in character, moral vision, and a fundamentally immaterial conception of social goods. Both of them came to reject the limited class perspective of Edwardian philanthropy. Yet both of them believed that good social relationships were inherently personal, that virtuous people and good citizens rather than well-contrived policies were the indispensable prerequisites of a well-ordered state, and that society was rooted in a reality that was ultimately transcendental. All of these views, though widely pervasive in late-Victorian and Edwardian social thought, were to fall catastrophically out of fashion in the philosophy, sociology and psychology of subsequent decades, which may help to explain the uneasy relationship that the study of social policy was to enjoy with other sectors of the academic community for the rest of the twentieth century.

Acknowledgement

Part of the research for this paper was carried out while I was on leave at the University of Sydney. I am very grateful to Dr Jill Roe, and to staff at the Fisher Library, Sydney University, and at the library of Macquarie University for their efforts in tracking down microfilm material on my behalf. I am also very grateful to Susan Crofton for extracting references from the London School of Economics's archives on my behalf, and to Sandra den Otter who did the same from the Bosanquet papers in the library of the University of Newcastle-upon-Tyne.

Notes

1   W. H. Dickinson, 'The Royal Commission on the care and control of the feeble-minded (1909) notes upon the Report', *Charity Organisation Review*, n.s., XXV, (149), May 1909, p. 248.

2   Charles Loch Mowat, *The Charity Organisation Society 1869–1913. Its Ideas and Work* (London: Methuen, 1961) pp. 112 and 171. See also the report of the Executive Committee on Social Education submitted to the COS Council, 8 June 1903 (cited in Marjorie Smith, *Professional Education for Social Work in Britain. An Historical Account* (London: George Allen & Unwin, 1965, originally published as an FWA pamphlet 1953), p. 39.

3   Madeleine Rooff, *A Hundred Years of Family Welfare. A Study of the Family Welfare Association (Formerly Charity Organisation Society)* 1869–1969 (London: Michael Joseph, 1972), p. 239.

4   Helen Bosanquet, *Social Work in London 1869–1912* (1914; 1973 edition with introduction by C. S. Yeo, Brighton: Harvester), pp. 404–5.

5   Bernard Bosanquet to Frank Peters, 18 July 1890, in J. H. Muirhead (ed.) *Bernard Bosanquet and His Friends* (London: Allen & Unwin, 1935) pp. 73–4.

6   Bernard Bosanquet, 'The Meaning of Social Work', *International Journal of Ethics*, XI, April 1901, pp. 291–306. On the multifarious strands of COS thought, see *Charity Organisation Review, passim*. The strong current of idealism in COS theories has been usefully explored in Andrew Vincent and Raymond Plant, *Philosophy, Politics and Citizenship, The Life and Thought of the British Idealists* (Oxford: Basil Blackwell, 1984), Chapter 6.

7   Gustav Spiller, *The Ethical Movement in Great Britain. A Documentary History* (privately printed, 1934) pp. 1–10; I. D. MacKillop, *The British Ethical Societies* (Cambridge: Cambridge University Press, 1986) pp. 90–8.

8   Helen Bosanquet *The Strength of the People. A Study in Social Economics* (London: Macmillan, 1902); *Charity Organisation Review, passim*. In outlining COS ideas I have avoided using the much-debated and much-misunderstood terms 'deserving' and 'underserving', which were formally abandoned by the COS in the 1890s, precisely because they were so much misunderstood. See also A. W. Vincent, 'The poor law reports of 1909 and the social theory of the COS', *Victorian Studies*, spring, 1984.

9   Alfred Marshall, *Official Papers* (ed. J. M. Keynes, London: Macmillan, 1926) pp. 211–12; J. A. Hobson, 'The social philosophy of charity organisation', *Contemporary Review*, 70, (November 1890), pp. 710–27.

10 See e.g. Gillian Wagner, *Barnardo* (London: Weidenfeld & Nicolson, 1979), pp. 157–8 and 268–70.
11 *Charity Organisation Review*, I (6), June 1885, p. 242; n.s., XXV, May 1909, p. 263.
12 On the impact of Barnett's move, see B. Webb *My Apprenticeship* (1926, reprinted in 1979 with an Introduction by Norman Mackenzie, London: Cambridge University Press and LSE) pp. 207–8.
13 Cited in Bosanquet, *Social Work in London*, op. cit. p. 402.
14 Margaret Sewell, 'The education of public opinion on charity', *Charity Organisation Review*, n.s., IX, (54), June 1901, pp. 285–95.
15 Mowat, op. cit., pp. 103–13; Rooff, op. cit., pp. 234–7; COS *Annual Report*, 12 March 1897, pp. 18–19.
16 Spiller, loc. cit., p. 10ff.; Muirhead, loc. cit., pp. 91–3.
17 E. J. Urwick, 'Social education of yesterday and today', *Charity Organisation Review*, n.s., XIV, July–December 1903, pp. 254–64.
18 *Charity Organisation Review, passim*. Unfortunately I have been unable to trace the institutional records of the School of Sociology, which have not survived in the archives of either the COS or the LSE.
19 Mowat, op. cit., p. 112; Margaret Sewell, loc. cit., pp. 285–95. Lectures and classes were held on premises owned by the COS at Edward Denison House. In addition the COS Council made a donation of £50 p.a.
20 E. J. Urwick, *Luxury and Waste of Life* (London: J. M. Dent & Co., 1908l), pp. 225–33. Urwick, like Keynes and other later writers, criticized Hobson for being too little concerned with maintaining adequate levels of investment.
21 For example, Philip Abrams, *The Origins of British Sociology 1834–1914* (Chicago: Chicago University Press, 1968) Part I, especially pp. 107–13. The opposite view was clearly expressed by the infant Edwardian Sociological Society (see Sociological Society, Report of the Council 1903–4, pp. 23–7).
22 Muirhead, op. cit., p. 91, misleadingly implied that the 'School of Ethics' set up by the London Ethical Society in 1897–1900 and the 'School of Sociology' set up by the COS in 1903 were one and the same institution – which 'with its director, E. J. Urwick, was in the end taken over by the London School of Economics'. I have found no evidence of direct continuity between the two institutions. But certain prominent figures such as Bernard Bosanquet and the historian of economic thought, Dr James Bonar, were active in both. The *International Journal of Ethics*, published in Philadelphia but edited by a committee which included many English idealist philosophers, provides a mass of evidence on the very close connections between philosophical idealism, the late nineteenth-century ethical movement, and the origins of professional training for social work. See also MacKillop, loc. cit., Chapter 3.
23 Bernard Bosanquet, 'A question of method', reprinted in *Charity Organisation Review*, n.s., XXX, June–December 1911, pp. 287–302.
24 Madeleine Rooff, p. 238; *Charity Organisation Review*, n.s., XXV,

(149), pp. 278–82, report of a conference on 'The teaching of social science', 13 February 1909.

25 LSE Records, extracts by Mr Headicar from Hutchinson Trust minute books; Minutes of Court of Governors, 14 December 1911; 'The teaching of social science', loc. cit., 13 February 1909. COS archives; A/FWA/C/A3.47/1, Administrative Committee minute book, 23 November 1911. Beatrice Webb had addressed joint audiences of LSE and COS members on social research methods in the late 1890s (COS archives A/FWA/C/A1/11/1, COS Council minutes, 7 February, 1898).

26 E. J. Urwick 'The development of training', *Charity Organisation Review*, n.s. XXXVI, (211), July 1914, pp. 79–81; J. H. Muirhead, loc. cit., pp. 9–13 records that Bernard Bosanquet and others had applied for incorporation of the School of Ethics into London University in 1897, but this had been rejected on financial grounds.

27 Since I wrote this sentence the bias has been substantially redressed by A. M. McBriar, *An Edwardian Mixed Doubles*; (Oxford: Clarendon Press, 1987) Chapters 7–10, which adds greatly to our knowledge of the Commission's internal work.

28 J. A. Hobson in *The International Review*, August 1909, cited in the *Charity Organisation Review*, n.s. XXVI, (154), October 1909, p. 247.

29 John Burns Papers, B.M., Add. Ms. 46301, f.121, John Burns to H. G. Wells, 16 May 1910. By 'archivists' Burns meant, of course, not the innocent persons who preserved the LSE archives, but those notorious grubbers among historical records, Sidney and Beatrice Webb. See also Austen Chamberlain, *Politics from Inside. An Epistolary Chronicle 1906–1914* (London: Cassell, 1936), pp. 238–9.

30 COS Archives, A/FWA/C/A3/47/1, f.132, Special Report of the Finance Committee, 21 December 1911; *The Reporter*, July 1909, pp. 21–2 (bound in *Charity Organisation Review*, XXVI); COS archives, A/FWA/C/A1/14/1, minutes of Council meetings, 4 May 1908, 11 May and 5 July 1909.

31 On the stormy and largely abortive relationship between the COS and City of London philanthropists see COS archives, A/FWA/C/A1/14/1, minutes of the COS Council, 14 March 1910 and 'Note on the City Council and Association of Subscribers'.

32 *Charity Organisation Review*, XXVI and XXVII, *passim*.

33 COS archives, A/FWA/C/A3/47/1, f.28. 'Notes drafted for the consideration of the Finance and Propaganda Committee', by C. S. Loch, 24 June 1912; and f.300, 'For the consideration of the Administrative Committee on Thursday 11 July 1912, suggestions with a view to arrangements for dealing with black spots'.

34 LSE Archives, minutes of Court of Governors, 4 July 1912.

35 *The Letters of Sidney and Beatrice Webb* (ed. Norman Mackenzie), Vol. II, *Partnership 1892–1912*, (Cambridge: Cambridge University Press for the London School of Economics, 1978) pp. 350–7.

36 Ken Young, *Local Politics and the Rise of Party: the London Municipal Society and the Conservative Intervention in Local Elections 1894–1963*, (Leicester: Leicester University Press, 1975) pp. 104–10.

37 F. A. Hayek, 'The London School of Economics 1895–1945', *Economica* n.s., XIII, (49), 1946, p. 16; Keith Sinclair, *William Pember Reeves: New Zealand Fabian* (Oxford: Clarendon Press, 1965) pp. 320–1.

38 Bosanquet archives (University of Newcastle), Trunk 1 A(5), Bernard Bosanquet to Robert Carr Bosanquet, 1 August 1912.

39 LSE Archives, minutes of Court of Governors, 4 July 1912.

40 The Committee included the Director, Professor Hobhouse, Dr C. S. Lock, Mr Frank Morris, Miss Florence Eleanore Powell, Mrs Reeves, Mr Lees Smith, Professor Urwick, Sidney Webb and The Rev. J. C. Pringle.

41 Miss Rosalie Bosanquet, an Oxford history graduate, daughter of the first secretary of the COS, C. P. Bosanquet and niece of Bernard Bosanquet. Not Helen Bosanquet, the social and economic theorist and leading figure on the Poor Law Commission, as some accounts have suggested. Rosalie Bosanquet appears to have soon left the department and I have found no further trace of her in COS or LSE records. In the 1920s and 1930s she was living in Northumberland, where she edited *In the Troublesome Times. The Cambo Women's Institute Book of 1922* (Newcastle upon Tyne: Northumberland Press, 1929).

42 COS archives, A/FWA/C/A1/14/1, minutes of COS Council, 22 July 1912, 44th Annual Report of the COS, 1911–12, p. 33.

43 Bosanquet archives, Trunk 1 A(5), Bernard Bosanquet to Robert Carr Bosanquet, 1 August 1912.

44 Helen Bosanquet, 'Methods of training', *Charity Organisation Review*, n.s., VIII, (44), August 1900, p. 103; COS archives, A/FWA/C/131/9, forty-fourth annual report of the COS, p. 33.

45 See Frank Harris, *J. N. Tata. A Chronicle of His Life* (2nd edition, London: H. Milford, 1958); Sir Frederick James, 'The House of Tata – sixty years of industrial development in India', *Asiatic Review*, 44, 1948, pp. 251–63; R. M. Lala, *The Creation of Wealth. A Tata Story* (Bombay: IBH Publishing Co., 1981) and R. M. Lala, *The Heartbeat of a Trust. Fifty Years of the Sir Dorabji Tata Trust* (New Delhi: Tata McGraw Hill Publishing Co Ltd., 1984); Sunil Kumar Sen, *The House of Tata 1839–1939* (Calcutta: Progressive Publishers, 1975).

46 Sir Frederick James, loc. cit., p. 252.

47 Lala, *The Creation of Wealth*, op. cit., p. 13.

48 Morris D. Morris, 'The growth of large-scale industry to 1947', in D. Kumar (ed.), *The Cambridge Economic History of India* (Cambridge: Cambridge University Press, 1983), Vol. 2, pp. 588–92. The Tata Iron and Steel Co. was refused finance by the City of London; it was floated with the help of Indian princes, Parsee merchants, and over 10,000 small savers in Bombay.

49 Lala, *The Hearbeat of a Trust, passim*, op. cit.; cf. Barry D. Karl and Stanley N. Katz, 'The American private philanthropic foundation and the public sphere 1890–1930', *Minerva*, XIX, (2), summer 1981, pp. 236ff. Lala notes that there were eventually nine separate Tata philanthropic trusts. By 1983 they owned capital of 100 million rupees,

and had given away 200 million rupees since the beginning of the century. 80 per cent of the profits of Tata firms is devoted to these trusts.

50 Lala, *The Creation of Wealth*, op. cit., p. 138.

51 Passfield Papers, B. Webb's typescript diary, vol. 31 ff.3214–15 and vol. 35, f.3701. Beatrice's speculation that the veto on the institute in Bangalore stemmed from the Indian government's hostility to the social sciences seems not wholly convincing, since the same Indian government had been sending a stream of students to study at the LSE since 1909 (LSE archives, minutes of the Court of Governors, 2 June, 9 and 16 December 1909). In fact the refusal was merely an episode in a much more prolonged controversy between the Tatas, who wanted to convert the institute into a broadly based, multidisciplinary university, and the Institute's director, Professor Morris Travers, who wanted to concentrate exclusively on advanced scientific research. Travers was on leave in England at the time of the visit of the Webbs. For details of this controversy, see Kim P. Sebaly, 'The Tatas and university reform in India, 1898–1914', *History of Education*, 1985, 14, (2), pp. 130–3.

52 Passfield Papers, B. Webb's typescript diary vol. 35, 5 June 1919. On B. J. Padshah's background, see Sebaly, loc. cit., pp. 117–36.

53 Passfield Papers, B. Webb's typescript diary, vol. 31, 10–15 April 1912:

> These millionaire financiers, merchants and manufacturers are attractive, cultivated persons – enlightened and discreetly patriotic – the women attractive, good-looking, charmingly dressed and highly educated, and the men able and refined. They live in sumptuous palaces and bungalows with a plenitude of motors, and make frequent journeys to Europe. The Tatas have houses and flats in London and Paris and are completely cosmopolitan . . . Compared to other plutocracies, these Indians are aristocratic, in appearance, manners and cultivation; and far superior, in personal distinction, to Government House or the English Indian official world – not to mention the Anglo-Indian commercial man – who is a very distinct commoner in body and mind.

The published version of the diaries is Sidney and Beatrice Webb, *Indian Diary*, edited N. G. Jayal, Oxford: Oxford University Press, 1988 especially pp. 198–208.

54 Frontispiece to R. H. Tawney, *Poverty as an Industrial Problem* (University of London: Ratan Tata Foundation, Memoranda on Problems of Poverty, No. 2, 1913).

55 Sir Frederick James, loc. cit., p. 259. Lala, *The Creation of Wealth*, op. cit., p. 34.

56 More probably the impetus came from B. J. Padshah who had himself worked on statistical surveys and was an admirer of the techniques of Charles Booth, Seebohm Rowntree and Patrick Geddes (Sebaly, loc. cit., p. 133, fn.58).

57 R. H. Tawney, *The Establishment of Minimum Rates in the Chain-Making*

Industry (London: G. Bell, 1914) and *The Establishment of Minimum Rates in the Tailoring Industry* (London: G. Bell, 1915); M. E. Bulkley, *The Feeding of Schoolchildren* (London: G. Bell, 1914); F. W. Kolthammer, *Some Notes on the Incidence of Taxation on the Working-Class Family* (University of London: Ratan Tata Foundation, Memoranda on Problems of Poverty, No. 1, 1913), Arthur Greenwood, *The Health and Physique of School Children* (London: P. S. King, 1913); Arthur Bowley and Burnett-Hurst, *Livelihood and Poverty* (London: G. Bell, 1915). V. de Vesselitsky *The Homeworker and Her Outlook* (London: G. Bell and Son, 1916). Later studies sponsored by the Ratan Tata foundation included A. R. Burnett-Hurst, *Labour and Housing in Bombay: A Study of the Economic Conditions of the Wage-earning classes at Bombay* (London School of Economics and Political Science, Studies in Economics and Political Science, No. 25, 1925) and S. P. Dobbs, *The Clothing Workers of Great Britain* (London School of Economics and Political Science, Studies in Economics and Political Science, No. 96, 1928).

58 *Changing Course, A Follow-Up Study of Students taking the Certificate and Diploma in Social Administration at the London School of Economics,* 1949–1973 (London: LSE, 1981).

59 LSE Archives, minutes of the Court of Governors, 2 July 1914, 1 July 1915, 9 December 1915, 6 July 1916. J. St. John Heath, director of the Ratan Tata foundation from 1914 to 1917, simultaneously held the post of Warden of Toynbee Hall. A Quaker and a pacifist he was virtually driven out of the East End in 1917 by the strength of local anger about Zeppelin raids. He died in 1918 (Asa Briggs and Anne McCartney, *Toynbee Hall: The First Hundred Years* (London: Routledge and Kegan Paul, 1984) pp. 86–8.

60 LSE Archives, minutes of the Court of Governors, 27 January 1921.

61 LSE Archives, minutes of the Court of Governors, 5 July 1917; Director's Annual Report for 1916–17, para. 110.

62 LSE Archives, minutes of the Court of Governors, 4 July and 19 December 1918, 3 July 1919, and 27 January 1921.

63 LSE Archives, minutes of the Court of Governors, 19 December 1918, copy of letter from Street Martland, W. P. Reeves and C. S. Mactaggart to the President of the Board of Education, December 1918.

64 LSE Archives, minutes of the Ratan Tata Benefaction Committee, 21 March 1919.

65 Passfield Papers, B. Webb's typescript diary, vol. 35, 5 June 1919, ff. 3701–4.

66 Lala, *The Creation of Wealth*, op. cit., p. 127; A. R. Burnett-Hurst, *Labour and Housing in Bombay*, op. cit. pp. 109–120.

67 LSE Archives, minutes of the Ratan Tata Benefaction Committee, 29 September 1918.

68 Daniel Houston Buchanan, *The Development of Capitalistic Enterprise in India* (London: Cass, 1966 edition) p. 162; Vera Anstey, *The Economic Development of India*, (1929, London: Longman, 4th edition 1952), pp. 244–52; Sunil Kumar Sen, op. cit., Chapter 6.

69 LSE Archives, minutes of the Ratan Tata Benefaction Committee,

19 December 1921. The Ratan Tata research grant appears to have continued until 1929, then came to an end almost certainly for economic reasons.

70   It is worth noting that when the fortunes of the Tatas revived in the late 1930s one of their first major philanthropic ventures was the establishment of a Graduate School of Social Work which eventually blossomed into the Tata Institute of Social Science (Lala, *The Creation of Wealth*, op. cit. pp. 153–5 and *The Heartbeat of a Trust*, op. cit. pp. 29–51). Like the Social Administration department at the LSE, the Tata Institute experienced certain recurring tensions between the academic and vocational aspects of its work.

71   R. H. Tawney, *Poverty as an Industrial Problem* (The Ratan Tata Foundation, 1913), pp. 10–12.

72   *Charity Organisation Review*. n.s. XXXVI, (211), July 1914, p. 81, Urwick defended himself against this claim by pointing out that many of the department's students were already highly experienced COS caseworkers before they came to the LSE.

73   Bedford College Archives AR 330/1, file on 'Social Studies – COS'. I am grateful to Jane Lewis for supplying me with this reference.

74   *Charity Organisation Review*, n.s. XXXVI, (215), November 1914, pp. 336–7, W. G. on 'Minimum rates in the chain-making industry'; XXXVII, (222), June 1915, pp. 315–17, A. M. H. on 'The feeding of schoolchildren'; and XXXVIII, (225), September 1915, pp. 309–12, E. Brabrook on 'Livelihood and poverty'.

75   *Charity Organisation Review*, n.s. XXXV, January 1914, p. 60. If the tie with the COS were to be broken, the scholarships were to revert to students studying history.

76   J. A. Hobson and Morris Ginsberg, *L. T. Hobhouse. His Life and Work* (London: Allen & Unwin, 1931) pp. 55, 65, 69, 170.

77   *Charity Organisation Review*, XLIII, January 1918, p. 29.

78   COS archives A/FWA/C/A3/47/1, f.28 'Notes drafted for the consideration of the Finance and Propaganda Committee', by C. S. Loch, 24 June 1912.

79   See e.g. Clement Attlee, *The Social Worker* (London: G. Bell & Sons Ltd., 1920).

80   Marjorie Smith, op. cit., p. 58, notes that the COS 'made no pretence of being primarily concerned with case work until World War I', but by 1920 case work had become its 'major function'.

81   For biographical details see John A. Irving, 'The Social Philosophy of E. J. Urwick', printed as an introduction to Urwick's posthumous *The Values of Life* (Toronto: University of Toronto Press, 1948), pp. xi–lxv.

82   E. J. Urwick, *Luxury and Waste of Life* (London: Dent, 1908).

83   E. J. Urwick, *A Philosophy of Social Progress* (London: Methuen, 1912, new edition 1920), Chapter ix.

84   E. J. Urwick, *The Message of Plato* (London: Methuen, 1920), especially pp. 220–60.

85   E. J. Urwick, *The Social Good* (London: Methuen, 1927) pp. 63–4.

86   The revival of the teaching of the Vedas was also a cause espoused by
     Sir Ratan Tata. But I have found no evidence to connect this with
     Urwick's directorship of the Ratan Tata Foundation.
87   John A. Irving, loc. cit., p. lix–lxi.
88   J. M. Winter and D. M. Joslin (eds) R. H. Tawney's *Commonplace
     Book*, Economic History Review Supplement 5 (Cambridge: Cam-
     bridge Univerity Press, 1972) *passim*. Tawney's affinity with Urwick
     was acknowledged in *The Message of Plato*, op. cit., p. viii, where
     Urwick remarked that Tawney had 'read the whole book in manu-
     script, and suggested several important alterations and additions.'
89   Tawney's successor, J. St. John Heath, wrote in the *Toynbee Record* that
     'There is a greater need than ever in Social Reform for mystics who can
     not only be practical but content to labour away at humble things. All
     social organisation need to be perpetually reinterpreted in terms of
     social beings'. Cited in Briggs and McCartney, loc. cit., p. 88.

3 *The academic tradition in social policy: The Titmuss years*

RAMESH MISHRA

Social Administration – as the study of social policy in general and social services in particular is known in Britain – became established as an academic subject in British universities in the 1950s and 1960s. In 1967 the Social Administration Association was formed and in 1971 its academic forum, the *Journal of Social Policy*, was launched. By the early 1970s social administration had 'arrived'. Subsequent years saw its further institutional development in British universities.

What was the nature of the academic tradition of social administration as it developed in the 1950s and 1960s? What contribution did it make as a new social science to the intellectual life of Britain? What, if any, were the academic aspirations of the discipline and how far were they realized? What follows is an attempt to answer these admittedly large questions within the confines of a limited space.

The post-war academic tradition

Social administration's main inheritance was the British tradition of social investigation and reform which goes back to the last century. It is represented by the work of public officials such as Chadwick and Simon, philanthropists such as Octavia Hill, social researchers such as Booth and Rowntree, and Fabians such as the Webbs. Social administration was deeply rooted in British history.

During the 1950s and 1960s, which were the formative years of the subject, its academic approach was dominated by the LSE tradition as articulated by Richard Titmuss. Titmuss held the Chair in Social Administration at the LSE from 1950 until his untimely death in 1973. With his outstanding originality and moral passion, Titmuss played an important part in giving the new subject academic visibility and wide social relevance. The Titmussian approach itself falls within the tradition of British collectivism associated with such eminent figures as the Webbs, Beveridge and Tawney, all of whom had close connections with the LSE.

A convenient label for this British genre of collectivism is 'Fabian'. The hallmark of Fabianism was its pursuit of national amelioration in order to enhance efficiency, social justice and equality through systematic investigation, public debate and legislative reform. The Fabian approach is noted for its distrust of theory and speculation and its preference for an empirically based, commonsensical study of social and economic issues. For example, as founders of the LSE, the Webbs wanted to 'break-up' the theoretical economics pursued at Cambridge by 'replacing analysis of concepts by collection and examination of facts'.[1] In the 1930s, Beveridge was also highly suspicious of Keynesian economics because it was speculative and had scant foundation in data. When retiring as director of the LSE in 1937, he regretted his failure to convert 'sufficiently to the new gospel of Sidney and Beatrice the heathen in Cambridge and other outlying places, who still cling to theory untested by facts'.[2]

Fabianism has relied generally on influencing the elites, and has seen professionals and administrators, in particular, as important allies in the struggle against *laissez-faire*. On the whole, Fabian reformers placed their trust in the educated middle- and upper-classes, seeing manual workers and the mass of the people more as objects of reform than as active subjects who made history. If not openly elitist, the Fabian tradition was certainly not populist. Enlightened paternalism may be an appropriate description. In any case it was firmly rooted in British history and nationalism and its frame of reference was nation, not class.

Undoubtedly, this is an over-simplified view of Fabianism but its main purpose is to highlight an elusive but recognizable and important influence on British social development. Fabian socialists such as Titmuss represented its egalitarian and democratic wing, compared with the more elitist and authoritarian wing of which Beveridge may be seen as representative. Apart from its Fabian heritage, social administration also inherited the mantle of the education of social workers and in particular the teaching of the social services. Moreover, it was largely a coincidence that it became established in the universities following the major reconstruction of social services after the Second World War, which gave rise to the popular phraseology of the welfare state. The vastly increased scope of social services and expenditures during this period underlined the need for their systematic study and for the training of social workers and others. These historical antecedents and contemporary influences tell us something about the nature of the soil out of which the new academic plant grew.

The dominant influence on post-war social administration was Fabian socialism, although other influences such as the philanthropic tradition should not be overlooked. Social administration at that time was distinguished by the following characteristics: a focus on British social services; a problem-centred and meliorist approach; concern with statutory services; empiricism, or concentration on the factual study of social problems; and last but not least, the virtual absence of a theoretical approach to its subject-matter. Let us examine these more or less interrelated features in some detail.

It would be more accurate to describe the nature of the subject in the 1950s and 1960s as *British* social administration rather than as social administration or social policy. For it was concerned not with the study of Social Policy as such but primarily with the study of British social services – their history and their contemporary structure and functions. Thinking about the social services was largely historical in that they were understood primarily, if not exclusively, as an integral part of British history. The over-arching idea that gave meaning to this historical exploration with the rise of *laissez-faire* in the nineteenth century, with the Poor Law reform of 1834 as a major signpost, and its subsequent decline which culminated in the arrival of the welfare state. The triumph of collectivism over individualism was generally seen as due to a growing social conscience, although a variety of influences were recognized. Such concepts as were in use at the time, for example, the Poor Law, deterrence, collectivism and the 'five giants' (of the Beveridge Report) were almost entirely drawn from British history. Grounding in British history, then, was one of the hallmarks of the subject.

The focus on Britain was the result of the main objective of the discipline, which was the improvement of life in Britain through a study of social needs and problems, formulation of proposals for reform, and assessment of the effectiveness of social services in meeting needs. Social progress, as revealed by national history, provided the backdrop of ideas, traditions and even methods to help to carry on the 'good work'. Social administration included two overlapping traditions of reform and amelioration. The primary one involved major alterations in socio-economic arrangements and the redistribution of life chances (chiefly a Fabian preoccupation). A secondary tradition was concerned with personal social services which involved social work and the philanthropic tradition.

Reform and amelioration naturally involved a critical viewpoint towards existing arrangements but this perspective of change was located within a broad consensus about the nature of social welfare itself, as well as the means and prospects of its advancement in Britain. Interest in social services and their past was from the point of view of their usefulness as a vehicle for the betterment of national life. Thus a 'commitment to welfare' as the art of possible reforms was the fundamental project of social administration.

History had shown that advancements in social welfare consisted essentially in the recognition of the failure of *laissez-faire* and its remedy through state collectivism (typically through the provision of services). Statutory social services therefore formed a natural focus of attention for the subject. Moreover, Beveridgian reforms and the post-war welfare state had resulted in the vast growth of public social services which eclipsed the voluntary sector and the friendly societies of an earlier era. Not surprisingly then, the focus of attention was entirely on public social services. Later, Titmuss was to question this limitation (see below) and extend the conception of social welfare to include a rapidly growing occupational welfare sector as well as the vastly expanded fiscal benefits of the post–war years.

Social administration's empirical orientation, rooted in British history, was chiefly concerned with meeting social needs through piecemeal reform within a broad framework of consensus. In short, fact-finding, that is, gauging the quantitative dimensions of social problems, was the major activity. This approach has been described somewhat uncharitably as 'social book-keeping'. But social demography or sociometry may be a more accurate description (the

delineation and measurement of poverty is a classic example).
Moreover, concern with welfare of the individual meant that the
fine print of social services became all important. Since the field of
social welfare has typically been rich in symbolism – political and
ideological rhetoric about new social services and provisions –
detailed knowledge of individual needs, level of benefits and actual
administration of services was essential in order to gauge the real
effectiveness of the presumed services. Titmuss's work exemplified
the mastery of such details coupled with a healthy scepticism about
stereotypes which often mistook symbol for reality. In short, such
was the nature of social administration's brief that it *had* to immerse
itself in facts. Given its basic objective and orientation to bring about
change within a broadly consensual framework, an obsessive
concern with fact-gathering, and a relative unconcern with social
and political theory, begin to make sense. When assumptions are
shared, facts speak for themselves and soon only facts need speak.
Thus the collection and dissemination of facts about social problems
within a shared national framework of amelioration distinguished
social administration's approach to social welfare development

As a result, a striking characteristic of social administration was the
virtual absence of a body of theory or even concepts. The subject was
seen as a 'field' of study and not as a discipline, that is, a fundamental
branch of knowledge with its own concepts, theories and methods (in
the manner of economics, political science or sociology). Problems of
social welfare were to be analysed and solved with the help of the
relevant social science disciplines, singly or in combination, depending on the problem in hand and the interests and competencies of the
scholar.[3] Social administration itself did not consciously strive to
develop concepts or theories of its own. This 'theory-free' nature is
surely the most striking thing about the subject and makes it virtually
impossible to assess it as an academic enterprise. For the logic of the
'field' concept is to turn social administration into a series of problems
and their practical solution with no other axe to grind. This theoryless
character of the subject also harks back to shared beliefs about the
nature of 'problems' and their solution. Problems and their resolution
were situated within a common-sense universe where everyone took
for granted what was meant, for instance, by poverty, homelessness
or child neglect, and what would constitute their amelioration. I shall
return to the question of theory later. Let us note, however, a major
implication of the absence of theory. It is that social administration

tended to operate with an *implicit* theory or range of assumptions about the nature of social welfare, the prospects of social reform in modern capitalist society and the nature and distribution of power. These assumptions shaped academic practice but were not available for scrutiny within the scholarly community.

However, apart from theory pertaining to the contextual or background assumptions of the subject, there were a number of concerns, for example, poverty, need, and stigma, which were specific to social welfare. One might have expected some conceptual and theoretical development around these issues. Traditional social administration, however, operated with very little recourse to explicit theories or concepts of social welfare.

Needless to say, I have presented a somewhat simplified and schematic view of the subject. Moreover it is a static view, seen from the perspective of the mid-1950s. In fact, social administration was gradually changing throughout the 1950s and 1960s albeit within the framework outlined above. On the basic theme of the subject as a study of British social services, Richard Titmuss provided an important variation, giving it a much wider scope and relevance. With Titmuss there was analysis and greater awareness of the basic values and principles underlying the services. Overall, however, the British-centred, concrete approach remained firmly in place throughout the 1960s. There was still no general or conceptual analysis of social policy to complement the specific historical and contemporary study of the British situation.[4] The absence of a conceptual apparatus, however rudimentary, hindered the accumulation and refinement of knowledge. The 1960s was a time of explosive growth of ideas, perspectives and methods in the social sciences. Yet social administration managed to retain a remarkable level of immunity from the epidemic of ideas and theories raging at the time. Therefore by the late 1960s (and to change the metaphor) the theoretical 'poverty gap' of social administration became very wide. It was not until the 1970s that an awareness of perspectives on social welfare other than Fabian began to find their way into the literature. But that is another story and we must return to the Titmuss years.

SOCIAL ADMINISTRATION AS SOCIAL CRITIC: THE TITMUSSIAN VARIATION

The characteristics of social administration outlined in the previous section of this chapter show clearly that it was not an academic discipline of the traditional sort. It was more socially oriented, combining a 'mission' component with a practical or 'applied' social science component. The first points to its value-orientation, a commitment to welfare which might range from amelioration at a 'micro' level to reform at a 'macro' level. The second points to social administration's involvement with the social services, the government and public sector – in short, the world of public policy and administration. Of course, these two aspects of the discipline are closely related and overlapping. Overall, social administration has been orientated towards 'practice' rather than 'theory' or academic analysis per se. Its missionary and practitioner role could therefore be in conflict with its role as an academic subject. These characteristics of the discipline have to be kept in mind when assessing its strengths and weaknesses. Indeed, it could be argued that in a discipline of this nature the 'academic' component as such cannot be separated easily from its overall character as a 'hybrid' discipline, which includes social and practical components.

At any rate, in this chapter I examine social administration, first, mainly as a social discipline and, second, mainly as an academic discipline. Under the leadership of Richard Titmuss, social administration played an important part as a critical social science in the late 1950s and early 1960s. The discipline made important contributions, both social and intellectual – though perhaps not academic – which in my view have received insufficient attention. Since at the time Titmuss exercised an important influence both on the discipline and on these developments I look at the contribution of social administration through his themes and emphases. These are: (1) a wide view of the subject-matter of social administration; (2) emphasis on values in social science; (3) emphasis on the importance of empirical research; and (4) an uncritical Fabian value-stance. Let us examine each of these in turn.

A wide view of social policy   Titmuss's influence on the study of social policy began to grow from about the mid 1950s. At that time social services were still mainly studied as a set of institutions with a minimum of reference to the wider social and economic context of British society. Whether outlining their history or current provision, the approach was descriptive. Titmuss drew attention to the connection between the social services and the social and political structure of the society of which they were a part. Instead of being viewed as the unfolding of the social conscience they began to be seen as having a variety of causes and consequences.[5] Secondly, although along with other social administrators Titmuss also focused on statutory social services, nonetheless in his celebrated essay 'The social division of welfare' he argued that in order to understand and debate social policy meaningfully, one had to look much further afield than the formally constituted social services.[6] As is well known, he singled out occupational welfare and fiscal benefits as parallel forms of social provision performing functions similar to those of the social services, although based on principles very different from the latter. In a major study of income distribution he traced the submerged welfare state which was operating through a vast array of tax concessions and allowances for the middle-and upper-classes.[7] By defining social policy in terms of latent function rather than manifest purpose Titmuss was able to widen its scope (at least in principle) far beyond the conventional social services. By extending the scope of social administration in this way, Titmuss gave it a controversial and polemical edge. Although the study of occupational welfare was neglected, taxation and fiscal welfare received more attention and entered the social policy debate. At any rate, armed with this wider view of social policy, social administration could join the debate then raging about the nature of post–war Britain and, in particular, about the apparently excessive equality that had already been brought about by the social services and progressive taxation. A wide-angled view of social policy, as interpreted by Titmuss, Townsend and other Fabian socialists, gave social administration a central place in the contemporary debates about income distribution and equality in Britain.

The importance of the normative Titmussian social administration affirmed the role of values in social science. For an academic subject defined by reformist and interventionist concerns, the stress on values made eminent sense. Titmuss, however, dramatized the role of values in social action. In his view the study of social policy, as indeed of society, was not, and could not be, a value-free enterprise.[8] At a time when value-freedom was so much in vogue in the academic world of social science, Titmuss's boldness in rejecting value-free social science was a considerable achievement. In those days value-freedom meant at least two things. First, the belief that social sciences should emulate the natural sciences in the search for general laws through an objective and detached approach. This involved a scientistic stance which banished value concerns and judgments from social science. Secondly, the idea of value-freedom was connected with the thesis of the 'end of ideology' and the coming of advanced industrial society. Put simply, it was claimed that the nature of social institutions was somehow predetermined by industrial technology and its inherent requirements. There was little to do, therefore, but to discover and follow these 'trends' and 'tendencies'. Against this double-bind and value-freedom Titmuss posited the role of value concerns and judgments in social sciences and the place of choice in social action. It is also from this standpoint that Titmuss rejected a technicist view of social administration. Social policy analysis was not simply a matter of finding appropriate research methods and techniques with which to solve pre-given problems. It involved the choice of ends as well as means. These choices implied particular forms of social and distributive relations – integrative or alienative, egalitarian or inegalitarian. Value choices may be implicit but they are always present in social action. It was the task of social policy studies to spell out the options available and their implications.[9] Social administration, then, appeared as a critical social discipline which was not afraid to take a stand on values, and was prepared to study and debate issues of public concern, such as income distribution, health care and pensions. This gave it a great deal of social relevance and a strong vantage point from which to contribute to the debate about the nature of British society and its social priorities.

The role of evidence in social criticism and debate The obverse side of Titmuss's emphasis on the normative was his insistence on grounding assertions and propositions in facts or verifiable evidence.[10] If social science was not value-free, neither could it be a fact-free endeavour. Rational debate over policy, which kept the possibility of choice open, was conditional upon being able to demonstrate the connection between means and ends, between the course of action chosen and the results that flowed from it. In this the role of evidence was crucial. In any case, informed social criticism and debate required factual knowledge about society and this, too, made the role of data crucial. Post–war social administration, therefore, continued the tradition of investigating social problems in detail, seeking to raise social awareness, acting as moral witness and as advocate for the underprivileged, and using 'social facts' as ammunition to make the case for a particular social policy. Overall, social administration seems to have performed this role remarkably well. The work of Abel-Smith and Townsend on poverty, Donnison on housing, Townsend's work on the relative and relational meaning of poverty and his survey of the life of the aged in institutions – all this and much more – attest to the contribution that the empirical tradition made towards focusing public attention on social issues and making an informed and enlightened debate possible.[11]

Single value orientation Titmussian social administration was firmly anchored in the values of Fabian collectivism. Its leading practitioners were women and men of the Centre-Left. There was therefore little by way of a normative debate, not to say dissent among social administrators. It must be remembered, too, that these were years of steady economic growth, which nourished a broad political consensus around the goals of full employment and universal social services. Marxism and the New Left were as yet only groping their way towards an understanding of post-war capitalism. At the other end of the political spectrum the Radical Right was strong on rhetoric but lacked intellectual and political credibility. Overall, there was a strong sense that the slow but sure advance of collectivism over *laissez-faire* represented evolutionary progress and that this progress would continue. These conditions gave the Centre-Left a high degree of legitimacy. In any case Titmuss's own outstanding position in the world of social administration also encouraged the hegemony of the Fabian perspective. With Titmuss's outright rejection of value-free social science and open espousal of values, social administration took on the character of a social reform movement (a 'value-committed' rather than a 'value-critical' or 'value-neutral' standpoint, to use Rein's distinction) rather than an academic enterprise.[12]

To sum up: Among the distinctive features of social administration as it developed in the Titmuss years were a wide-angled view of social policy, emphasis on the role of values and choices in social action, concern with social facts, and grounding in Fabian ideology of welfare. These interwoven strands gave Titmussian social administration a distinct identity and the role of a critical social science in the 1950s and 1960s. The nature and distinctiveness of this role merit a further comment.

Post–war Britain, along with other Western countries, was difficult to comprehend as a social system. The mixed economy, full employment, universal social provision and heady economic growth represented an entirely unprecedented situation. Pre–war notions of capitalism and class conflict seemed increasingly inappropriate. Ideas such as 'post–capitalism', 'industrial society', and 'end of ideology' gained wide currency as they captured the sense of a qualitative transformation of Western societies into something much more affluent, egalitarian and democratic. The conventional wisdom was that social levelling and egalitarian distribution of income had proceeded quite far. One source of this new equality was presumed to be the welfare state with its extensive 'cradle to grave' social provision for the masses financed out of progressive taxation. Titmussian social administration met these arguments head on. At a time when much of sociology and economics accepted the view that a great deal of social and economic levelling had taken place Titmuss had the audacity to look beyond official statistics of taxation and income distribution and to challenge this view of growing equality.

It must also be remembered that the welfare state was crucial to the debate about socialism at the time. Revisionist social democracy was looking more and more towards creating an equal society through progressive taxation and social services – in short, 'the strategy of equality'. Universal social provision, which embraced education, health care, income support services and more – represented a new and major development in the assumption of collective responsibility. In particular, the British National Health Service was a unique institution in the Western world, having divorced access to health care almost completely from income. The right to receive the best possible health care had become a right of citizenship. This 'decommodification' (to a greater or lesser extent) of a range of services looked like the prefiguration of the socialist principle of 'to each according to [their] needs'. Against this, however, theorists of industrial society and also Marxists (still few and far between) argued that there was nothing socialist about the social services, which were to be found in all modern capitalist societies. To this debate over the nature of the welfare state as socialist or as a by-product of industrialism and capitalism, Titmussian social

administration brought a sceptical dimension. It rejected the auto-
matism and determinism implicit in the arguments of convergence
theorists and Marxists, and affirmed that politics, that is, value
choices, matter. On the other hand, arguing on the basis of its
considerable empirical knowledge of British society and social
welfare, it cautioned against the assumption that the 'welfare state',
whether in its origins or consequences, was a socialist institution. In
demonstrating the multiple origins and consequences of the social
services, Titmussian social administration questioned their facile
identification with the labour movement or with socialism. [13]

There is one last point to be made about the role of social
administration as a critical social science. In the post–war years,
sociology and other social sciences were aspiring to achieve the
status of 'sciences'. This meant distancing themselves from social
reform and other value-laden activities in order to pursue value-
free theoretical and conceptual concerns. Economics had already
established itself as a discipline closer to the exact sciences and
others wanted to do the same. Social administration, therefore,
arrived on the scene just as economics, sociology and political
science were tending to withdraw from 'society' in order to attend
to their own intellectual puzzles. In any case, in the 1950s and
early 1960s sociology was dominated by Parsonian functionalism,
with its quietistic, if not conservative bias. On the other hand,
radical sociology and neo–Marxism (more a product of the late
1960s) had yet to make their mark. In such an environment,
dominated by academic specialization and scientism, social administration took on the role of a generalist, missionary social science;
a sort of Robin Hood with no fixed address, ready to move in and
out of academic territories of all kinds in pursuit of justice and
equality.

In focusing on the role of social administration as the keeper of
social conscience and as social critic, my intention has been to point
out that it was a good deal more than a problem-centred, practical
study of the social services. The Titmussian variation on its basic
theme enabled social administration to play the part of a socially
relevant and critical social science at a time when other social
sciences were either unable or unwilling to do so. True, it was a
particular conjuncture that made this possible and it was not to last.
But that should not detract from the fact that social administration
had something of importance to say about some of the major issues

of the time concerning the nature of British society, post–war capitalism and the extent of social change.

Social administration: academic orientation

Social administration, as we saw in the last section of this chapter, seems to have had considerable success in its 'missionary' role as a critical social discipline. The same cannot be said of its development as an academic subject.

THE PROMISE OF TITMUSSIAN SOCIAL ADMINISTRATION

In the light of its intellectual heritage of pre–war reformist and social work traditions, post–war social administration showed a considerable advance. The Titmussian approach furthered the academic study of social policy in at least three ways. First, the very idea of policy analysis, that is, that there were general principles and objectives behind the vast array of social services and that they were both important and accessible to analysis, began to emerge clearly with Titmuss's analytical and value–centred approach. Second, it was again Titmussian social administration that began to look at the social services as more than simply the unfolding of the social conscience or as an aspect of evolutionary progress, seeing them as social institutions shaped by a variety of influences and having diverse consequences. In other words, the germ of a sociological and political approach to the analysis of social services began to appear. Third, Titmuss extended the notion of social policy beyond the social services to other forms of welfare systems operating on the fringes or outside of statutory social services. This could be seen as prefiguring the idea of social welfare as a generic form of social institution of which social services were only one species. Lastly, social administration's role as social critic and its engagement with the debate about the welfare state suggests a promising advance towards an understanding and expectation of social welfare in relation to the social structure at both macro and micro levels.

Yet it cannot be said that this promise – and it is implicit in Titmussian social administration – was in any way fulfilled. The most impressive contribution of social administration remained empirical and specific rather than conceptual and general. The detailed study of problems and services, the exploration of the technicalities of social research, sociographic 'community studies', and historical studies of particular services, were its forte. Sociologists such as Townsend, working within the area of social welfare, explored the relations between the changing family and kinship structures and their implications for social services.[14] Despite its impressive contribution in these ways, the subject remained undeveloped in academic and conceptual terms. While the basic texts in use in the late 1960s show some advance towards an analytical approach to the subject–matter, they fall short of a conceptual and theoretical treatment of the subject.[15] The organizing frame remained historical, that is, the social services were seen as part of the unfolding of British history, and institutional, i.e. focused on the study of specific services such as health, housing and pensions, with largely a 'social conscience' view of the development of collective social provision. In 1967 Titmuss felt it necessary to claim that, as an academic subject, social administration was not a 'messy conglomeration of the technical *ad hoc*'.[16] Four years later, in a critical study of the theoretical and academic aspects of the discipline, Robert Pinker discussed the 'poverty of Social Administration as a theoretical discipline' extensively.[17] In short, it would not be unfair to conclude that at the beginning of the 1970s, two decades after Titmuss had assumed the Chair of Social Administration at the LSE, social administration remained in a state of academic 'underdevelopment'. In what ways and why?

IDEALISM AND A VALUE-COMMITTTED APPROACH

As we have noted, the missionary aspect of the discipline was very prominent during this time. The field of social policy came to be defined in terms of a struggle between the forces of good and evil – the institutional and residual approaches to social policy. With its predominantly collectivist values social administration was on the side of the 'good', while individualism and *laissez-faire* represented the 'evil' side. With the arena of social policy defined in this way, 'moral rhetoric and fact-finding' (in Pinker's useful phrase) in the pursuit of equity and justice loomed large. Academic development, on the other hand, seems to have received less attention.

More generally, the value-committed approach of the discipline meant a refusal to examine 'social welfare' and 'commitment to welfare' as problematic or contested notions which required clarification. This gave rise to the paradoxical situation in which social administration, the critical social science which emphasized the importance of values and choice and saw its main contribution as making society more aware of the choices available and their consequences, paid scant attention to its own value-orientation as a discipline. The uncritical equation of collectivism and state welfare with the idea of 'welfare' itself tended to give social administration an ideological character which was scarcely recognized. The same could be said of a range of other assumptions on which this particular view of welfare was based.

Social administration: 'field' or 'discipline'?

The lack of critical self-awareness as a discipline is connected with its definition as a 'field', that is, an area of study which uses basic social science disciplines to analyse and solve its own problems but does not have any theories and methods of its own.[18] But what *are* its problems? How does the discipline identify them? Clearly other disciplines cannot help social administration in doing that. The field approach cannot address this issue. It follows that the subject-matter of social administration itself has remained untheorized, that is, outside of its own field of operations. The approach to social welfare has therefore been pragmatic and, at bottom, ideological. The discipline took for granted the pre-given idea of a 'mission' or commitment to welfare – reform, amelioration, betterment, etc., – and a set of institutions – the social services. Once these were in place it followed that the problems arising within the discipline, for example, concerning the efficiency of the social services, were largely practical and applied – whether value-related or pragmatic – and were self-evident. By implication, the nature of social welfare, and therefore the nature of the discipline itself, remained unexamined and unclarified.

Perhaps, however, the idea of a 'field' should not be interpreted too narrowly. Clearly what was meant at the time was that 'social welfare' represented a clutch of variegated problems rather than a fundamental approach or 'mode of thinking' and therefore did not require the elaboration of specific concepts, theories and methods which could be peculiar to it. This raises the intriguing question: how can social administration as an academic subject *develop*? What constitutes intellectual and academic development? What sort of understanding does social administration seek as a subject? True, it can accumulate knowledge about techniques and practices, but to do that would be to accept virtually a technicist role for itself which the discipline has rejected.[19]

In this context it is interesting to note that on the occasion of the formation of the Social Administration Association in 1967, Titmuss, while accepting the multidisciplinary (that is, 'field') nature of social administration, at the same time envisaged considerable potential for its theoretical development. He states:

> I happen to believe that as a subject, social administration has begun to develop a body of knowledge and related set of concepts and principles. It is in the process of knowledge–building which is one of the attributes of science. In doing so, it has borrowed heavily from different disciplines in the social sciences, and now faces the task of refining, extending and adapting insights, perspectives and methods so as to further our understanding of ... the roles and functions of social services in contemporary society.[20]

This is a remarkably clear statement of the academic task and direction for social administration. Yet there is little evidence that this statement was taken very seriously within the discipline. In any case, Titmuss's own practice in this respect was not likely to help matters. Although remarkably original and incisive in his analyses, Titmuss was not a systematic thinker. It is clear that he had little patience for theorizing and did not care much for a schematic study of welfare.[21] It may be that in the above statement he recognized, as a matter of principle, the direction in which the discipline should go, even though he himself did not feel able to undertake or initiate such a task.

I should like to conclude this section by looking briefly at developments within the discipline in the 1970s and 1980s in the light of Titmuss's agenda for a theoretically advanced study of social policy. Since the mid-1970s, a number of new departures can be seen. There has been a small but steady output of theoretically orientated literature which has (1) widened the normative perspective on social policy far beyond the implicit Fabian framework of Titmuss's days; (2) tried to order the field conceptually; and (3) elaborated the view of social policy from new perspectives, for example, Marxist and feminist.[22] With the diversification of its normative and explanatory perspectives, social administration is becoming less of a missionary and pragmatic enterprise dominated by a single value perspective and more of an academic enterprise which recognizes a plurality of normative and explanatory perspectives on social welfare and seeks to analyse them. The literature of social administration is now more informed theoretically. There is a good deal more of comparative work while 'abstracted empiricism' is less in evidence today. As well there is perhaps a greater awareness of the political economy of social welfare, in part because the conditions and assumptions of economic growth are no longer valid. Yet the academic purpose and task of social administration itself still remain to be clarified and, I believe, Titmuss's agenda still remains to be addressed.

Conclusions

Post–war social administration began as a study of British social services and the human needs and social problems to which they were a response. Given its focus on concrete British problems and practices, the idea of the study of the 'social policy' underlying them was slow to develop. During the Titmuss years, social administration did not differentiate between the study of social welfare policy *in general* (theory) and the British social services *in particular* (practice). At the end of the 1960s the focus of attention was still very much on Britain.

Overall, the academic tradition of social administration has been pragmatic, Britain-centred, socially concerned, and empirical. The political, economic and social context in which the social services functioned was recognized as important in a general way but was not seen as a part of the subject, which was primarily concerned with the policies, provisions and practices of specific social services. Under Titmuss's influence, some inroads into the wider context were made, but largely in an ad hoc way. The meliorist-Fabian framework remained hegemonic if not monopolistic, and the boundaries of the discipline remained narrowly circumscribed.

In terms of developing a theory of social welfare, Titmuss's contribution was probably the most significant feature of this period. His originality, inventiveness, and ability to make connections where others saw none, opened up new horizons and created a sense of excitement around a subject not exactly renowned for that quality. At the same time, much of Titmuss's work was ad hoc, eclectic, and above all, improvized. Many of his insights and contributions had a 'will-o'-the-wisp' quality; after a sudden flare-up, the darkness returned. His work was truly exploratory and pioneering in nature. There is often the sense of a commando-style raid on some uncharted territory with improvized equipment and ammunition. But after a successful and sometimes spectacular raid, the party would invariably withdraw. The new territory was seldom annexed and rarely colonized. From a disciplinary perspective, then, there was a great deal of charisma but little routine.

The social administration tradition has not been systematic or theoretical. It did not seek to locate the study of social welfare within a broader social structure, much less attempt to investigate the political economy of democratic-welfare-capitalism. Its approach was idealist and reformist, with little grounding in economic, political or social structures of society. No wonder it was difficult for the discipline to cope with the political and economic problems of the British welfare state when times got worse.

New tasks need new orientations. But of what kind? Perhaps the lesson of the Titmuss years is that commitment to welfare and social change needs to be matched by an equally strong commitment to conceptual and theoretical development. Given the exigencies of academic division of labour and other institutional considerations, however, can social administration really take up such a challenge?

Notes

1 Quoted in D. Winch, *Economics and Policy: A Historical Survey* (London: Fontana Books, 1972), p. 64.
2 ibid., p. 206.
3 Richard Titmuss, *Social Policy* (London: Allen & Unwin, 1974), pp. 57–8; D. V. Donnison and V. Chapman *et al., Social Policy and Administration* (London: Allen & Unwin, 1965), pp. 26, 27.
4 See e.g. M. Brown, *Introduction to Social Administration in Britain* (London: Hutchinson, 1969), and T. H. Marshall, *Social Policy* (London: Hutchison, 1965) both of which are excellent introductions to the field in their own right and were far more analytical than was usual in the literature of the 1950s.
5 See e.g. 'Trends in social policy: health' (1959) in R. M. Titmuss,

Commitment to Welfare (London: Allen & Unwin, 1968). See also Donnison *et al.*, op. cit., Chapter 2 for an excellent overview of the variety of influences on the development of social welfare in Britain.

6   In R. M. Titmuss, *Essays on 'The Welfare State'* (London: Allen & Unwin, 1959), pp. 34–55.

7   R. M. Titmuss, *Income Distribution and Social Change* (London: Allen & Unwin, 1962).

8   D. A. Reisman, *Richard Titmuss* (London: Heinemann, 1977), pp. 9, 14–15, 173–4.

9   Titmuss, *Social Policy*, op. cit., and Chapter 2.

10 Reisman, *Richard Titmuss*, op. cit. pp. 173–4.

11 See e.g. B. Abel-Smith and P. Townsend, *The Poor and the Poorest* (London: Bell, 1965); P. Townsend, 'The meaning of poverty' *British Journal of Sociology* XIII (3), 1962; P. Townsend, *The Last Refuge* (London: Routledge & Kegan Paul, 1962).

12 M. Rein, *Social Science and Public Policy* (Harmondsworth: Penguin, 1976), pp. 78–9.

13 See e.g. Titmuss, *Income Distribution and Social Change*, op. cit. Chapter 9; Titmuss, 'The irresponsible society' in *Essays on 'the Welfare State'*, op. cit.; Titmuss, 'Introduction' to R. H. Tawney, *Equality* (London: Allen & Unwin, 1964); B. Abel-Smith, 'Whose welfare state?' in N. Mackenzie (ed.), *Conviction* (London: McGibbon and Kee 1958).

14 See e.g., P. Townsend, *The Family Life of old People* (London: Routledge & Kegan Paul, 1957); E. Shanas, P. Townsend *et al.*, *Old People in Three Industrial Societies* (London: Routledge & Kegan Paul, 1968).

15 See note 4 above.

16 Titmuss, 'The teaching of social administration' in *Commitment to Welfare*, op. cit., p. 22.

17 R. Pinker, *Social Theory and Social Policy* (London: Heinemann, 1971), p. 5.

18 See note 3 above.

19 On the 'field' vs. 'discipline' debate see J. Carrier and I. Kendall 'Social administration as social science' in H. Heisler (ed.) *Foundations of Social Administration* (London: Macmillan, 1977), pp. 25–32, which rejects the view of the subject as a 'field' and looks at it as a 'social science' concerned with the study of welfare activity of societies; A. J. Culyer, 'Economics, social policy and social administration: the interplay between topics and disciplines' *Journal of Social Policy* 10 (3), July 1981, pp. 311–29, for an enlightening discussion of relevant issues which sees topic (i.e. a field or area of study) and discipline as more like roles rather than attributes of an academic subject.

20 'The teaching of social administration' in Titmuss, *Commitment to Welfare*, op. cit. p. 23.

21 P. Wilding, 'Richard Titmuss and social welfare', *Social and Economic Administration* 10 (3), autumn 1976, pp. 147–66; R. Pinker 'Preface' to Reisman, *Richard Titmuss*, op. cit. p. xvi; H. Rose, 'Rereading Titmuss', *Journal of Social Policy* 10 (4), October 1981, p. 480.

22 V. George and P. Wilding, *Ideology and Social Welfare* (London: Routledge & Kegan Paul, 1976); A. Forder, *Concepts in Social Administration* (London: Routledge & Kegan Paul, 1974); I. Gough, *The Political Economy of the Welfare State* (London: Macmillan, 1979); J. Parker, *Social Policy and Citizenship* (London: Macmillan, 1975); G. Room, *The Sociology of Welfare* (Oxford: Martin Robertson, 1979); E. Wilson, *Women and the Welfare State* (London: Tavistock, 1977).

4 *Social work and social policy in the twentieth century: retrospect and prospect*

ROBERT PINKER

Introduction

The relationship between social administration and social work has been more like a marriage of convenience than a case of love at first sight, and their relationship with other social sciences is reminiscent of the Reverend Sydney Smith's description of marriage as a relationship which 'resembles a pair of shears, so joined that they cannot be separated; often moving in opposite directions, yet always punishing anyone who comes between them'.

It is in the nature of an applied social science to put ideas to practical use in the study and resolution of social problems and the enhancement of social welfare. The intellectual history of social administration and social work has been shaped by the process of developing the various policies which led to the creation of the protective institutions known as the welfare state. There have also been times when policy-making has been influenced by social investigation.

It is difficult to give precise dates for the historical transition from the safety net system of residual welfare agencies to the institutional system of statutory social services, but by the time the First World War broke out a basic framework of statutory welfare institutions was firmly established in Britain. This process vastly extended the subject field of social policy and administration.

By contrast, social work at the end of the nineteenth century was already a major force, albeit in a modest welfare system, but subsequently, even though it acquired a statutory dimension, its growth rate was dwarfed by the rapid expansion of the other major social services. The significance of these developments can be gauged from their effects on the client constituencies of social administration and social work. Social security, health care and education became universalist services and they directly affected the lives of almost all citizens, and public housing provided accommodation for nearly one in every three households. Growth on this scale made these statutory services an integral part of the nation's political economy, thereby strengthening the intellectual links between institutions of work and institutions of welfare and also between economic and social policies. Social work, on the other hand, is still almost exclusively concerned with the most depenent and least economically successful minority groups in the population and British social work, like its clients, has become steadily more isolated from the political economy of the nation.

The historical perspective

The discipline of social administration developed alongside the first of the organized empirical inquiries into the social problems of the early nineteenth century. In reviewing the history of applied social research in Britain, Martin Bulmer settles on the 1830s as the period when 'adequate scientific methods for social enquiry were first developed' (Bulmer, 1981, p. 37). Although the Royal Commision on the Poor Laws of 1832–34 was methodologically deficient in most respects, it served nevertheless 'to distinguish social enquiry from policy-making', thereby giving the former 'an impetus within the sphere of government which was soon followed up' (Bulmer, 1981, p. 40). Thereafter the findings of successive social inquiries into the sanitary conditions and housing of the urban poor or the relationship between disease and destitution, for example, added authority to the case for increasing government intervention and stirred the pragmatic inclinations of leading utilitarian thinkers and administrators.[1]

Empirical methods and a general distrust of theory characterized the development of applied social research throughout the nineteenth century, and from the 1880s onwards there was a 'strong historical continuity' which ran from the pioneering surveys of Booth and Rowntree to the major undertakings of the Webbs and Bowley and the early initiatives of the General Register Office and on into the present (Bulmer, 1982, p. 9 *et passim*).

The closeness of the links between social reform, political activity and social policy research gave the emerging discipline its strongly empirical character. It also helps to explain why the subject took so long to develop a range of testable theories. This trend has changed in recent years; social administration has added theoretical awareness to its methodological strengths and it has entered into a closer relationship with the other social sciences.

Although social work, like social administration, is closely identi-fied with the growth of the British welfare state, there are two important differences. First, despite its longstanding institutional links with social administration, social work was slow to develop a scientific research capability, and social work theory is rarely presented in testable forms. Secondly, although most social workers are employed in welfare bureaucracies, the profession has always been ill at ease with the administrative ethos. Its relationship to bureaucracy is as equivocal as its relationship to the academic community, particularly where other social sciences are concerned. At some point in its history, unlike social policy, social work appears to have drifted away from the tradition of scientific and administrative rationality which figures so strongly in the develop-ment of the British welfare state.

Yet there was a time when social work had a powerful voice in the arena of social welfare on questions such as the delineation of collective, familial and individual responsibility. The history of modern social work begins with the foundation of the Charity Organisation Society (COS) in 1869, a time when voluntary giving was dramatically on the increase (Mowat, 1961). The Society's approach to social policy is sometimes associated with doctrines of classical political economy and competitive individualism, but these persuasions could not be attributed to the Bosanquets who were the philosophical driving force of the COS. If there was any coherent theory informing the Society's hostility to government interven-tion, it came from Bernard Bosanquet's conceptualization of the role of the state. This, he felt, should be limited to 'creating the conditions in which individual citizens would be able to develop their own characters and thereby discover a collective sense of purpose'. In his opinion 'the potential power of the human mind was such that, given the right incentives, it would usually enable the individual to rise above adverse circumstances' (Pinker, 1987; McBriar, 1987; Bosanquet, 1925).

The Bosanquets' views on the relationship between character and social structure brought them into conflict with the Webbs, 'who believed that, while character was important, the greater part of poverty was caused by deficiencies in the social structure'. 'There was substance in both approaches to the problem of poverty, although the Webbs perhaps came closer to striking the right balance between character and social structure.' A. M. McBriar does not see the debate between the Bosanquets and the Webbs as a conflict between individualists and collectivists, and I agree with him. 'The Bosanquets and the Webbs were equally critical of neo-classical economics and eager to develop new forms of sociology and social economics which would express a more organic and co-operative view of social life' (Pinker, 1987, p. 1185).

In stressing the importance of self-help and familial responsibility the COS was in step with the economic values of late nineteenth-century Britain. At the same time there was a collectivist dimension in the Society's approach to social welfare which is exemplified by its participation in the Settlement movement and its confident assumption that the social classes would find common cause in public service and community work (Meacham 1987). This tradition has survived in modern social work, along with the development of individualized forms of social casework, in which the COS had a pioneering role.

Nevertheless the Society contributed little of any lasting value to social research. Its leading members were stronger on moral theorizing than on scientific method and their claim to be practitioners of 'scientific charity' rested on a combination of general ethical principles and a record of practical experience derived from agency work of various kinds. The opprobrium which the COS finally incurred is largely attributable to the Society's preoccupation with the personal causes of need at a time when the structural causes were so manifest and when there was no such thing as a safety net of social services. Indeed I would say that the fundamental defect in the society's approach was its assumption that personal deficiencies of character were the *major* cause of dependency. The mass of evidence so meticulously collected in the course of its 'casework' investigations was used not to test the Society's hypotheses about the causation of need but to vindicate them.

It can be argued that in the subsequent development of social administration and social work the old COS prejudices about people's characters and personal causes of need have been replaced by new ones – a profound reluctance to attribute personal responsibility or blame to anyone who is in need and undue preoccupation with the structural causes of need. The merest suggestion that there may be people with a marked preference for idleness and improvident lifestyles who run the risk of destitution – and deservedly so – is enough to send a shiver of apprehension through the collective psyche of social administrators and social workers.

The influence of the COS survived, however, in the development of the earliest forms of training in social work. In 1903 a School of Sociology was established under the Society's direction. This new institution was in fact a school of social work. In 1912 – on the brink of closure – it was transferred, with a generous grant from the Ratan Tata Foundation, to the London School of Economics. There it became the chief concern of the Department of Social Science. When the LSE assumed complete responsibility for it in 1919, the department became the Department of Social Science and Administration (Woodroofe, 1974, p. 24 and 47; Titmuss, 1958, p. 15).

It is unclear why the new department was not named after social work, which was by then its main subject. Nevertheless this pattern was copied in other universities during the inter–war years, social work was incorporated into higher education largely under the aegis of social administration, although it was not until the early 1960s that social administration was widely taught as a degree subject in its own right. Within this strange marriage of academic convenience the two disciplines followed increasingly divergent courses. The academic reputations of the new university departments were built on research in social administration, while the social work courses concentrated on raising standards of professional practice and establishing close working relations with employer agencies.

Despite its lack of background research, social work teaching drew on a growing range of theories which were relevant to professional practice. By contrast, social administration generated an impressive research capability, while its leading teachers remained indifferent or even hostile to theory – with the exception of T. H. Marshall, who was Head of Department at the LSE from 1944 to 1950 (Marshall, 1981, p. 15 *et passim*). Only recently has social work begun to develop its own research tradition.

From social casework to genericism

Early forms of casework intervention rested on a model of human nature in which the will to recovery and the capacity for self-determination are universal human characteristics. In that context the science (or art) of good social work was to locate or revive those attributes when they appeared to be missing or enfeebled. The collapse of this orthodoxy began in the late nineteenth century with the development of the settlement movements, which drew many social workers and community workers into direct and continuous contact with the realities of working-class life. New perspectives on the causes of poverty and social injustice were also offered by Marxism and democratic socialism, but at the time they gained little purchase on the imagination of social workers. The gradual metamorphosis of social work from interventions based on confident moral judgements and positive assumptions about human rationality into a less judgemental form of therapeutic intervention was an altogether more complex and subtle process.

Take, for example, the work of Mary Richmond in the United States during the second and third decades of the present century. In Richmond's view of social casework, the process of intervention took account of both social and personal causes of need, and the process itself was carefully structured in accordance with the functions and capacity of the social worker's agency. Richmond's *Social Diagnosis*, which was published in 1917, describes not only the first steps towards integrating the knowledge and skills pertaining to social work but even more ambitious attempts to incorporate sociological knowledge and research methodology into the therapeutic enterprise (Richmond, 1965). Nevertheless Richmond's approach has been criticized for its lack of a psychodynamic dimension and the attendant benefits of Freudian insight.

In her comments on the psychodynamic schools of thought after the First World War, when they took hold, Woodroofe suggests that in the United States they encouraged 'a swing away from the socio-economic determinism of the previous era to the psychological determinism of the 1920s, and in England a decade later, were to temper the content and emphasis of social workers' thinking about family and individual problems' (Woodroofe, 1974, p. 121). In retrospect, however, it is clear that Woodroofe exaggerated the impact on British social work practice of what she calls 'the psychiatric deluge'.

We should remember that throughout the inter-war years the links between scholarship and practice in social work were tenuous and in many parts of the country non-existent. As Younghusband pointed out, as late as the 1950s 'No training was available for the vast majority of social workers in the health and welfare fields unable to go to university' (Younghusband, 1978, p. 218; Seebohm Report, 1968, Appendix M, p. 336; Birch Report, 1976; Leaper Report, 1980).[2]

Before Seebohm, social work was a fragmented occupation in terms of the main centres of training, the division of training responsibilities, the variety of specialized qualifications and the numerous employment and agency settings. As Brian Heraud points out, these factors constituted 'a barrier to the passing on of an integrated set of attitudes to the profession' and to the creation of what he describes as 'a full professional culture' (Heraud, 1970, p. 237).

It is therefore misleading to talk about a 'psychiatric deluge' affecting the practice of social work as a whole. More accurately, certain very small but highly specialized and relatively influential groups of social workers became the major exponents of psychodynamic theories in British social work during the inter–war years. Their impact on the development of British social work has, in turn, been exaggerated, partly because the leading members of these groups dominated the key professional associations and partly because the psychodynamic paradigm was not seriously challenged within social work at the time.

Freud's findings and the subsequent development of his theories offered a new range of insights and therapeutic possibilities to lay practitioners working in many different welfare settings. Freud's mechanistic theory of the mind, for example, as a piece of psychic apparatus was essentially deterministic and, in so far as it attributed an important role of unconscious mental processes, it was a challenge to traditional forms of social work intervention which took rationality and free will for granted, and hence the attribution of praise and blame (Woodroofe, 1974, pp. 124–5; Freud, 1955; Wollheim, 1971; Rycroft, 1972; Yelloly, 1980). Yelloly distinguishes between the period before the Second World War when, in her view, the extent of the psychoanalytic influence was exaggerated and the years after the mid–1950s in which it has probably been underestimated. She defines psychoanalysis and psychodynamic theories as theories deriving from Freud 'which stress the import-ance of unconscious mental processes and which involve acceptance of such central psychoanalytic concepts as transference and resist-ance' (Yelloly, 1980, pp. 2–3 and 4 *et passim*).

The new respect for unconscious processes and subjective experi-ence constituted a psychodynamic legacy which still determines the orientation of social casework, holding it apart from the empirical tradition of social administration and also keeping it separate from the academic community. For many years psychoanalysis provided the major theoretical frame of reference for social work, but it also put the emerging discipline in double jeopardy. In the first place the most telling criticism of psychoanalysis itself is that its claim to scientific status is undermined by its failure to comply with Popper-ian standards of falsifiability or at least to develop testable theories based on experimental methods. Secondly, the long association between psychoanalysis and social work has tended to distance social work from social administration and even from social psy-chology.

Rycroft argues that Freud was misguided in calling psychoanaly-sis a 'scientific' form of psychology since psychoanalysis is not causal theory and it is not carried out on the basis of experimental methods and representative samples of patients. Nevertheless he suggests that the whole question was approached in the wrong way: 'The analysts are claiming that analysis is what it is not and Eysenck is attacking it for failing to be what it has no need to be. And both parties are assuming that it is only the natural sciences which are intellectually respectable' (Rycroft, 1985, pp. 43–9). Rycroft refuses to make any sharp divisions between reason and the imagination or to construct a hierarchical model of knowledge and understanding in which one must be inferior to the other.

There were other post-Freudian revisionists who had greater influence than Rycroft on social work teaching and practice in the post–war years, notably John Bowlby and David Winnicott, who provided new insights into the processes of separation, loss and change. (Bowlby, 1982; Winnicott, 1958). There were also other theoretical developments within social work during the two decades following the Second World War. Apart from the work of Bowlby and Winnicott, the contributions of Robinson, Taft and Smalley and Perlman's formulation of the 'problem-solving' approach all add a stronger social dimension to traditional casework. Although they had the effect of broadening the role and tasks of social work, these new approaches were sufficiently specific in aim to act as conceptual forerunners of subsequent forms of task-centred social work and the case review methods of intervention pioneered by Goldberg, Fruin and others in the early 1970s (Robinson and Taft, 1944; Smalley, 1967; Perlman, 1957; Roberts and Nee, 1970). However, the effectiveness of the practice based on this social work theorizing was insufficiently evaluated. The continuing lack of an empirical research tradition in social work left an intellectual vacuum which was all too readily filled with abstract models and macro-theories which became increasingly grandiose as they paid less and less attention to the relationship between ends, means and resources. This split between theory, practice and research methodology created a climate in which policy-making in social work became a needs-led rather than a resource-determined enterprise.

The new theoretical initiatives of the 1950s and 1960s became the intellectual raw material of the generic movement, which was already gaining influence in the early 1950s. The essence of the generic approach is that there is a range of common needs and 'universal human realities' (Younghusband, 1978, Vol. 1, p. 247) which call for the development of a common core of knowledge, values and skills with which to equip social workers to practise all the main methods of intervention, with reference to all the major needs groups and in all the major practice settings as required. Genericism is not so much a theory as a voyage of discovery in search of the essential core and boundaries of a professional identity. The generic notion of a boundary, however, is rather nebulous because it is unrelated to mundane considerations such as the finite nature of resources, administrative capacity and professional effectiveness.

In most other applied social sciences knowledge advances in a piecemeal way; theories are put to the test and modified or disposed of accordingly. In social work during the 1960s and 1970s various theories were advanced, amplified and merged into each other on syncretic principles in the search for an all-encompassing ideal. The Seebohm-inspired reforms of 1970–71 had the twofold effect of creating a new administrative framework to serve as a testing ground for the generic agenda and of revolutionizing the institutional relationship between social administration and social work in the context of social welfare outside higher education. Within the universities the marriage of convenience between the two disciplines had been characterized by the partners leading separate lives in the same establishment; after Seebohm – in daily practice at least – they were compelled to share the same bed.

The prologue to Seebohm

The intellectual prologue to the Seebohm Report begins in 1947 with the publication of the first Carnegie Report, undertaken by Eileen Younghusband, who was by then already on the staff at the LSE (Younghusband, 1947). Younghusband formulated three over-riding policy objectives, to create a university-based centre for social work education and research, to convert social work into a research-led profession and to identify what Kathleen Jones describes as 'a core and a periphery' defining the intellectual and professional character of social work (Jones, 1984, p. 51).

Younghusband had long been critical of the administratively fragmented and specialized character of social work and she was searching for a conceptual framework on which to build a unified profession. In 1951, when her second Carnegie Report was published, she was already engaged in introducing a new kind of social work training programme into her department (Younghusband, 1951). At that time the social work section of the department accurately reflected the divided nature of professional social work training on specialist lines throughout the country. There was a mental health course, established since 1929, and a separate child care course, established since 1948. (Probation students took their training at Rainer House.) The department was also home to a personnel management course which was later transferred to the Industrial Relations Department.[3]

There were other features of the organization and status of the department which made it fairly representative of fellow departments throughout the country. Donnison reminds us that in the mid–1950s social administration did not enjoy high academic standing as a university subject. This was particularly evident at the LSE, where it suffered from being associated and sometimes confused with social work. The good reputation of the social work staff was based on their professional expertise outside the school, not on their scholarly publications, and while teaching in social administration increasingly involved co-operation with other departments in the school, the social work courses were not fully integrated into their own departmental activities, let alone those of the rest of their academic community (Donnison *et al.*, 1975, pp. 256–7).[4] As Donnison observes, the continuous liaison between social work staff and external practice agencies and central and local government departments also reinforced the impression that social work 'led a precarious existence within the School' and that its centre of gravity lay outside academic life (Donnison *et al.*, 1975, p. 257).

Titmuss's decision to back Younghusband's plans for a new applied social studies course and to make her its director was taken in the knowledge that other social work teachers, notably Kay McDougall who ran the mental health course, and Clare Britton, who ran the child care course, were hostile to the scheme. Although McDougall and Britton were as committed as Younghusband to the idea of a unified profession, they also believed in the effectiveness of specialist training. McDougall thought that case conferences and the institution of a professional association were the key to fostering co-operation within social work. Once she had secured a grant from the Carnegie Trust for a short-term experimental course, however, Younghusband took study leave at the Chicago School of Social Work. There she came under the influence of Professor Charlotte Towle, whose work was centred round the identification of a core of basic social work skills and social knowledge which were generally relevant to a wide range of human needs and crises. It was this emphasis on a common core of skills and knowledge which gave generic social work – and the new course – their distinctive character. As Donnison suggests, it represented 'a new kind of professional education which would equip students to work in a variety of fields, rather than specialist training to work (often as junior partners) in one field' (Donnison *et al.*, 1975, p. 270).

Younghusband also attached great importance to the need for training in agency management and research for social work students and, as Jones points out, these interests 'brought her much closer to the Social Administration viewpoint than to the preoccupations of the casework teachers, which were primarily psychoanalytic' (Jones, 1984, p. 58). It may be that Titmuss had planned to back the new applied social studies course in the hope that it would increase the academic unity of the department, yet there was a sense in which Younghusband had no real affinity with either side of the department. She was not a qualified social worker and other members of the social work staff rejected her views on professional training. At the same time, as Jones observes, she was never truly a part of the social administration tradition either. 'She was, herself, uniquely a specialist in the social policy of social work' (Jones, 1984, p. 72).

The outcome of the conflict which followed is part of the folklore of social work. Titmuss eventually decided on the advice of his colleagues to merge the three social work courses into a single generic programme under the direction of Kay McDougall. Younghusband resigned and her course co-tutor, Kate Lewis, also resigned within the year. However, not only did the new applied social studies course survive but the generic approach which it pioneered was to become the cardinal principle in the teaching and practice of professional social work throughout the UK. The fact that the Central Council for Education and Training in Social Work decided, soon after its establishment in 1971, to hinge course validation on acceptance of the generic approach led to the rapid adoption of genericism, which became universal in the UK by the end of the 1970s.

Some good may have come out of the 'long drawn out agony of debate' which temporarily split this department during the mid–1950s. For example the fact that our social work courses are now so closely integrated into the activities of the department and of the school perhaps owes something to our shared memory of the upheavals which can be caused when a sub-discipline isolates itself from the mainstream of academic life. When we look beyond the personalities to the underlying academic principles, Titmuss's compromise appears inevitable – a single course leading to a common qualification, with specialist endorsements for different branches of social work. Given the resources needed to run three small, separate programmes, it might have been possible to carry out a controlled study of the respective merits of the generic course and the two specialist courses. As it is, neither side in the dispute had sufficient evidence to match the partisanship of its claims.

After more than thirty years in the universities the advocates of traditional specialists casework had failed to produce any convincing evidence as to the effectiveness of their approach. The path-breaking evaluative studies of Meyer, Borgatta and Jones, Mullen and Dumpson and J. Fischer were yet to come and, when they were published in the late 1960s and early 1970s, they proved highly critical of most of the interventive methods studied (Meyer *et al.*, 1969; Mullen and Dumpson, 1972; Fischer, 1978). Research on the effectiveness of generic social work was similarly sparse and the literature on the subject amounted to little more than a number of interesting and optimistic but untested hypotheses. In effect the department had been given a choice between two pigs in two separate pokes.

The lessons learned were not forgotten thereafter. Social work research in the department steadily increased and improved, and new common courses were developed to suit both the social work and social administration programmes. By 1978 when a Chair of Social Work Studies was created at the school, much of the recovery and reintegration of the social work side of the department had been accomplished, and in such a way as to preserve the distinctive character of the professional courses, thanks largely to the exemplary leadership of Zofia Butrym, the senior social work tutor during the difficult years of transition.

The postscript to Seebohm

The Seebohm Report gave social work a new mandate whose potential scope more than matched the optimism of the period, and the subsequent reorganization of the personal social services created an administrative structure within which all things seemed possible. However, in addition to its failure to address the resource implications of its proposals, the Report was largely devoid of guidance on the types of theory and practice skills needed for the tasks ahead. Nevertheless there was not much likelihood that social casework and its various psychodynamic offshoots would fit easily into the activities of the new social services departments, which were dominated by an administrative ethos and committed to a wide range of objectives involving groups and local communities and the provision of material support as well as personal counselling.

The post-Seebohm gap between aims and resources was never to be closed but a fortuitous stream of new social work theories soon purported to fill the intellectual vacuum in genericism. In 1973 Alan Pincus and Anne Minahan published *Social Work Practice: Model and Method* and Howard Goldstein published *Social Work Practice: A Unitary Approach* (Pincus and Minahan 1973; Goldstein, 1973). Both of these books by American scholars were enthusiastically received by social work academics in Britain and it was not long before Specht, Vickery and others began to popularize the 'integrated' approach to social work (Specht and Vickery, 1977). Pincus and Minahan conceptualize social work in terms of 'systems theory', in which the potential scale of social work intervention encompasses four main systems – a change agent system including the social worker and his agency and employing authority; a client system including the client's family and all the other groups, organizations and local communities which might conceivably be direct or indirect beneficiaries of the social work intervention; a target system including the individuals, families, groups and local communities which are the potential objectives of the 'change agent' (social worker); and the action system, which describes all the people and the processes involved in bringing about change. The range of skills required by the social worker to meet this ambitious mandate includes social casework, group work and community work, with the emphasis throughout on the worker as an agent of *social* change.

Goldstein's book is also based on a systems model but his approach relies more explicitly on social learning and problem-solving. A three-dimensional frame of reference for social work intervention with no less than twenty-seven component parts makes up his 'unitary approach' to social work practice, and that by no means exhausts the complexities of Goldstein's grand design.

In commenting on these two major contributions to the conceptual framework of generic social work, Heraud observes that: 'A fundamental emphasis is ... placed upon the interdependence of variables in the system so that no one element is of greater significance than others, or is in any way a determining variable.' (Heraud, 1979, note 4, p. 123). It was this feature which limited the utility of these new approaches, both diagnostically and in the ordering of task priorities. It was not long before individual social workers found that they did not have the time, the skills or the resources to meet the daunting range of needs and tasks presented by these theories.

Nevertheless, because they extended the repertoire of social workers, systems theory and integrated methods had great appeal in the 1970s, when the British personal social services seemed to be on the brink of becoming accessible to every family and community in the land. More significantly, systems theory and integrated methods gave a semblance of intellectual credibility to the generic principle and a sense of professional unity to local authority social workers, and they were equally acceptable to senior local authority administrators, who had to make sense of the growing mixture of mandatory and permissive activities heaped on them by new legislation. It was a time in which expectations raced ahead of available resources and the Babel of universalist aspirations over-whelmed the language of priorities. When in the late 1970s economic realities began to intrude, serious damage had been done to the reputation of practical social work. Contrary to the confident expectations expressed in the Seebohm Report, the needs of long-neglected priority groups such as the elderly, the mentally ill and the physically handicapped had not been met, and a succession of tragic cases in child care had demonstrated that the precarious legacy of specialist expertise in that field had been dissipated in the pursuit of a generic utopia.

Systems theory and the integrated approach were welcomed by the Central Council and by many social work teachers, on the supposition that theories can be used to give a 'sustaining' frame-work to a curriculum. Although it is possible to put theories to this type of use, if it is done, the theories in question lose their provisional nature and turn into doctrines which are defended against all comers. At the same time Marxist theory became popular in some social work courses. The Marxist critique of conventional casework theory began in the late 1960s. Casework was accused of reprehensible activities such as 'political quietism', 'pathologizing the client' and 'sustaining unjust systems of social control and repression'. This was the beginning of 'radical' social work, in which the model of the social worker as an agent of change went further than it did in systems theory: this time it represented a direct challenge to the 'system' itself (Pinker, 1983, p. 163; Pateman 1972, pp. 7 and 261; Brake and Bailey, 1980; Bolger *et al.*, 1981; *Critical Social Policy*, 1981, p. 1; C. Jones, 1983).[5]

Although the radical approach has lost credibility in recent years it has had one unfortunate effect. In any system of social work practice the attribution of authority and accountability is based in law. The Marxist model of radical social work encourages resistance to definitions of social work which revolve around its statutory functions. This hostility is coincidentally shared by the traditional caseworkers, although their objections rest on the very different premise that social work is basically concerned with relationships. These elements of resistance to a legal emphasis in social work largely account for the persisting confusion over the definition of social work. The profession is torn between two equally diffuse paradigms: the casework model comprising a heterogeneous diversity of personal and professional relationships and the radical model which betokens an ever-widening range of social interventions.

The radical approach to social work has also introduced a spirit of egalitarianism which conflicts with professional 'elitism', except in the case of pay levels and terms of employment. Whatever the methodological deficiencies of the old casework tradition might have been, it was firmly committed to an idea of professional practice which was at the same time a central objective in Younghusband's view of the future. The marked change in professional attitudes over the past twenty years can be inferred from a comparison of the considered definition of social work given in the Younghusband Report of 1959 and the cursory dismissal of social casework in the Barclay Report of 1982 (Younghusband Report, 1959, paras 615–33; Barclay Report, 1982, paras 10–19). The trend towards the diffusion and dilution of skills is equally manifest in the Parsloe Report of 1983, in which it is argued that 'The distinction between social work and social services which has been relevant in the past now seems to us inappropriate'. (CCETSW, 1983, p. 3).

Nevertheless the Parsloe Report at least recommended that its proposed unitary system should be divided into an upper and lower level of qualification. The Younghusband Report, of course, had recommended a three-tier training hierarchy for work with 'straightforward and obvious needs', work with the 'more complex problems requiring systematic help from a trained social worker' and work with 'problems of special difficulty requiring skilled casework' (Younghusband Report, 1959, paras 558–602). This overtly elitist proposal would incur anathema now but, had it been adopted, it might have infused social work education and practice with just enough specialization to give backbone to the generic experiment.

Conclusion

There are, however, some more encouraging signs that social work is beginning to move away from a diffuse generic model to more focused forms of practice, that its research capability is steadily improving and that these two trends are interactive and mutually supportive. For example, there has been a gradual development of interest in task-centred social work practice deriving from Perlman's 'problem-solving' approach. Task-centred social work was pioneered by Reid, Shyne and Epstein in the late 1960s and early 1970s and it provided the conceptual basis of the work done throughout the 1970s by Goldberg and her colleagues on the development of a case review system . (Goldberg and Fruin, 1976; Goldberg and Stanley, 1979; Goldberg *et al.*, 1977; Goldberg and Warburton, 1979; Goldberg *et al* 1980; Goldberg *et al.* 1985).[6]

The growing acceptance of behavioural techniques in British social work is another cause for optimism. These techniques are exemplified in the work of Brian Sheldon and others (Raynor, 1984; Sheldon, 1984; Pinkston *et al.*, 1982; Bloom and Fischer, 1982; Sheldon, 1983) who use single case experimental designs in evaluation studies. Similar studies in behavioural social work have been conducted by Roger and Patricia McAuley with distressed children and their families, and by Barbara Hudson in the field of mental health (McAuley and McAuley, 1977; McAuley and McAuley, 1980; Herbert, 1981; Brown and Christie, 1981; Hudson, 1982). There have been normative objections to these behavioural initiatives, of course, on the grounds that social work is essentially a qualitative activity and that its effectiveness cannot be objectively measured. Also genericists have been quick to condemn the lack of a 'holistic' perspective in the therapeutic techniques of behaviour modification.

In answer to these objections there is no harm and possibly some good to be found by at least finding out what can be measured and the 'holistic' approach, far from complementing the principle of 'respect for persons', is all too often used as a licence for intrusion into the private lives of clients. In any event 'It is generally acknowledged that (behavioural) techniques are least effective in helping people with very longstanding problems of a chronic nature, the delinquent and poorly motivated and people who have severe personality problems. Similar limitations apply in the case of task-centred work' (Pinker, 1985, pp. 38–9). Nevertheless, both approaches encourage clearer thinking and greater specificity and realism in the definition of tasks and objectives, and are therefore more amenable to the systematic evaluation which is needed before the quality of practice can be improved. The work of the Personal Social Services Research Unit at the University of Kent should also be mentioned. The unit pioneered a major evaluative study of social work practice which has clearly demonstrated the positive links between specialization and improved effectiveness.

Unless resource units and the personal rule and tasks of social workers are clearly defined, their effectiveness in operation cannot be evaluated, in which case resources may be wasted and needs left unmet. As Brian Sheldon claims on the basis of twenty-eight controlled experiments, 'When social workers clearly identify target problems, work extensively with them, apply task-centred or behavioural approaches; help co-ordinate the other services concerned with an agreed and definite policy; adopt a contractual style with people they are trying to help; rehearse possible solutions to problems rather than just talking about them . . . then social work is likely to be effective' (Sheldon, 1985).

In the universities the intellectual links between social work and social administration are at last being reinforced and the bridge joining them in a common enterprise is the research tradition. There are still two reasons why social work may not survive as a university subject. First, there is the Seebohm legacy of administrative structures and policy objectives which were basically unhelpful to the development of good social work practice and evaluation. Secondly, there is the pervasive influence of the Central Council, whose virtual sanctification of genericism and whose insistent inroads into the work schedules of social work departments have constituted the biggest single impediment to social work's chance of becoming a research-led profession. It may be that the new Qualifying Diploma in Social Work will spark off a revival of specialist expertise in the final training year, although it seems doubtful that the curriculum of the first two years will be suficiently focused to provide the basis for it.

In conclusion I have no intention of limiting my definition of social work to measurable roles and tasks, but I would argue that in the interests of accountability, efficiency and the welfare of clients there are certain functions which call for precise definition and objective evaluation. We can begin by defining as core tasks of social work those which stem from legal duties and administrative requirements, without prejudice to the traditional counselling and supportive roles of social workers.

If we could reorganize social work on the basis of specialization by client group, the arbitrary distinctions between social work tasks and social service tasks and between field work, day care and residential care might become a thing of the past. It would then be feasible to construct a manageable two-tier programme of social work education which was logically related and made sensitive to the changing pattern of welfare needs and the progressive development of practitioner skills. As long as there is growth in the area of social work research, the association between social work and social administration will be strengthened and the possibly insulating effects of specialization outweighed.

Finally, we should consider what is perhaps the quintessence of social work: like social administration, social work is concerned with issues of collective justice and fairness, but above all it is a personal social service. Social workers spend a high proportion of their time working on problems affecting their clients' personal feelings to which standards of justice and fairness cannot usefully be applied. These include the irreversible losses and tragedies of human life, and those who deal with them obviously need special qualities and skills.

In the same way the primary focus of social work practice must be individuals in the context of their immediate kin and their personal problems, some of which are insoluble. In recent years continuous pressure to extend the remit of social work into communities and society as a whole and an increasingly structural view of social problems have distracted social workers from this central concern. If social workers continue to exaggerate the importance of community action and social change, we will need to reinvent the social work profession.

It seems obvious – to me at least – that problems of a personal nature do exist and that people are quite capable of being the architects of their own misery. If these propositions are false, the principles of 'self-determination' and 'respect for persons' are without foundation.

Social workers are used to coping with the conflicting tasks of care and control, but they also need to give equal attention to the uses of reason and imagination in both practical work and research. The relationship between social administration and social work suffered when the two disciplines fell victim to what the late Sir Peter Medawar described as the 'two widely prevalent diseases' of 'scientism' and 'poetism' (Medawar, 1984, p. 17). Medawar takes the Popperian line in his argument that reason and imagination are not alternative 'accounts of *one* process of thought' but 'accounts of *two* successive and complementary episodes of thought which occur in every advance of scientific understanding' (Medawar, 1984, p. 33).

There are signs at last that social administration and social work are developing a common research tradition which will uphold the complementary claims of reason and imagination, without impairing the distinctive character of their respective intellectual concerns. In this combined endeavour the universities can make a unique contribution to the betterment of the personal social services.

Notes

1 As I have suggested elsewhere, 'Many of those who sought to promote the principle of utility in legislation were soon drawn to favour the extension of state intervention in order to combat vested interests and cope with the new problems of industrial and urban growth. Leading public figures such as Senior, John Stuart Mill and Chadwick, who were to varying degrees of utilitarian outlook, did not hesitate to modify their individualism in response to practical considerations' (Pinker, 1971, p. 53).

2 The total number of people employed as social workers was low: as late as 1967 the Seebohm Committee found that there were just over 11,000 social workers employed across the whole range of the health, probation and personal social services, of whom roughly 40 per cent were professionally qualified. (These figures should be treated as approximations.)

3 There is scarcely a reference to the personnel management course in the several papers written about this period in the history of the department. Had personnel management drawn attention to itself as a related subject, the future pattern of social work education might have been

radically changed – if, for example, the traditionally exclusive relationship between social work and the social market had been extended to include the world of work and the economic market.

4 According to Donnison the social work courses 'were left almost entirely to the staff concerned with them: it was they who provided most of the teaching and arranged for the contributions made by other lecturers, who were drawn mainly from outside the School.'

5 Pateman's *Counter Course* is an interesting set of papers illustrating the growth in the range and variety of Marxist critiques of teaching in the social sciences which had taken place by the early 1970s. The preface begins by stating that 'We have produced this handbook for the use of students in higher education who find their courses boring, cramped by exams, methodologically unsound or with content politically obnoxious in its only possible real-world uses. In short, for students who find that their education consists of being processed for a particular niche in the class structure of society' (p. 7). The chapter on social workers by Crescy Cannon indicts both 'casework' and 'community' as reactionary, but argues that 'community work' is 'a better alternative to traditional casework' because it is a potential 'foundation for militant action' (p. 261).

In 1981 a new journal, *Critical Social Policy*, was set up to 'serve as a forum to encourage and develop an understanding of welfare from socialist, feminist and radical perspectives' and it invited support from 'the academic social science community' and from 'workers and practitioners in the Welfare State, particularly social workers, advice workers and the increasingly wide range of activists in all social services'. (p. 1).

6 The key paper formulating the Case Review System was published by Goldberg and Fruin in 1976.

References

Barclay Report, *Social Workers: Their Role and Tasks* (National Institute for Social Work: Bedford Square Press/NCVO, 1982).

Birch Report, *Manpower and Training for the Social Services*, Working Party Report: DHSS, 1976).

M. Bloom and J. Fischer, *Evaluating Practice: Guidelines for the Accountable Professional* (London: Prentice Hall, 1982).

S. Bolger, P. Corrigan, J. Docking and N. Frost, *Towards Socialist Welfare Work* (London: Macmillan, 1981).

B. Bosanquet, *The Philosophical Theory of the State* (London: Macmillan, 1925).

J. Bowlby, *Attachment and Loss*, Vol. 1, *Attachment* (London: Hogarth Press, 1982).

M. Brake and R. Bailey, *Radical Social Work and Practice* (London: Edward Arnold, 1980).

B. Brown and M. Christie, *Social Learning Practice in Residential Care* (London: Pergamon, 1981).

M. Bulmer, 'The British tradition of social administration: moral concerns at the expense of scientific rigour', *The Hastings Centre Report*, April 1981.

M. Bulmer, *The Uses of Social Research: Social Investigation in Public Policy-Making* (London: George Allen & Unwin, 1982).

Central Council for Education and Training in Social Work, *Report of the Council Working Group: Review of Qualification Training Policies* (Parsloe Report), paper 20.1, 1983.

D. Donnison, V. Chapman, M. Meacher, A. Sears and K. Urwin, *Social Policy and Administration Revisited* (London: George Allen & Unwin, 1975).

J. Fischer, *Effective Case Work Practice: An Eclectic Approach*, (London: McGraw Hill, 1978).

S. Freud, *The Complete Psychological Works*, Standard edition, (London: Hogarth Press, 1953).

E. Goldberg and D. Fruin 'Towards accountability in social work: a case review system for social workers', *British Journal of Social Work*, 6, (1), 1976.

E. Goldberg, R. Warburton, R. Lyons and R. Willmott 'Towards accountability in social work: one year's intake to an area office', *British Journal of Social Work*, 7 (3), 1977.

E. Goldberg and J. Stanley 'A task-centred approach to probation', in J. King, *Pressures and Changes in the Probation Service* (Cambridge: Institute of Criminology, 1979).

E. Goldberg and R. Warburton, *Ends and Means in Social Work: The Development and Outcome of a Case Review System for Social Workers* (London: Allen & Unwin, 1979).

E. Goldberg and S. Stanley with J. Kenrick, *Evaluating Task-Centred Casework in a Probation Setting* (London: National Institute for Social Work, 1980).

E. Goldberg, J. Gibbons and I. Sinclair, *Problems, Tasks and Outcomes: The Evaluation of Task-Centred Casework in Three Settings* (London: George Allen & Unwin, 1985).

H. Goldstein, *Social Work Practice: A Unitary Approach* (Columbia: South Carolina Press, 1973).

B. Heraud, *Sociology and Social Work: Perspectives and Problems* (London: Pergamon, 1970).

B. Heraud, *Sociology in the Professions* (London: Open Books, 1979).

M. Herbert, *The Behavioural Treatment of Problem Children* (London: Academic Press, 1981).

B. Hudson, *Social Work with Psychiatric Patients* (London: Macmillan, 1982).

C. Jones, *State Social Work and the Working Class* (London: Macmillan, 1983).

K. Jones, *Eileen Younghusband: A Biography*, Occasional Papers in Social Administration, 76 (London: Bedford Square Press/NCVO, 1984).

Leaper Report, *Setting a Target Date*, Report of a Study Group, Personal Social Services Council, 1980.

T. Marshall, *The Right to Welfare and Other Essays* (London: Heinemann Educational, 1981).

R. McAuley and P. McAuley 'The effectiveness of behaviour modification with families', *British Journal of Social Work*, 10, (1), 1980.

A. McBriar, *An Edwardian Mixed Doubles: The Bosanquets Versus the Webbs: A Study in British Social Policy, 1890–1929* (Oxford: Clarendon Press, 1987).

S. Meacham, *Toynbee Hall and Social Reform, 1880–1914: The Search for Community* (Yale: Yale University Press, 1987).

P. Medawar, *Pluto's Republic* (London: Oxford University Press, 1984).

H. Meyer, E. Borgatta and W. Jones, *Girls at Vocational High* (London: Sage, 1969).

C. Mowat, *The Charity Organisation Society, 1869–1913: Its Ideas and Work* (London: Methuen, 1961).

E. Mullen and J. Dumpson, *Evaluation of Social Work Intervention* (New York: Jossey-Bass, 1972).

T. Pateman, *Counter Course: A Handbook for Course Criticism* (Harmondsworth: Penguin, 1972).

H. Perlman, *Social Casework: A Problem Solving Approach* (Chicago: University of Chicago Press, 1957).

A. Pincus and A. Minahan, *Social Work Practice: Model and Method* Itasca, Illinois: Peacock, 1973).

R. Pinker, *Social Theory and Social Policy* (London: Heinemann Educational 1971).

R. Pinker, 'Social welfare and the education of social workers', in P. Bean and S. MacPherson, *Approaches to Welfare* (London: Routledge & Kegan Paul, 1983).

R. Pinker, 'The role of social work in dealing with societal stress', in *Social Work's Role in Dealing with Societal Stresses: Capabilities and Aspirations*, a Symposium, Paul Baerwald School of Social Work, the Hebrew University of Jerusalem, 1985.

R. Pinker, 'For the good of others', *The Times Literary Supplement*, 30 October–5 November 1987.

E. Pinkston, J. Levitt, G. Green, N. Linsk and T. Rzepnicki, *Effective Social Work Practice: Advanced Techniques for Behavioural Intervention with Individuals, Families and Institutional Staff* (New York: Jossey-Bass, 1982).

P. Raynor, 'Evaluation with one eye closed: the empiricist agenda in social work research', *British Journal of Social Work*, 14 (1), 1984.

M. Richmond, *Social Diagnosis* (New York: Free Press of Glencoe 1965).

R. Roberts and R. Nee, *Theories of Social Casework* (Chicago: University of Chicago Press, 1970).

V. Robinson and J. Taft, *A Functional Approach to Family Casework* (Pennsylvania: University of Pennsylvania Press, 1944).

C. Rycroft, *A Critical History of Psychoanalysis* (London: Nelson, 1972).

C. Rycroft, *Psychoanalysis and Beyond*, edited by P. Fuller (London: Chatto & Windus / Hogarth Press, 1985).

Seebohm Report, *Report of the Committee of Local Authority and Allied Personal Social Services*, Cmnd 3703, HMSO, 1968.

B. Sheldon, 'The use of single case experimental designs in the evaluation of social work', *British Journal of Social Work*, 13, (5), 1983.

B. Sheldon 'Evaluation with one eye closed: the empiricist agenda in social work research: a reply to Peter Raynor', *British Journal of Social Work*, 14 (4), 1984.

B. Sheldon, 'Yes, and the prospects are good', *Social Work Today*, October 1985.

R. Smalley, *Theory for Social Work Practice* (Columbia: Columbia University Press, 1967).

H. Specht and A. Vickery *Integrating Social Work Methods* (London: George Allen & Unwin, 1977).

R. Titmuss, *Essays on the Welfare State* (London: George Allen & Unwin, 1958).

D. Winnicott, *The Child, the Family and the Outside World* (London: Tavistock, 1958).

R. Wollheim, Freud (London: Fontana, 1971).

K. Woodroofe, *From Charity to Social Work in England and the United States* (London: Routledge & Kegan Paul, 1974).

M. Yelloly, *Social Work Theory and Psychoanalysis* (London: Van Nostrand, 1980).

E. Younghusband, *The Employment and Training of Social Workers* (Dunfermline: Carnegie United Kingdom Trust, 1947).

E. Younghusband, *Social Work in Britain* (Dunfermline: Carnegie United Kingdom Trust, 1951).

Younghusband Report, *Report of the Working Party on Social Workers in the Local Authority Health and Welfare Servcies* (Ministry of Health, Department of Health for Scotland: HMSO, 1959).

E. Younghusband, *Social Work in Britain, 1950–1975: A Follow-Up Study* (London: George Allen & Unwin, 1978).

5 Swimming against the tide: the prospects for social policy

HOWARD GLENNERSTER

One might be forgiven for producing a gloomy prognosis at this point in the subject and the Department of Social Science and Administration's history. Here is a subject and a department which many would see as embodying the very essence of collectivism at a time when the political climate has moved decisively against collective or social action. There may be a place for the study of social policy amongst historians, in the home of lost causes, but what real future does it have as a lively field of applied social science when the welfare state, its real focus of inquiry, is a wasting asset? That would, I believe, be a mistaken prognosis.

Rolling back the frontiers of the state?

First, although the rhetoric of a Conservative government has been that it is aiming to reduce the role of the state, in practice the scale of government intervention seems to be growing rather than diminishing. Let us take housing as an example. From the late nineteenth century governments have sought to fix minimum standards for human habitation above levels that a free market would generate. In Britain, for particular political and administrative reasons, this produced large-scale municipal housing projects, though it did not in other Western countries.

The present Conservative government sought to rid the state of this costly and poorly executed responsibility for owning a third of the nation's housing stock. It tried to sell houses at knock down prices to the tenants. It found to its surprise that two-thirds of these tenants had no income of their own and many others had very little hope of buying even at very low prices. They turned instead to a policy of diversified ownership. Tenants are to be able to opt for other landlords – 'approved' by central government, like housing associations. Even that may not be enough, so central government will step in to take over estates itself and create 'Housing Action Trusts' (Cmd. 214, 1987). Housing associations are now building at least as many houses as local authorities under a bewildering regime of grants (Hills, 1987). The state remains involved in setting the legal regime for private landlordism and, through its tax concessions, is a dominant force in the owner-occupied market. So, far from removing the state from the housing market, this government has steadily woven a more and more complex web of involvement.

Much the same story can, I think, be told of the government's social security policy. A major review was instituted aimed at reducing the scale of public expenditure by abolishing the state earnings-related pension scheme, extending the role played by private individual pension schemes and occupational or firm based ones, within statutory limits. Now we have *both* the state earnings-related pension scheme and an even more complex set of pension arrangements which are subject to government rule making.

The extension of private and voluntary provision in the personal social services is already requiring more monitoring and inspection. The interweaving of publicly provided social work services with informal neighbourly care, if it happens at all, will widen and complicate the net of statutory involvement. In education, the government's new proposals will centralize and extend political control (Glennerster, 1987).

What we are witnessing in Britain, I suggest, is not a rolling back of the frontiers of the state, but merely an elaboration of the forms which government intervention takes – a process government hopes will enable it to reduce actual public expenditure. Whether it will succeed remains to be seen. No country in Europe has been able to reduce its share of the gross national product devoted to social protection significantly in the last ten years since the oil crisis and in most this has increased (EEC, 1987). We may be seeing the break up of old forms of welfare statism (Johnson, 1987) and a more pluralistic form of welfare, but that is involving more extensive and complex kinds of social policy. The scale of the non-statutory, non-profit sector is growing. The scale of expenditure already matches the whole of the statutory personal social service sector without counting in the value of volunteers' time.

The central concern in this paper is the subject of social policy rather than its substance. The second strand of my argument is that this growing complexity of government has been matched by the academic study of social policy. It has been transformed in the past twenty-five years in a way that admirably fits it to analyse the new diversity we see emerging in the world of government.

Nevertheless, and this is my third theme, such academic variety has its dangers. If social policy is no longer merely the study of the welfare state, what is it? Hence, in the last part of this chapter I try to answer that question.

The transformation of a subject

It is possible, crudely of course, to distinquish four phases in the post–Second World War literature on social administration: pre-Titmuss; the influence of Titmuss; the critical reaction; divergence and reassessment.

THE PRE-TITMUSS TRADITION

The pre-Titmuss tradition, which chronologically continued long after he took up his Chair at the LSE contained three main kinds of writing.

(1)   Empirical work on social conditions, such as the extent of poverty, poor housing conditions, the problems of old age and dependency.
(2)   Accounts of the administrative and legal structures that delivered social services.
(3)   Historical descriptions of the development of services – mostly in the Whig tradition, explaining how the 1944–8 legislation had reached the summit of human achievement.

THE INFLUENCE OF TITMUSS

Titmuss influenced the subject both by the liberating power of his ideas and his position as head of the largest department of social administration in the country. He influenced the subject in three ways:

(1) He shifted the whole focus of policy analysis from a primary concern with public provision to the complementary and contradictory effects of the tax system and to a lesser extent occupational or firm-based welfare.
(2) He initiated critical and sceptical evaluations of the real policies of government, measuring performance against promise. How much income distribution was there? Did the 1957 Rent Act achieve its objectives? And many more.
(3) He and his followers were not afraid to be policy prescriptive. Most of the social policies of the 1960s and 1970s in Britain were influenced by one part of the LSE or the other.

THE CRITICAL REACTION

The critical reaction came in the years after Richard Titmuss's death, not least from people such as Professors Mishra and Pinker. Social administration, they argued:

(1) was not sufficiently grounded in the theoretical disciplines of sociology or economics;
(2) it was too ideologically narrow – Fabian to the core;
(3) it was narrowly ethnocentric – as two of our leading European experts put it: 'English analyses despite their descriptive richness are in a curious sense "culture bound".' (Flora and Heidenheimer, 1981);
(4) it took no account of the economic effects of welfare provision or of economic constraints.

Yet, as so often when such academic criticisms are made, it was precisely then that the subject was changing fast. A large body of theoretical literature drawing on sociology, social history, economics and political theory came to dominate our reading lists. The ideological frameworks diverged as Marxists, New Right, and pluralist advocates rewrote the texts. The economic changes of the mid 1970s made a large impact so that almost every book you picked up seemed to have some variant of 'crisis' in the title. International comparative treatment of the subject blossomed, and feminist work turned many of the old assumptions on their heads and produced a whole new set of questions.

DIVERGENCE AND REASSESSMENT

Looking back at the first social policy reading lists I compiled for students in the mid 1960s shows how very different a subject we taught then. Reading was dominated by Royal Commission and Advisory Committee Reports, a fairly narrow range of authors, Fabian and the occasional Institute of Economic Affairs pamphlets. The study of State Welfare in Britain dominated. Of course, we propounded Titmuss's threefold division of welfare, (Titmuss, 1958) the effect of tax allowances and the scope of occupational welfare, but they were still seen as secondary. Child tax allowances were a problem precisely because they were not statutory cash benefits.

Today we look back on Titmuss's categories and see that they were only a partial glimpse at the full spectrum of social policy. It is not simply that the tax system provides a parallel form of benefits to cash welfare, but that, as Piachaud's work has shown, the tax structure and the income-related benefit structures interact, become cumulative, and both interact with work as a source of income and welfare. Both affect the economic behaviour of individuals and households. It is a story that becomes even more complex when we take into account work *in* the home as well as *outside* it, yet we have to do so if we are to gain any real understanding of what consequences may follow changes in tax or benefit levels (Piachaud, 1987).

It is not just that firms provide their own sickness and pension schemes. What we are concerned with is a multitude of ways in which individuals' income streams are manipulated through time to try to ensure a degree of income security in times of adversity, all of which are affected by the government's tax regimes, regulations and benefit provisions. Moreover some individuals' capacity to arrange their incomes to gain security is vastly greater than others, especially in periods of much higher unemployment than those we thought tenable in the 1960s.

I can find no reference to unemployment on my reading lists of twenty years ago. Now it features in a large way. A multiplicity of government agencies and programmes seek to make and regulate work for the young and we discuss the relationship between benefit levels and incentives to seek employment. Once again government's withdrawal from Keynesian macro-economic policy has vastly increased the scale and complexity of potential and actual governmental intervention. The distribution and creation of work in our societies is now a major social policy issue. It cannot be left to either economic planners or to the markets alone.

Again, take the concept of community care. Twenty years ago there was little or no reference on our syllabus to the family as carer, or who it was in the family who did the caring. Now we have a rich and growing literature: in this tradition Jane Lewis and Barbara Meredith (1988) have just produced a study that examines some of the motives, the strains and the rewards of caring as described by daughters who cared for their mothers.

Sally Sainsbury has just completed a fascinating account of the way in which a local authority discharged its duty (or failed) to inspect standards in a private home for the deaf over twenty years. Martin Bulmer (1986, 1987) has given us considerable cause for reflection in his analysis of the opportunities for and constraints upon care and support by neighbours and 'the community' and the problems involved in interweaving family, professional and informal care. Not only are we concerned with diverse forms of providing care but also with the diverse ways we can finance it (Glennerster, 1985).

Or take the issue of poverty which the LSE was founded to study. To consider poverty excluding a Third World perspective is now inconceivable. The adjustment of the world economy to the two successive oil price shocks and the subsequent world recession has thrust many developing economies and more of their population into deprivation of a kind that makes our debates about how to define poverty seem mere academic nit-picking (Cornia, Jolly and Stewart, 1987). European governments' economic and social policies interact in ways we have only begun to appreciate.

Too wide a canvas?

The subject has come far in the last twenty years and has exploded its original boundaries – both intellectual and geographical. Explosions can be destructive as well as liberating. To change the metaphor, perhaps the canvas has become so vast as to become incomprehensible. The definition of social policy may have become 'the world, the universe and everything', and is consequently nothing. There is a real danger that the subject will become too vast and incoherent. Yet the answer should not lie in any attempt to draw restrictive boundaries round the subject at this point. I recall John Stuart Mill's attempt to define the boundaries of 'Political Economy' in the middle of the nineteenth century. A useless task, he concluded. It was like trying to build a city wall around a prosperous town. Once you succeed you knew the city was dead. Yet though we may not want to draw predetermined boundaries for the subject we do need a set of questions which provide the starting point for our intellectual journeys.

Redefining our starting point

The starting point *cannot* be the study of a set of institutions at a point in time in a particular country. Yet in his inaugural lecture as the first Professor of Social Administration in 1951, Richard Titmuss, came pretty close to saying just that. 'Social Administration may broadly be defined as the study of the social services' (Titmuss, 1958, p. 14). Yet, Titmuss, as I have shown, set in train a process that invalidated his own first definition. What, then, are the basic questions with which social policy begins?

Social policy, I wish to argue, is essentially concerned with the question: what is the appropriate scope for social, as distinct from individual, action? What are the limits to individualism and what are the limits to collectivism in our different societies in a changing world? Utopian collectivists and utopian individualists will say there are no limits to either collective or individual action. In between lies the territory most of us in this department have occupied. The second-order question then becomes: in so far as social action is appropriate, what is the most effective way of achieving its purposes?

If I am right in identifying these as the central questions then the present political climate should be enormously exciting. Politicians are debating these issues afresh. Moreover, it becomes easier to see why those in social policy departments concentrate their attention on some topics rather than others.

What I wish to argue is that the last twenty years have taught us both the limits to the individualist justification for limited social action, but they have also taught us the deficiencies of large-scale collective provision. We are thus provided with a large but coherent body of work to undertake. One way to structure that agenda is to consider the theoretical and practical limits to liberal individualism and then the limits to utopian collectivism. There is, of course, enough material for two books at the very least, but the following skeleton agenda may be enough to provide a basis for discussion.

The limits to individualism

Individualists have logically to accept that for individuals to make choices in a free market and to exercise their democratic rights and obligations of citizenship, certain conditions must be satisfied. It is in determining what these necessary conditions are and how to achieve them that social policy as an academic inquiry begins its quest.

THE INDIVIDUAL'S PROTECTION OF THE LAW

The normal starting point for individualist political theory is the responsibility of the state to safeguard individuals' life and property from the unwanted attention of other individuals, thus freeing them to pursue their own life plans. Even Nozick (1977) concluded that there were difficulties with a free market in policemen! Yet the definition of crime, who suffers most from what crimes and the interaction of crime with a whole range of other social deprivations, brings the subject of law and order firmly within the ambit of social policy. We must, for example, ask ourselves why it is that tenants on deprived housing estates are many times more likely to be burgled or assaulted than the average householder. (Hope, 1986). Members of the LSE department are currently undertaking a research project jointly with the Home Office on deprived housing estates. The early results suggest that on one estate 93 per cent of residents suffered from some kind of criminal behaviour in the past year. The theoretical model we are testing to understand this kind of phenomenon involves an interaction between social factors, low income, the housing market, housing allocation policies, poor housing management and design features, as well as policing. The courts and police, 'law and order' on its own, seem weak instruments to ensure the protection of these tenants.

SECURING AUTONOMY

The second necessary condition for a liberal democracy is, as Weale (1983) puts it: 'The principle of autonomy (which) asserts that all persons are entitled to respect as deliberative and purposive agents capable of formulating their own projects.' That is surely a necessary condition for both political and economic individualism.

Such autonomy and self-respect will not be guaranteed without some form of collective action to ensure that citizens possess sufficient resources to be self-respecting, literate, numerate and healthy individuals, capable of acting autonomously or collectively if they choose to do so. It also contains the implication that it is necessary to ensure that individuals' self-respect, freedom of action and access to resources is not circumscribed by systematic prejudice or discrimination. How much autonomy do individuals from different social groups actually have?

Principled individualism, as opposed to sheer populist Conservative politics, requires, I suggest, social action to limit racial, religious or sex discrimination.

THE PROBLEM OF AUTHORITY

Individualists require a state that can exercise authority to ensure freedom, but they have thrown over other traditional or superstitious reasons for accepting its authority. Others may ask us to accept the authority of the state because of religious belief, through fear, through belief in the Party, or the customs of the tribe. But for the individualist the only convincing reason is that the state will ensure his or her autonomy and that the rules of the game are fair. It is only our 'public sense of justice (that) makes (our) secure association together possible' as Rawls (1972) put it. Free societies built on pluralist principles cannot be seen to be denying autonomy, self-respect and fair treatment to their citizens without losing legitimacy.

Rawls, of course, argued that the shared sense of justice of which he talked not only existed but rested on certain principles of distribution which could be deduced by those individuals occupying his 'original position'. Most individualist libertarians accept that there is *some* level of human existence at which a collective responsibility must be exercised by a nation state to preserve its citizens' lives if it is to retain moral legitimacy. The last ten years have taught us that society will tolerate large-scale unemployment and widening incomes without questioning the legitimacy of government. Whether benefits should carry obligations of work or repayment or enforced contributions from the extended family is all a part of social policy debate in the United States today and will be here tomorrow. In both Britain and the United States, market generated incomes of the poorest fifth have been declining compared to the richest fifth (Burtles, 1987; CSO 1987). Labour market changes and new family patterns seem to be making more people vulnerable to low incomes. Why and what to do about it must be high on our agenda.

In this country the average *annual* income of the poorest 20 per cent of the population (excluding state benefits) was £120 in 1985. (*Economic Trends*, July 1987) As Professor Sen said in one of his Robbins Memorial lectures at the LSE in 1987 on the 'Political economy of hunger', without a social security system during the past seven years Britain would have experienced one of the worst famines the world has ever seen. Without any form of collective action ten million people might be starving in Britain today. Such an outcome would not be a good way of ensuring allegiance to any political system, let alone one that rests on principles of individual autonomy. Whether the social security system we have could be better structured and administered is a second-order question to which we shall return. The necessity of its objective should be plain.

PROTECTING VULNERABLE INDIVIDUALS

Some of the earliest social legislation concerned the protection of children. Adam Smith and John Stuart Mill accepted that children were not yet full individuals capable of rational choice, and they adapted their theories to take account of the fact. Today we seem more uncertain about the proper boundary between parental rights and the rights of the child and society's collective responsibility to ensure children are not harmed, abused or their lives endangered (Lewis and Cannell, 1986). How society performs the caring function when the parent does not and what rules and safeguards to apply must be matters for more academic discussion and research. Rose Rachman's work on the history of child abuse shows that there has been a remarkable stability in the recorded cases of child abuse

Howard Glennerster

pei 1,000 population since the early years of the century, despite growing affluence, education and popular knowledge about child-care and contrary to much popular mythology.

Economic incentives, and women's desire for economic indepen-dence are leading to a gradual but apparently inexorable trend to equalize men's and women's participation in the labour market. Yet alternative provision for child care outside the home has failed to keep pace, notably in Britain. Only 18 per cent of five-year-olds have nursery provision, compared to 90 per cent in Belgium and there is no tax relief for child care as there is in Canada or the United States. Ensuring minimum standards of childcare and education, however provided, must be a collective responsibility. So must the care and protection of those incapable of sustaining their own independence – the mentally ill and the mentally disabled, the elderly mentally impaired and frail. John Stuart Mill (1848) made the point long ago:

> The individual who is presumed to be the best judge of his own interests may be incapable of judging or acting for himself; may be a lunatic, an idiot, or infant; or though not wholly incapable, may be of immature years and judgement. In this case the laissez-faire principle breaks down entirely. The person most interested is not the best judge of the matter, nor a competent judge at all ... In the care of children and young persons, it is common to say that though they cannot judge for themselves, they have their parents or other relatives to judge for them. But this removes the question into a different category; making it no longer a question whether the government should interfere with individuals in the direction of their own conduct and interests but whether it should leave absolutely in their power the conduct and interests of somebody else.

How can we inspect, regulate and motivate carers where market incentives and public bureaucracies seem to have performed equally poorly? This leads on to the next category of problems market advocates have to face.

INDIVIDUALS' WEAKNESS IN CERTAIN MARKETS

All individuals, not just the most vulnerable, are at a disadvantage in certain kinds of market, not least those pertaining to medical and social care. Most economists have come to recognize that the consumer of health care is at a major disadvantage compared to the professional provider. This may be overcome by various forms of collective activity, by health care consumers grouping together in various ways, for example. The comparative advantage of these kinds of collective action remains to be studied in more depth. In all societies the distances between what could be spent on health and what is economically feasible is growing. It is even more manifest in privately funded or insurance-based health care systems than it is in public ones. There is, therefore, a growing ethical dilemma about how to ration health care. Can we draw distinctions between life-saving procedures and those which reduce pain and inconvenience? If so, who draws them? Can we make judgements about the quality of life? (Gudex, 1986) We have to make collective decisions about these issues, even if these issues would seem to suggest that access to human life is just a commodity transaction like any other. If we do not take that view then a range of increasingly difficult collective rationing decisions have to be taken. Neither can they be avoided by privatizing or introducing markets to do the rationing. Even if these steps did produce a once and for all increase in efficiency and there-fore health care output (itself unproven), the rationing dilemmas will grow inexorably as medical technology gains in sophistication. Social policy research in these circumstances has to address itself to the question of how we can better inform such rationing decisions and make them more publicly accountable. We have already made considerable strides in this direction (Mays and Bevan, 1987).

MARKET FAILURES

As Barr (1987) has argued, while the case for market exchange on certain conditions is powerful, these conditions are frequently not met – especially in insurance. Private insurers must know that the risks of individuals claiming are small and that the overall risk must be calculable. I must not be able to keep from the insurance company that I am a bad risk. I must not be able costlessly to affect the likelihood of my suffering loss or the size of the loss. These conditions break down in all kinds of situations: health and sickness, unemployment and marital separation.

MARKET AND SOCIAL SEGREGATION

Much market activity actually helps to level social differences. Over 90 per cent of us in Britain, I am told, are clad in underwear from the same shop. The market can be a great leveller, but it can also be a great divider just where the consequences for the stability of the social order are greatest. Let us take the government's current education policy as an example. Current proposals permit schools to opt out of local authority control and the eventual aim of Conservative reformers is to finance parents with a cashable voucher which can be used to buy education in the market place. The threat that schools may opt out could exert a sanction on the local authority to improve its efficiency, but in practice schools are already largely independent entities and will become even more so under the government's other proposals to give them their own budgets. Once independent, however, schools will be dependent on the cash brought in by a child attending the school. Schools will compete to capture and keep students and revenue.

It is here that the peculiarly perverse characteristics of the economics of schooling come into play. What is unique about schools and other educational establishments is that the consumers are also the producers. *The* major determinant of the output of any school is the ability and motivation of its children, and the interest and support of parents. No school, however good, actually contributes anything like as much as the children and parents. (See several library shelves of references from educational research in the 1960s and 1970s.) Thus in a competitive situation it will always be easier and more rational for schools to raise the average quality of their output – their exam results – and hence keep and attract custom by selecting out the less academically able, the less motivated, those with least parental support and the slow learner. The analogy with the private insurance industry is very close. Any pension or health insurance scheme will try to exclude the bad risk and will try to cater for a highly selective group of clients. This tendency will be encouraged if the government, as they have suggested, gave a flat rate per pupil grant to schools that opt out. That would encourage any school to select pupils who needed less special tuition or help. The new independent direct grant schools will be under strong market pressure to accept only the able, the motivated and the child with the acceptable parent. There will thus be a systematic tendency for institutions to respond to the threat of exit and to the pressure of competition once independent, by becoming academically and socially selective. That in its turn has implications for the social cohesion of society.

Many will dispute my analysis but the importance of the debate can scarcely be exaggerated.

THE LIMITS TO SELECTIVITY

One common argument of those who wish to limit collective action to a minimum is to argue for greater 'selectivity', which is usually interpreted to mean providing cash rather than services only to low-income households. The case is forcefully argued not just by Friedman (1962, 1979), but by more moderate analysts such as Dilnot, Kay and Morris (1984). Surely they must be right? Concentrating a given sum of tax payers' money only on the poor will enable us to give them more than by spreading the same sum over everyone. That essentially begs the question, as Titmuss himself argued. Will the generality of tax payers be prepared to pay as much if the recipients are the poor rather than their own children or themselves albeit later in life? It is a complex question, though susceptible to comparative and historical testing. What really sets the limits to selectivity, however, is the problem of incentives. The UK has already devised one of the most selective and complex systems of assistance to the poor of any European country. (Walker, Lawson and Townsend, 1981) The consequence is that a couple with two children who drew housing benefit in the summer of 1987 could see its gross income rise from £60 a week to £160 a week, and yet be no better off. That was perilously close to the average earnings level. What would one of our upwardly mobile city slickers say of such penal levels of taxation? By any test of individualist motivation this must be mad. Yet that is a situation that holds with a universal child benefit, with universal free education and with universal free health care. At a seminar last year given by someone from the Institute of Economic Affairs who was advocating income-related help with health insurance and schooling, I asked what range of incomes he thought would be caught in a near 100 per cent poverty trap under such a regime? It was something to which he had no ready answer. I do not believe we can do without income-related benefits, but where the limits to selectivity lie involves a complex piece of economic and political analysis. Something else to add to our agenda.

OUR GROWING INTERDEPENDENCE

A central theme of Richard Titmuss's work was his attempt to define those parts of human existence where individual action on its own, however favoured those individuals are, is simply not enough to achieve their ambitions or their safety. He learned this lesson watching the consequences of world war on an isolated island community (Titmuss, 1950). He went on to describe the way economic change can have unpredictable and devastating consequences against which individuals can never secure themselves. We have just learned this afresh in the activity of stock markets. We may now be about to learn just as harsh a lesson of international interdependence in the AIDS epidemic. We have been through an unusual period in the medical history of the world in the past half century when we have been free of major epidemics that called for a collective response. Hazards to health and safety in the environment are other examples. I still find Fred Hirsch's work (1977) of a decade ago the most convincing analysis of the growing importance of interdependence in modern society.

The market for the mass media is another fascinating example of interdependence (Ferguson, 1987). New technologies have effectively destroyed our capacity to monitor and ration the quality and content of what people see in their living rooms. On one level people favour their new freedom; at another they worry about their childrens' exposure to video nasties – parents losing control of the culture and standards their children acquire just at the point they are demanding more control over the less significant impact schools make.

The case so far

What I have tried to establish so far is that even if we begin within a framework of liberal political theories and traditional economics we find there are many difficulties for the naive individualist. The limitations to pure individualism are growing, not declining. Equally we have also learned the deficiencies to naive collectivism.

The limits to collectivism

THE LIMITS TO A COMMAND ECONOMY

Alex Nove (1983), as a sympathetic and knowledgeable socialist, is probably a more effective critic of the command economy than any free market economist. Central economic planners can never have the detailed knowledge that would enable them to make sound investment and production decisions. Marxist theory, as Nove shows, just docs not provide us with any clue as to how these collective decisions can be made. Thus the scope for market allocations for many goods and services is considerable. One central question for social policy is: where do we draw the boundary line between market and non-market allocations? The other is how do we plan resource allocation in that sector of the economy where we have decided to abjure the market? We have a long way to go to develop adequate tools for such social planning (Midgley and Piachaud,1984; Walker, 1984; Robertson and Osborn, 1984).

THE LEAKY BUCKET

One of the most sloppy characteristics of social policy writing in the 1960s (and later!) has been its tendency to ignore the effects of raising the levels of taxation required to finance collective provision. Assuming there is some positive relationship between income received and work effort, it is reasonable to assume that higher taxes may depress work incentives and so may high benefit levels relative to earnings in work. Restrictions to the market may produce a loss of efficency – a welfare loss as the economists put it. Now all of this is mere first-year economics. The loss of welfare that derives from such redistribution was what Okun (1975) called the 'leaky bucket': you lost income as you tried to transfer it. The pure individualist suggests leakage is total or worse – not so much a hole, more a case of no bottom to the bucket. Social administrators tend to assume a pure copper-bottomed bucket – no holes at all. Neither seems likely. What we really want to know is how big is the hole? Remarkably little work has been done on this question until very recently. As one might expect, some economists in the United States have suggested the effects are rather big (Browning and Johnson, 1984). Others have suggested that though there is an effect, it is surprisingly small.

David Piachaud, who has done more than any other social administrator to make us face up to these unpleasant facts, has recently suggested, I think rightly, that the whole issue is a good deal more complicated than economists believe. They ignore unpaid work in the home. They assume all work is a pain and not a pleasure and ignore the extreme pain that some work undoubtedly is. 'Discussion of the distribution of income and work in Britain is trapped in past conceptions of the issues ... the distribution of income and work need to be thought about together' (Piachaud, 1987). There is much mileage in pursuing these thoughts.

PERVERSE INCENTIVE EFFECTS

Social policy, like any other policy, tends to produce unintended consequences. Giving benefits to those who suffer misfortunes may well make people less careful to avoid such misfortunes. It is a kind of moral hazard. Murray (1984) blames most of America's ills on the state's attempts to relieve distress. It is, however, a problem for private charity just as much as state provision. The Victorians and Edwardians were much concerned with that problem. One might say, indeed, that that is where the LSE department began 75 years ago trying to train those admirable young ladies how to minimize the perverse consequences of generosity. The same problem applies with even greater force to private insurance, indeed any kind of insurance. It is only the ideologically blinkered that would fail to see that. Social scientists need to examine just what perverse side effects social policies can and undoubtedly do have, but to put them in perspective.

THE EFFICIENCY OF PUBLIC SECTOR ORGANIZATIONS

We come finally to one of our major failings as an academic profession. Rarely, did scholars take time to analyse in depth or theorize about how welfare bureaucracies actually worked (Billis, 1984). David Donnison (1963) had done so but few followed. One who did, and to great practical as well as academic effect, was Anne Power (1987a, 1987b, 1987c); she has shown how it came about that many local authority housing estates came to be so poorly managed.

In the end social services have lost public support not because we failed to make the equity case with sufficient conviction and eloquence or reveal depths of poverty with sufficient rigour in the pages of the *Journal of Social Policy*, but above all because ordinary people's experiences of the services have often been demeaning and downright inefficient.

It is not enough to say that this is because the consumers are poor and that you can't do better with this side of a socialist utopia. I spent some time recently walking up and down filthy blocks of flats with rubbish shutes that don't work; lifts full of garbage and racist graffiti on walls of Bangladeshi homes. The tenants who live on these estates, where nothing works or ever seems likely to work, have never seen the caretakers or cleaners who are employed by the council and actually live on the estate. It is difficult not to ask fundamental questions about the nature of the bureaucratic incentives which make this a way of life.

Economists have a powerful answer. Social service consumers can exercise no power of 'exit'. They cannot bring sanctions to bear by taking their service elsewhere. 'Voice', consumer participation, (Hirschman, 1970) is incapable of producing a real incentive for efficiency. Public servants merely maximize their own self-interest (Niskanen, 1971). These individualist attacks on public bureaucracies have force, not because they provide a wholly convincing account – they do not (Dunleavy, 1981) – but mainly because there is no coherent alternative view about what makes public bureaucracies work, or could make them work better. That is our fault. If we had worried less about critical theory and more about ensuring people's rubbish was cleared we would have served humanity better.

That is not to say that social administrators should run courses in waste disposal, but it does mean we should devote more thought to understanding the nature of public sector and non-profit social service organizations. How do we provide appropriate structures to respond to consumers' demands, and ration scarce resources in ways that reflect political and professional preferences too? How do we maintain the motivation for efficiency in the absence of profit or the test of competition? It is our failure to grapple successfully with these issues, I believe, that could condemn our subject.

What we must do next is to undertake the same kind of work in other areas of social administration so that we can build up a better theoretical understanding of how welfare organizations work, and of ways of making them work better.

In conclusion

The prospects for social policy, as an area of academic study defined as I have tried to do, are enormously exciting. So far from being gloomy we should be elated. That is not to say that the ideas or policies that many of us hold dear will not be rejected, but that as a field of debate and inquiry social policy has never been more alive or had more to do.

The question, then, is not whether there will *be* social policy of one kind or another to study. There will be, with more complex mechanisms and outcomes to analyse than before. The question is whether it will be in the government's interests to permit us to continue to expose social ills and the limits to individualism, the consequences of government in action as well as service inefficiency. Here, the answer must be much more depressing and negative. In a political climate that favoured social action, governments were not adverse to funding research that justified more intervention or improved the effectiveness of social institutions. Now we have seen governments here and abroad which are opposed to collective action cutting back on social research, on regular monitoring of social conditions because they fear it will provoke calls for more public spending.

Monitoring and performance indicators have been developed not to show us where unmet need or hidden demands exist, but how to reduce unit costs. The challenge will be to set our own agendas and gain the resources to do so.

References

N. Barr, *The Economics of the Welfare State* (London: Weidenfeld, 1987).

D. Billis, *Welfare Bureaucracies* (London: Heinemann, 1984).

E. K. Browning and W. R. Johnson, 'The trade off between quality and efficiency', *Journal of Political Economy*, vol. 92, 1984.

M. Bulmer, *Neighbours: The Work of Philip Abrams* (Cambridge: Cambridge University Press, 1986).

M. Bulmer, *The Social Basis of Community Care* (London: Allen & Unwin, 1987).

G. Burtles 'Inequality in America: where do we stand?', *Brookings Review*, summer 1987.

Cm 214, *Housing: the Government's Proposals* (London: HMSO, 1987).
(For a discussion of the issues, see L. Bonnerjea, *The Future of Social Housing*, Department of Social Administration Discussion Paper no. 1, October 1988, London School of Economics.)

G. A. Cornia, R. Jolly and F. Stewart (eds) *Adjustment with a Human Face: Protecting the Vulnerable and Promoting Growth* (Oxford: Oxford University Press, 1987).

CSO 'The effects of taxes and benefits on household income 1985', *Economic Trends*, July 1987.

A. W. Dilnot, J. A. Kay and C. N. Morris, *The Reform of Social Security* (Oxford: Oxford University Press, 1984).

D. V. Donnison, *Social Policy and Administration* (London: Allen & Unwin, 1963).

P. Dunleavy, *The Politics of Mass Housing in Britain, 1945–1975: a study of corporate power and professional influence in the welfare state* (Oxford: Clarendon, 1981).

European Economic Community, *Basic Statistics of the Community* (Luxembourg, 1987).

M. Ferguson, 'Broadcasting in a colder climate', in a special issue of the *Political Quarterly*, 58, (1), on new technology and the mass media, 1987.

P. Flora and A. Heidenheimer, *The Development of Welfare States in Europe and America* (New Brunswick: Transaction Books, 1981).

M. Friedman, *Capitalism and Freedom* (Chicago: University of Chicago Press, 1962).

M. Friedman, *Free to Choose* (Harmondsworth: Penguin Books, 1979).

H. Glennerster, *Paying for Welfare* (Oxford: Blackwell, 1985).

H. Glennerster, 'Goodbye Mr. Chipps', *New Society*, 9 October, 1987.

C. Gudex 'QUALYS and their use in the health service', Centre for Health Economics Discussion Paper no. 20, York University, 1986.

J. Hills, *When is a Grant not a Grant? The Current System of Housing Association Finance*, Welfare State Programme paper no. 13, STICERD, London, LSE, 1987.

F. Hirsch, *The Social Limits to Growth* (London: Routledge & Kegan Paul, 1977).

A. O. Hirschman, *Exit, Voice and Loyalty* (Cambridge, Mass.: Harvard University Press, Cambridge Press, 1970).

T. Hope, Paper given to Home Office Cambridge Seminar, July, 1986.

N. Johnson, *The Welfare State in Transition: The Theory and Practice of Welfare Pluralism* (Brighton: Wheatsheaf Books, 1987).

J. Lewis and B. Meredith, *Daughters Who Care* (London: Routledge & Kegan Paul, 1988).

J. Lewis and F. Cannell 'Warnock, Gillick and feminists', *Journal of Law and Society*, vol. 13, 1986.

N. Mays and G. Bevan, *Resource Allocation in the Health Service*, Occasional Papers in Social Administration no. 81 (London: Bedford Square Press, 1987).

J Midgley and D. Piachaud. *The Fields and Methods of Social Planning* (London: Heinemann, 1984).

J. S. Mill, *The Principles of Political Economy* (1848, Harmondsworth: Penguin, 1970), p. 322.

C. Murray, *Losing Ground* (Lexington: Basic Books, 1984).

W. A. Niskanen, *Bureaucracy and Representative Government* (Chicago: Aldine-Atherton, 1971).

R. Nozick, *Anarchy, State and Utopia* (Oxford: Blackwell, 1977).

A. Nove, *The Economics of Feasable Socialism* (London: Allen & Unwin, 1983).

A. M. Okun, *Equality and Efficiency: The Big Trade Off* (Washington: The Brookings Institution, 1975).

D. Piachaud, 'The distribution of income and work', *Oxford Review of Economic Policy*, 3 (3), 1987.

A. Power, *Property Before People* (London: Allen & Unwin, 1987a).

A. Power, 'The crisis in council housing', Welfare State Programme paper, no. 21, STICERD, London, LSE, 1987b.

A. Power, *The PEP Guide to Local Housing Management*, Department of the Environment (London HMSO, 1987c).

J. Rawls, *A Theory of Justice* (Oxford: Oxford University Press, 1972), p. 5.

A. Robertson and O. Osborn, *Planning to Care* (London: Gower, 1984).

R. M. Titmuss, *The Problems of Social Policy* (London: HMSO, 1950).

R. M. Titmuss, *Essays on the Welfare State* (London: Allen & Unwin, 1958).

A. Walker, *Social Planning: A Strategy for Socialist Welfare* (Oxford: Blackwell, 1984).

R. Walker, R. Lawson and P. Townsend, *Poverty Lessons from Europe* (London: Heinemann, 1981).

A. Weale, *Political Theory and Social Policy* (London: Macmillan, 1983).

PART III

Social Policy and the Family

6 *Introduction*

JANE LEWIS

The last decade has seen an explosion in the literature on all aspects of the family and its relationship to other institutions and structures which contrasts strongly with the relative silence of social scientists and policy-makers on the family during the peak growth years of social administration as a subject in the 1960s and early 1970s. Titmuss wrote one short but influential essay on the position of women, delivered as the Fawcett Lecture in 1952, in which he perceived the way in which demographic changes had altered the lifecourse expectations of women,[1] but thereafter he largely ignored both the provision of welfare by, and the needs of, the informal sector.

The subject of the family was not completely neglected in academic work, rather, discussion of it was severely confined within unimaginative boundaries. The dominant approach established in the 1950s was that of the structural functionalists (most importantly Talcott Parsons), who perceived the modern family of breadwinning husband and dependent wife as providing an harmonious, organic unit best able to meet the needs of an industrial society. Studies such as those of the Institute of Community Studies provided an alternative, empirically-based approach, which was supported by Richard Titmuss. However, recent research has criticized much of this work, especially the classic studies of Bethnal Green, both in terms of their generalizability and lacunae, particularly in respect of gender.[2] Feminist writers such as Viola Klein and Alva Myrdal, made a determined attempt to put the issue of married women's work on the policy agenda, but submitted to the structural functionalists' analysis of the distribution of tasks within the family by recommending that women consciously plan for and adopt an interrrupted career pattern, stopping work for the period of childbearing and rearing. The Parsonian view of the family, both in terms of its internal workings and in its relationship as a dependent variable to the wider society, became the accepted reference point and determined both the conceptual range and style of work on the family for the best part of two decades.[3]

In large measure it was feminist analysis that brought the study of the family back to life. Particularly crucial have been the distinction between sex (the biological) from gender (the social) and the conceptualization of women's labour as wives and mothers as unpaid work. Both have had major implications for the development of social policy analysis. Feminist work has made clear that it is impossible to talk of 'the' family in the manner of the 1950s sociologists.[4] In the first place, there are many different kinds of families not least as a result of the threefold increase in the divorce rate since 1969 and the (largely) consequent increase in both the number of lone parent families from 570,000 in 1971 to 940,000 in 1984, and the number of 'blended' families; one third of all marriages now involve a remarriage for one partner. Second, the experience of family members and particularly of husbands and wives, differs because the allocation of obligations as well as of work and resources are profoundly gendered. Furthermore, feminist work has stressed that without adequate consideration of gender as a variable that is as significant as social class or race or age, policy analysis is likely to be fundamentally flawed. It should, for example, be impossible to write about equality solely in terms of only one of these variables, or of inter-generational responsibilities, currently the subject of intense debate among political philosophers and sociologists,[5] in a language that is gender neutral.

Much of the early work of feminist policy analysts was devoted to exposing the assumptions about the place of men and women in the private sphere of the family and in the public world of work and citizenship on which social policies were based. For example, Hilary Land returned to the issue of the problems raised by the wage paid as a reward for individual effort and its role in reproducing labour power, which had first attracted the attention of Eleanor Rathbone in the early 1920s.[6] Rathbone commented in her famous text, *The Disinherited Family* (1924) that economists had singularly failed to take seriously the nature of the relationship between the family and the wider eonomy, something that remained true until a group of American economists began to address the apparently mysterious allocation of time and resources in their work on the new home economics which began to appear at the begining of the 1970s,[7] but which relied for its explanatory framework on Parsonian ideas as to the roles and responsibilities of family members. Feminist work, such as Land's, pointed out that the bourgeois family model of wage-earning husband and dependent wife and children represented an ideal for policy-makers and also for family members including many women. But it nevertheless did not accurately represent the real world in which increasing numbers of women combined paid and unpaid work. Irrespective of ideals, problems arose when polices were implemented in which assumptions were embedded as to the way families worked that owed more to an ideal than the reality. As Land's most recent work points out this remains true in respect of the way in which the tax and social security systems provide incentives for particular kinds of support within the family.[8]

An increasing volume of feminist work in the 1980s has focused on the unequal division of power and resources which follows in large measure from the unequal division of paid and unpaid work. Policy-makers have recently begun to talk (especially in the USA) of the 'feminization of poverty', albeit that as great a proportion of the poor were women at the end of the nineteenth century as now. The largest groups of poor women are old, reflecting women's lesser entitlement to occupational pensions and lesser propensity to accumulate wealth during their lifetimes as well as greater longevity; or they are divorced, reflecting women's economic dependency on men, especially when there are children; or they are adult and able-bodied, but are in low status, low paying 'women's work', or unemployed.[9] Less visible are, for example, the full-time housewives who do not obtain a fair share of the family income. Many studies of battered wives separated from their husbands have shown them to be better off drawing income support than when they relied on their husbands for maintenance.[10] The commitment of New Right governments in both Britain and the USA to bolster traditional family responsibility as a means of making individuals less dependent on the state effectively threatens to make women more economically dependent on men rather than on the labour market or on the state by increasing the amount of unpaid caring work they do.

In fact, family policy has become a major issue on the policy agenda of the 1980s, making the understanding achieved by feminist analysis of families and social policies, begun in the early 1970s, of particular significance. In Britain it is five years since the discussions of the government's Family Policy Group over ways in which to encourage parental responsibility were leaked to the press. From the government's point of view, the concern has been twofold: first, anxiety that the family is 'breaking up', with high rates of divorce and increasing numbers of one-parent families, and second, determination that the family, together with the voluntary sector and the market, should provide welfare rather than the state. Of this 'trinity', as Malcolm Wicks termed it,[11] the family was obviously intended to act as the first line of defence. The two concerns are thus intimately linked: for the family to perform its task effectively it is believed that it must be 'stable', that is, that it should conform to model of the male breadwinner with wife and child dependants.

In fact, the family has arguably always provided the greatest amount of 'welfare'. For example, a similar proportion (6 per cent) of elderly people (over 65s) receive institutional care today as did at the beginning of the century. There is no sign of the family abdicating its caring responsibilities. Nor is there any evidence to support the idea that there exists an unused pool of family carers.[12] Furthermore, pursuing the care of the elderly example, where the person in need of care is shown to have a family carer, there is much less likelihood that he or she will receive support from statutory services. Finally, and perhaps most significantly, 'family carers' are, of course, usually women. Thus it is that feminist analysis of social policy has argued that women are the major providers of welfare through their paid work as employees of the welfare state, but more especially through their unpaid work at home. As Caroline Moser points out in one of the chapters that follows, current efficiency models of economic development for the Third World also rely implicitly on similar assumptions in regard to the provision of welfare by women in the family.

All the chapters in this section of the book pursue the implications of the way in which concern to promote family responsibility is fundamentally based on the unequal way in which men and women experience family life. Hilary Land, in Chapter 7, makes clear how the statuses of dependent and independent are much more complicated than is implied by government policy. The woman caring for a dependent relative in the home is enabling the person-cared-for to remain relatively independent of state aid and support, but may herself require state maintenance. Government definition of dependency is confined to economic dependency on the state. It ignores dependencies other than the economic (most importantly the emotional), while implicitly encouraging economic dependency on sources other than the state: on the labour market in the case of men and on men in the case of women.

Expressions of anxiety about the family have been episodic responses to perceptions of actual or incipient family failure, often during periods of military or economic crisis. In the twentieth century, Edwardian commentators worried about both the physical welfare of children, because of the low quality of army recruits brought to light during the Boer War, and the economic instability of the family signalled by the increase in numbers seeking poor relief. Again, during the late 1940s, the social dislocation due to war, following hard on the 1930s Depression, was feared to have substantially destroyed family ties, with the rise in juvenile delinquency cited as proof. During both these episodes, the major concern was that the family showed signs of both an inability to nurture and maintain its members and an inability properly to socialize its young.

These two themes remain today. In 1981 Mrs Thatcher explained the significance of the family thus:

> It all really starts in the family, because not only is the family the most important means through which we show our care for others . . . It's the place where each generation learns its responsibilities towards the rest of society . . . I think the statutory services can only play their part successfully if we don't expect them to do for us things that we could be doing for ourselves. [13]

What is new in the 1980 formulation of anxiety about the family is the diagnosis of cause. In the early twentieth century, social investigators, philanthropists and government officials were likely to blame working-class parents: wives were deemed to be ignorant of the elementary principles of child care and housecraft, husbands were believed to be constitutionally lazy. The flood of literature on the need to rebuild the family after the Second World War showed considerably more faith in the working-class husband's willingness to fulfil his role of breadwinner and focused almost exclusively on the importance of the mother–child bond and the 'adequacy' of the particular mother. In both these diagnoses, expert intervention in the form of educating mothers or inculcating greater work discipline in fathers was applauded. In the 1980s however, in both this country and the USA, the perceived erosion of family responsibility has been blamed not on parents but on agents of the state. As one American commentator put it in 1983:

> Here then is the cliffhanger. Will society return control of children to the family . . . Can we return assurance to mothers and fathers, along with confidence in how they raise their young? Or is it too late to stop the inexorable movement led by professionals, justified by academics, funded by the government, and publicized by the media, that claims society knows best – and is ready to tell mothers and fathers how to do it, and even to do it for them?[14]

In this country in the same year, Ferdinand Mount similarly condemmed 'public visitors', including health visitors who were described as having at their 'ultimate disposal a Stalinist array of powers'.[15] Nor has suspicion of state interference in the private sphere of family life been confined to the Right. From George Orwell to Christopher Lasch the political Left has rebelled against the idea of professional middle-class agents of the state imposing essentially middle-class behaviours on the working-class family; in Lasch's words, extending capitalist control through 'the agency of management, bureaucracy and professionalisation'.[16]

As the chapters in this section make clear, the policy aim in the 1980s in this and many other First World countries has been to redraw the boundaries between the family, the market and the state. (In the Third World, where the state provision of welfare is but slight, it has been more a matter of deliberately factoring-in the contribution of the informal sector.) Thus, for example, the work of providing lunches for children, traditionally done by mothers whether as paid or unpaid workers, has in part been returned to the private sphere, just as care 'in' the community has increasingly become, as per the intentions of the 1981 White Paper, care 'by' the community, meaning care by women. Ideally the private sphere of the family is to be left free from public interference, thereby ensuring its autonomy. But when 'failure' is manifest, for example in cases of proven child abuse, intervention (often of a punitive nature) is considered justified.

The assumption behind this thinking is similar to that made by the sociologists of the family in the 1950s; as recent contributors to the debate about the family put it: 'The family and specifically the bourgeois family is the necessary social context for the emergence of autonomous individuals who are the empirical foundation of political democracy.'[17] This analysis echoes that of Mrs Thatcher in her 1981 speech to the WRVS quoted above. But paradoxically (like the classic sociological formulations of the 1950s), such an analysis treats the family as a dependent variable, which as the chapters in this section of the book show, is to be overly optimistic as to the amount of control that can be imposed on the family. Even when control takes the negative form of forcing the family to be free, upholding the idea of family privacy, the promotion of family responsibilities relies on particular ideas as to family form and gender roles which are no longer the social norm. Second, despite the greater play made with the concept of consumer choice in the government rhetoric of the 1980s, such an approach ignores the preferences of family members and the way in which these relate to the subtle ways in which family ties and obligations actually work.

In the first place, it would in fact be difficult to recreate the traditional roles and responsibilities of the two-parent family. In the case of anxiety about lone mother families, which is most explicitly born of concern to prevent economic dependency on the state, writers as ideologically far apart as Charles Murray and William Julius Wilson have seen the solution for the large numbers of black American lone mothers to lie ideally in marriage to black men in whom a sense of responsibility for maintaining their families has been rekindled, whether through coercion or provision of more equal opportunities.[18] In the meantime, US policy has swung back towards that of the nineteenth century of treating women with children and without men as workers rather than mothers and thereby inducing them, via workfare programmes, to seek support from the labour market rather than the state. The artificiality of treating the problems of lone parents separately from those of two-parent family arises from the assumption that the primary source of economic support for adult women is properly men. However, the complex issues arising from the effort to combine paid and unpaid work have increasingly affected *all* mothers in the recent past. Instead of seeking to put the clock back, policy initiatives would do better to make the gendered division of work central and to address the way in which adult women engage in paid and unpaid work over the lifecourse, rather than centring policies around the presence or absence of a male partner. As the need for care among dependent groups (particularly the over-85s) increases, *all* women will experience increasing tension in balancing their commitment to paid and unpaid work. Particularly striking in this regard has been some American research on the expectations of adolescent girls, who apparently anticipate fully equal opportunities in education and the workplace as well as expressing a commitment to caring for their mothers.

In the second place, as both Janet Finch in Chapter 8 and Kari Waerness in Chapter 9, stress, while government rhetoric stresses family autonomy and thereby choice, little attention is paid to the actual preferences of family members. The historical evidence suggests that the demands of Edwardian working people, male and female, did not ignore the issue of the provision of welfare by the state, as some have argued, but rather sought non-stigmatizing and non-intrusive provision to tide them over periods of misfortune.[19] So also, there is little evidence for Mount's conclusion that families do not require and do not want help to overcome, for example, the complex problems of disadvantage, which as the late 1970s studies of transmitted deprivation showed, result from a mixture of familial and socio-economic processes.[20] Similarly, both the elderly or disabled in need of care and their informal carers may state a preference for family care, but still view a service such as that provided by the home helps as furthering their independence: on the part of the carer by enabling her to pursue other activities including paid work, and on the part of the person-cared-for by enabling him or her to maintain a measure of independence from their families. As Janet Finch indicates, family ties and obligations are based on a delicate balance of reciprocal relationships that a measure of state intervention can actually help to sustain by preventing one party becoming too dependent.

Thus when government promotion of family responsibility as an alternative to the provision of welfare by the state is examined in relation to a gender–based analysis, it is seen to rely on a very traditional concept of the family, which in any case has not been demonstrated to have provided more care and nurture for its members in the past than present-day families. The first point to emerge from this session for the future agenda for the study of the family and social policies is, therefore, the need for more careful attention as to how families work and how their delicate interactions based on affection, reciprocity and obligation may best be supported. The second is to question the usefulness of such a crude framework as that of dependency and independency which, as the discussion following the papers given at the conference concluded, defied dichotomous definition. There may be more mileage in research on interdependency, emotional and economic, and on the choices or constraints that determine the quality and quantity of interdependent relationships.

Notes

1 R. M. Titmuss, 'The position of women', in R. M. Titmuss, *Essays on the Welfare State* (London: Allen & Unwin, 1958).

2 T. Parsons and R. F. Bales, *Family Socialization and Interaction Process* (Glencoe Ill.: Free Press, 1955). For the work of the Institute of Community Studies, see especially M. Young and P. Willmott, *Family and Kinship in East London* (Harmondsworth: Penguin, 1972), 1st ed. 1957; and P. Townsend, *The Family Life of Old People* (London: Routledge & Kegan Paul, 1963).

3 For example, Alva Myrdal and Viola Klein, *Women's Two Roles: Home and Work* (London: Routledge & Kegan Paul, 1956); and R. N. and R. Rapoport, *Dual Career Families* (Harmondsworth: Penguin, 1971).

4 Barrie Thorne and Marilyn Yalom, *Rethinking the Family: Some Feminist Questions* (London: Longman, 1982).

5 For example, R. E. Goodin, *Protecting the Vulnerable* (Chicago: University of Chicago Press, 1985).

6 Hilary Land, 'The family wage', *Feminist Review* 6 (1980).

7 For example, Theodore W. Schultz (ed.), *Economics of the Family* (Chicago: University of Chicago Press, 1974).

8 Hilary Land, 'Social security and community care: creating perverse incentives', in S. Baldwin, G. Parker and R. Walker (eds) *Social Security and Community Care* (Aldershot: Gower, 1988).

9 Caroline Glendinning and Jane Millar, *Women and Poverty in Britain* (Brighton: Wheatsheaf, 1987).

10 Jan Pahl, *Private Violence and Public Policy* (London: Routledge & Kegan Paul, 1985).

11 Malcolm Wicks, 'Enter right: the family patrol group', *New Society*, 24 February 1983. 24 February 1983.

12 Alan Walker, 'Community care: fact and fiction', in A. Walker, P.

Ekblom and N. Deakin (eds) *The Debate about Community: Papers from a Seminar on Community in Social Policy* (London: PSI, 1986).

13 Speech to WRVS Annual Conference, 1981.

14 R. Kramer, *In Defence of the Family* (New York: Basic Books, 1983).

15 F. Mount, *The Subversive Family: An Alternative History of Love and Marriage* (London: Allen & Unwin, 1983).

16 C. Lasch, *Haven in a Heartless World: The Family Besieged* (New York: Basic Books, 1977).

17 B. Berger and P. L. Berger, *The War over the Family* (London: Hutchinson, 1983), p. 172.

18 Charles Murray, *Loosing Ground: American Society Policy 1950–1980* (New York: Basic Books, 1984); William Julius Wilson, *The Truly Disadvantaged: The Inner City, the Underclass and Public Policy* (Chicago: University of Chicago Press, 1987).

19 Pat Thane, 'The working class and state welfare in Britain, 1880–1914', *Historical Journal* 27 (1984).

20 Muriel Brown and Nicola Madge, *Despite the Welfare State* (London: Heinemann Educational Books, 1982).

7 The construction of dependency

HILARY LAND

'The next step forward in the long evolutionary march of the Welfare State in Britain is away from dependence towards independence,' the new Secretary of State for the Social Services told us in a major speech in autumn 1988. 'This', he continued, 'is the principle which should guide the formation of social policy into the next century'.[1] In this Chapter I first want to examine the assumptions being made about the nature and desirability of different kinds of dependencies both within and outside the family. Second, I want to look at some of those policies, or lack of them, which create dependencies and question the assumption being made by John Moore and others that they are the sole product of a too powerful state. Finally, I want to look at ways in which we might challenge the assumption that relationships between the generations and between men and women within the family can only be described in terms of either dependence or independence.

In recent months there has been much discussion among politicans on the Right about the need to replace a 'dependency culture' with an 'enterprise culture'. It is asserted by the Prime Minister and the Secretary of State for Employment, Norman Fowler, for example, as well as by John Moore that the welfare state has spawned a debilitating 'dependency' or 'benefit' culture in which individuals have entitlements to benefit when in need and therefore feel under little obligation to work, (meaning to take a job however badly paid). As John Moore says, social policy reforms in general, and social security changes in particular, have been shaped by the desire to emphasize that everyone has an obligation to be a productive member of society. It is argued that state provision undermines both the self-respect and the capacity of individuals to become and to remain self-sufficient and must therefore only be used to relieve distress. Thus, for example, under the Income Support system which replaced the means-tested Supplementary Benefit Scheme in April 1988, claimants of exceptional needs payments have become applicants for discretionary loans.

This critique of the welfare state, which has been heavily influenced by the debate about welfare in the United States (both John Moore and Norman Fowler have visited the United States and met with Charles Murray and other leading proponents of this view) define 'dependent', 'work' and 'productive' in particular ways. First, production is defined as only taking place in the market place. All those activities occurring outside of the market which are nevertheless vital both to the maintenance and the future of society, such as those tasks associated with bringing up and caring for the next generation, are ignored. Second, it follows from this that care is not valued in the way that waged work is, indeed as will be discussed below, it is barely acknowledged; those who care do not work, are not productive, and are counted among the dependants in society. Third, it assumes that independence is a function of employment or investment incomes.

These definitions and assumptions do not, however, belong solely to right-wing analysts of the welfare state. Those on the Left make similar asumptions about the locus of productive work and hence the source of an individual's independence. For example, Peter Townsend and Alan Walker have argued that the dependent status of elderly people has been deliberately structured by the state and society by forcing them to retire from the labour market.[2] As Paul Johnson has argued in a recent paper 'as long as those who use the concept of structured dependency continue to make the automatic association of retirement with dependency, they will continue to bolster conservative notions of the competitive work ethic'.[3] He suggests that marginalization in production need not necessarily be equated with marginalization in consumption. Provided people are not plunged into poverty when they retire, they need not feel dependent. In contrast to John Moore and indeed to Peter Townsend and Alan Walker, he says 'there is no *theoretical* reason to suppose that a transition from labour market income to State benefit income induces the onset of dependency; indeed logically the reverse should happen' (my emphasis).[4] He therefore concludes that the development of State pensions has more than compensated for the reduction in employment opportunities for older workers and, at the same time, has made elderly people less dependent on the goodwill of their families – at least for financial support (like so many economists he only sees the financial dimension of dependence).

Paul Johnson's analysis pays no heed to differences in terms of class and sex, nevertheless he does draw attention to the link between the experience of dependency and the level of consumption commanded by a wage or benefit as well as to the relationship between reliability and source of income and whether or not an individual is regarded by others, as well as by him or herself, as dependent. But just as some men have found that dependence on a guaranteed pension, even if modest, is preferable to relying on the vagaries of the labour market and an exploitative employer, some women have discovered in the last twenty years that relying on a state benefit may well be preferable to relying on an unpredictable and ungenerous husband. Dependence in that sense is not an absolute state but a relative one.[5] John Moore and Norman Fowler, however, are quite clear that the state, even if the benefit received is one to which a direct contribution has been made, should *always* be seen as a less desirable source of maintenance than the labour market in the case of men, or the family in the case of women. Young people should choose between the labour market or their families, the state providing only benefit linked to a training scheme.

As John Moore (in the speech quoted at the beginning) cited the reform of social security embodied in the Social Security Act, passed in 1986 and fully implemented in 1988, to illustrate how he saw the shift from dependence to independence being achieved, it is worth examining briefly some of the detailed provisions in the new legislation for further clues, both about what he understands by dependence and independence and what lies behind the rhetoric. Who benefits from this emphasis on independence?

The first thing to note is that very different assumptions are being made about men and women. In discussing pensions, for example, like Norman Fowler before him, John Moore appears not to have noticed that the *majority* of pensioners are women; he refers only to men. 'Under the new Social Security Act it will be possible for the first time in Britain for an individual to have his own personal pension, which *he* owns himself and can transfer from one job to another' (my emphasis).[6] Although the earnings–related component

of the state scheme, SERPS, is not after all to be abolished, the
emphasis in the new legislation is on earnings-related pensions
acquired either through an employer's scheme or through a money
purchase scheme. But what of those who may not be able to
contribute enough over a sufficiently long period to purchase or
qualify for a worthwhile personal pension? There are growing
numbers of workers in this position. A recent study by the Department of Employment of what is called the 'flexible' labour force
(comprising those who are employed part-time, or full-time but on
temporary contracts or who are self-employed) showed that those
workers in 1986 included half of all women and a quarter of all men
in the labour force, that is one-third of the labour force.[7] For those
who earned enough to pay a national insurance contribution,
SERPS provided a guaranteed addition to their basic state pension
and of course it was transferable between jobs. But in future SERPS
will be worth far less, for its value will be based on total working life
earnings instead of the best twenty years. Those with periods of
interrupted or low earnings – mainly women – will be penalized just
as they are in money purchase schemes. Meanwhile the UK
government is the government opposing an EC draft directive
which would strengthen the rights of part-time workers to both
state and occupational benefits, because it would be too costly for
employers. The government, then, is not aiming to help women
enjoy more independence in old age because to do so would reduce
their 'flexibility' in the labour market. Thirty years ago, Richard
Titmuss wrote:

> Already it is possible to see two nations in old age; greater
> inequalities in living standards after work than in work; two
> contrasting social services for distinct groups based on different
> principles, and operating in isolation of each other as separate
> autonomous instruments of changes.[8]

The picture he would see now, and for the next thirty years, is even
starker.

Ignoring women's presence in the labour market is nothing new,
but at least in previous reforms of the British social security system
women have been recognized as wives and mothers within the
family. In the 1940s William Beveridge designed his scheme on the
explicit assumption that women once married would not normally

expect to earn their own pensions via their *own* contributions and must therefore depend on their husband's contributions. For him, work in the home was 'vital though unpaid'. Barbara Castle, thirty years later, began to recognize women as mothers and carers in their own right instead of as dependants of their husbands and protected their basic state pension rights when they had full-time home responsibilities. The 1986 Social Security Act *weakens* the extent to which women may acquire rights to a pension through their husband's contributions both to the state and occupational schemes, but does nothing more to recognize women as individuals in their own right within the family. Widows, for example, can only inherit half instead of all the SERPS component of their husband's pension. Personal pension schemes need not make *any* provision for a surviving spouse. A spouse does not even have the right to know what provision if any is made for a survivor's pension. Under the 1975 Social Security Act, provision for widows became mandatory in an occupational pension scheme if it was to satisfy the conditions necessary for contracting out of SERPS, and wives divorced over a certain age acquired claims for a state pension based on their former husband's contribution record. This remains the case, but during the Fowler reviews there was no discussion of the claims divorced spouses might have on each other's occupational pension entitlements. With one in four, or even one in three, marriages contracted in the 1980s, compared with one in ten in the 1950s, unlikely to last 20 years, this is an important issue for the future, especially as the value of an adequate occupational pension entitlement may be as valuable an asset as the matrimonial home. The Lord Chancellor's Department made a number of proposals in 1985, but these have yet to be incorporated in either social security or matrimonial law. Meanwhile, many women who leave their marriages run the risk of foregoing valuable pension rights.

Another example of the failure to recognize women's needs in the labour market but at the same time reducing their chances of acquiring some security through marriage, thereby trapping them into prolonged dependence on state benefits, can be found in the changes made to the means-tested social assistance called Income Support. The rules for earnings disregard (that is, the amount of money a claimant can earn before losing any benefit) has changed. Until April 1988 the earnings disregard was based on income net of tax and National Insurance and reasonable working expenses. The

latter included travel and child care expenses. Since 1980 all claimants and their spouses had the first £4 of their *net* earnings disregarded, with the exception of lone parents who could have a
maximum of £12 net earnings disregarded. The new disregard of £15
based on *gross* earnings will mean that lone parents with child care
expenses are likely to be worse off if they try to maintain contact
with the labour market while on benefit. The longer they stay out of
the labour market, the lower their future earnings – and pension
entitlements – are likely to be. This, then, is a recipe for increasing
poverty now *and* in the future. Disabled claimants who would incur
substantial travel expenses if they wish to earn will face a similar
problem.

At the same time, there are other changes which may make it
harder for lone parents to cease being dependent on state benefits by
finding another partner. The Social Fund, which in future will be
used to meet exceptional needs, will provide help in the form of
loans which will be recoverable not only from the claimant's own
benefit (the DSS will not wait until a claimant returns to paid
employment) but 'where that person is a member of a married or
unmarried couple, from the other member of the couple' (S33.
(7b)). If lone parenthood is considered to be an undesirable state of
affairs, especially if it involves dependence on the state, why provide
lone mothers with the equivalent of a negative dowry? Is the answer
that they should never have become lone parents in the first place?
Certainly changes such as reductions in the amount of help available
to cover a claimant's housing costs will make it harder for a woman
to leave a marriage, even if she succeeds in remaining in the
matrimonial home. Such policies do not appear at first sight to be
consistent with the belief, to use John Moore's words, that: 'the
well-being of individuals is best protected and promoted when they
are helped to be independent, to use their talents and take care of
themselves and their families and to achieve things on their own.'[9]

The picture becomes a little clearer when the other aspects of the
reforms are examined, and once again it can be seen that 'individuals' mean men. As I have argued elsewhere,[10] the changes
proposed in the benefits designed to support families with children
show very clearly how women's and children's needs are taking
second place to the desire to impose greater discipline on the male
work force. The means-tested family credit which is to replace
family income supplement (FIS) was to have been administered by

employers and paid in the men's wage packets, thus making it an instrument which could be used to reduce demands for higher wages among low paid workers. (It would also have made employers less likely to be willing to take on lone parents or men with large families.) The government, however, were defeated on this proposal and, like FIS, family credit is paid to the caring parent by means of an order book cashable at the Post Office.

Changes in support for young people can also be seen as a means of putting pressure on them to accept employment for lower wages. Until they are twenty-five years old, they will only be eligible for a lower rate of income support when sick or unemployed, their access to housing benefit has been reduced, and under the 1988 Social Security Act 16-and 17-year-olds will no longer be eligible for income support; neither will they be eligible for unemployment benefit, for in future eligibility will depend on *two* years of contributions, not one as at present. Instead, their parents will continue to receive child benefit but, if John Moore has his way, most families will not even receive that for he has plans to means-test child benefit. The possibility of young people being financially independent of their families has been reduced; the length of childhood dependency has been extended and state support for all children is diminishing.

There are many other examples where the changes embodied in the Social Security Act 1986 and the Social Security Act 1988 add up to a withdrawal of or reduction in rights to state benefits, the result of which will be to trap more people in badly paid jobs or, in the case of women and their children, in dependence within miserable, and possibly dangerous, marriages. Low wages may promote the economic welfare of employers and the owners of capital but not that of the recipient of those wages when it is only fear of unemployment or total dependence on their families which keeps them in those jobs. They will experience the state as having *more*, not less, control over their lives. It therefore does not follow that the *withdrawal* of state provision gives *everyone* more control over their lives. As Tawney wrote, just as the post-war welfare state, so maligned by John Moore, was beginning to take shape in legislation:

A society is free in so far, and only in so far as all the elements composing it are able in fact and not merely in theory, to make the most of their powers to grow to their full stature, to do what they conceive as their duty and – since liberty should not be too austere

– to have their fling when they feel like it. In so far as the opportunity to lead a life worthy of human beings is restricted to a minority, what is commonly described as freedom would more properly be called privilege.[11]

It also does not follow as is implied by so many critics of the welfare state, that only state policies create dependencies. The consequences of economic growth and increased consumption can do so, too. Richard Titmuss called this 'the theory that increasing private wealth (among all or part of the population) leads to an increase in social disservices'[12] and he used the growth of car ownership in urban societies to demonstrate this theory. Among what he called the disservices created by the car he included more roads and motorways and therefore more houses in their shadows; more road accidents; more noise, fumes etc. I want to examine a further disservice which reduces the independence of children, disabled and elderly people: namely, the resulting increase in danger to other road users.

In 1986 there were 320,583 road casualties including 5,397 who were killed and 68,565 who were seriously injured. Over one-quarter were cyclists or pedestrians and the majority (60 per cent) of cyclists killed or seriously injured were under twenty, 38 per cent were under fourteen and 11 per cent were under ten years old.[13] Traffic danger to young children means that they are less likely to be able to go safely to school unescorted, and their older brothers and sisters are less likely to use their bicycles. A large national survey in 1972 found that two-thirds of the youngest school children walked to school, and of these half were accompanied by an older person. The main reason given for escorting the children was the danger from traffic.[14] A number of surveys carried out in the 1970s showed that even in areas in which the majority of junior and secondary-school children owned bicycles, fewer than one in ten used them to cycle to school. Lack of safety on the roads was one of the main reasons given for such a low use of bicycles.[15] A more recent national study of pedestrians found that half the sample considered crossing roads to be more difficult than five years previously, so these figures are likely to be an underestimate of the restrictions experienced today.[16]

The need for children to be accompanied to school or to the local park not only restricts *their* independence but also places restrictions on their escorts. The 1975–76 National Travel Survey found that in households in which there were children under 15, 16 per cent of all trips and 27 per cent of all car trips made by the housewife in those households were to escort others.[17] Mothers are more likely than fathers to take their children to and from school, especially if the journey is made on foot,[18] and so the school journey and the school day structures their activities, including their availability for paid work and hence their ability to acquire a measure of economic independence. Helga Hernes has argued fragmentation of women's lives is one of the products of the development of public welfare services:

> The transfer of reproduction to the public sector has been accompanied by fragmentation . . . Women's roles as worker, paid or unpaid, as client of the State, and as consumer of public services, are much less cohesive and more fragmented than is the case for men . . . The lives of individual women are influenced not only by the husband's income but also by his and their own status as employees, and by their position as mothers. *For women with family obligations the time-budget is at least as influential as the financial budget and is often even more disjointed* (my emphasis).[19]

The growth in the use of the private car, associated with greater dangers for other road users, has also increased this fragmentation of women's lives. The Institution of Highways and Transportation put the number of people with what they call a 'mobility handicap', at any point in time, at ten million. It is a sad commentary on our society that this includes not only disabled and frail elderly people but 'people coping with children (with or without pushchairs or prams), carrying shopping or luggage, pregnant women . . .'[20]

Roads are also dangerous to elderly pedestrians, who have three times as many pedestrian accidents as other adults. Indeed, in 1985, one-third of all pedestrians killed were aged over 70 years.[21] They are more likely to make their journeys on foot or using public transport because the majority do not live in households with a car. (In 1984 only one in three households with an economically inactive head had a car.) Increased traffic density and a decline in public transport has increased the hazard facing these road users. At the same time they have had to travel increasing distances to shops, post offices, chemists, doctors, hospitals, etc. The number of retail outlets in Britain fell by 30 per cent between 1970 and 1980.[22] In particular, the number of chemist shops and sub-post offices has declined. General practitioners are now more likely to work from a health centre or group practice – a policy which increases the choice of doctor and range of expertise available to the patient, but may involve a longer journey as they are less widely dispersed within the community than solo general practitioners were. As a result, elderly people may have to rely on someone else to collect their pension or prescription, do their shopping and escort them to the doctor or the hospital. This makes them *more* dependent on others.

Some of these changes have occurred as the direct or indirect result of social policies, others are the outcome of the working of 'the market'. The impact of changes in the location of these services and amenities on the needs of elderly people have not been given much attention, let alone priority. The safety of old people on the street is much more likely to be discussed in terms of reducing the risk of being injured by a mugger than being injured by a car. Unlike some other countries, future policies concerning road safety in Britian give priority to making the environment, including the car itself, safer for the *driver*. Bob Davies, in a review of road safety policies, drew attention to the need to deal with

> the pervasive effects of an ideology which inevitably distracts attention away from driver restraint, and with the fact that increasingly well-protected motorists will feel less commitment to perceived restriction as they gain less benefit. The future for vulnerable road users, who generally pose little threat to others on the road, looks bleak.[23]

While not denying that the fear of being attacked is a very real one for old people and women of all ages, and this has to be addressed, tackling the road and car lobbies involves taking on very powerful and deeply entrenched economic interests.

One of the major challenges confronting those concerned with developing community care in the future is to think about policies which make the environment safer and more accessible and welcoming for children, disabled and elderly people. The current aim of policies for the care of the elderly is to enable them to stay at home rather than in an institution, but unless these environmental issues are confronted this too often will literally mean *at* home. That does not spell independence, either.

Developments in the service sector in general, and in new technology in particuar, have meant, as Jonathan Gershuny, for example, has argued that those employed in the service sector are not so much employed in providing direct services themselves as in providing goods through which the consumer can meet their own needs. Information technology could bring some services right into the home. For example, he describes home-based shopping thus:

> we would have a smart terminal at home (it would be much smarter than Prestel – full TV-quality moving images of products, perhaps with superimposed 'consumer association' evaluation of products and simultaneous dietary advice as well) – and the goods would be delivered to our doors.[24]

However, for this to happen on a scale widespread enough to reach everyone, priorities in economic policies would have to change. As Jonathan Gershuny himself points out, not only would public investment in appropriate telecommunication infrastructure be necessary, but 'it must also, if it is to be effective, be combined with the more tradition (sic) sorts of Keynesian redistributive policies – the potential new markets remain just that until the mass of consumers have the money to spend in them'.[25] If the pension policies outlined at the beginning of this paper are not radically changed in the future, then the majority of pensioners are *not* going to be able to benefit from these developments. In any case, they are no substitute for a safer environment in which young and old, able bodied or frail, feel free to make the *social* contacts of their choosing. Health, education and welfare services are not mere commodities like groceries; there is a limit to the value of self-service in these areas. Care can only take place in the context of a *social* relationship and it is the assumptions made about the nature of those relationships to which I now wish to turn.

Dependence and independence have many dimensions and the meanings and values placed on them vary with the context within which they occur. The first part of this chapter discussed economic independence, which in John Moore's terms can only be acquired in the labour market. It is therefore no accident that he was talking only of men and the effect state provisions might have on their incentives to take up, or stay in, paid employment, because men have an obligation to take paid employment in order to support themselves and their families. The second part of the paper discussed independence in a rather different sense: the freedom to travel safely in order to have access to community-based resources and services without depending on another's presence and help. When support is needed it is largely women who provide it and in so doing their ability to be economically independent is impaired. That however is acceptable because women's obligations are defined very differently; their obligations are primarily located within the family not the labour market, and once married, in return for caring for husbands, children and infirm relatives, they have claims to economic support from their husbands. As Hilary Graham concluded after discussing some of the complex ways in which caring and dependency are linked and showing that these links are different for children and old people as well as for women and men, 'for many women being dependent is synonymous not with receiving care, but with giving it'.[26]

The social security systems have always been designed so as not to undermine either men's incentives to take paid work or women's incentives to undertake the unpaid work of caring for their families. The current social security reforms are no exception, and examples of the ways in which the new measures are intended to put more pressure on young people and men to stay in jobs, however badly paid, have already been discussed. Other changes illustrate the enormous resistance to giving women claims to economic support from the state, thus weakening the link between dependency and caring.

For example, eligibility for the invalid care allowance (ICA) has recently been extended to include married women as a result of a European court ruling that to restrict it to single women and men contravened the EC Directive on equal treatment in social security. At the time the decision was made, the Social Security Bill was still going through Parliament, and immediately the government moved to limit the impact of the decision by making changes in other benefits for the disabled. In particular, eligibility for the additional premiums for disabled people receiving Income Support will depend on the severity of the disability. Those who are sufficiently ill or infirm to qualify for an attendance allowance (that is requiring a 'wakeful and watchful presence' day and/or night) will qualify for the highter premium. They will also, however, have to show that no one is getting an ICA in respect of the care they need. In other words, after April 1988 anyone who gives up their job to care for a disabled person and applies for an ICA will see that person's income support reduced by exactly the same amount. (£24.75 in April 1988). This is different from the rules which apply to overlapping benefits. In this case the claimants are different people, not necessarily living in the same household; one benefit is based on some recognition of loss of earnings and carries with it protection of basic state pension rights, the other on additional needs arising from chronic sickness or disability. The amount of care required to qualify for an ICA is thirty-five hours per week, but the person needing care must be receiving an attendance allowance which presumes the need for between 84 and 168 hours of care per week. In short, the state is forcing the carer to forgo the ICA and protection of their right to a basic state pension, or making the person dependent on another's care pay for it.

Of course, these rules save money in the short run, although in the long run they may not because, as the government's own social security advisory committee pointed out in 1984, extending the ICA to married women would give 'practical encouragement . . . to the growth of care in the community'.[27] But, by reducing the material incentives for carers to give up paid employment, at least in poorer families where eligibility for income support would be affected, the *capacity* of families to provide care is reduced. However, the rules also weaken the ideological message embodied in the European court's decision, namely that irrespective of their marital status women should enjoy some measure of financial independence in recognition of the work of caring in the home. In other words, the link between caring and dependency has been chipped a little but not broken. What has changed is that the married woman is expected to be less dependent upon her husband unless he happens to be the disabled person benefiting from her care. This is entirely consistent with other modifications to a man's obligation to maintain his wife, or former wife, for her claims to maintenance have become more contingent on her caring responsibilities both in practice and, since the Matrimonial and Family Proceedings Act 1984, in law.

The discussion so far has contrasted meanings of independence and dependence for men and women of working age. It is legitimate for a man not to care for others at this time and indeed to rely on others to care for him because he should be giving priority to his work in the labour market. He is the breadwinner. If he does have responsibilities for caring for an adult dependant or a child in the absence of a wife he will be given far more support in the shape of domiciliary care as well as informally by neighbours. He will also be able to purchase more substitute care than a woman because of his higher earnings. Moreover the person being cared for will try to do far more for himself or herself if the carer is male than if the carer is female. Women as well as men find it easier to accept care from a woman. Fay Wright, for example, in her study of single carers describes how one woman spent nearly all day preparing and cooking an evening meal for her working son. Working daughters did not receive nearly as much help from the disabled person for whom they were caring.[28] As Hilary Graham has very cogently argued: 'the concept of dependency, although carrying no apparent gender tag, has a very different meaning for men and women'.[29] This is as true for those dependent on others for care as it is for the care-givers.

In future however, some of the material pressures which sustain these gendered meanings are likely to be reduced, at least for some men. In particular, growing numbers of men are retiring from the labour market in their middle fifties, rather than their middle to late sixties as was the case only a decade ago. For example, in 1973, 82 per cent of men of working age were economically active, by 1984 this had fallen to 75 per cent. The decline was most marked for 16-and 17-year olds and those over the age of fifty five. In 1984 fewer than three-quarters of men aged 55–59 years and only half of those aged 60–64 years were working compared with 94 per cent and 85 per cent ten years earlier.[30] Changes in the 1988 Social Security Act disqualify anyone over the age of 55 from claiming unemployment benefit if they have an occupational pension of £35 or more. This limit was set in 1981 when the government introduced the regulation that anyone over 60 years old with an occupational pension would not qualify for unemployment benefit if the pension was as much or more than the basic level of unemployment benefit. (The comparable figure today would be £48.) This, of course, saves the DHSS money but it also confirms that men who retire early from one occupation should consider themselves permanently retired unless they wish to join the 'flexible' labour force. In John Moore's terms such men should still feel economically independent because they have earned their own pension and this is preferable to relying on state benefits. (This begs major questions about the extent to which private pension schemes are in fact subsidized by the state via the tax system.)

This means that one important legitimate reason not to care, namely that priority should be given to their paid work, is being removed very rapidly from growing numbers of middle-aged men. In addition, the opportunity costs to men and women in the family are changed. Clare Ungerson has rightly argued that 'however state benefits are arranged in future the relative difference in men's and women's earning power will continue to ensure that married women, if they perceive that someone who needs their constant care and attention, are subject to powerful incentives to stay there'.[31] If *both* men and women are out of the labour market, the possibility of sharing care with the family differently is at least opened up.

At this stage of their lives, men are unlikely to have either dependent children or dependent elderly relatives. At least they will not be in the same household, and the little research that has been done regarding the study of male carers shows that if men do care, they are most likely to be looking after someone with whom they have lived for a long time. In particualr, they may have a wife who needs care. In 1984, 43 per cent of women aged 45–64 reported long-standing illness, and for 26 per cent of them this illness restricted their activities in some way.[32] Moreover, the proportions of middle-aged men and women reporting chronic illness increased in the 1970s, and for women continued to increase in the 1980s. The prevalence of chronic sickness is greater for men and women in manual than in non-manual occupations. In addition, more women than men reported experiencing acute illness which restricted their activities, and on average they also reported more incidents of this kind during the year.[33]

Demographic changes also make it more likely that spouse care will become more, rather than less, important in the future. More men and women are marrying than in the past, and although divorce rates have risen, re-marriage rates are high, especially for men, who are three or four times as likely to re-marry than women. We do not yet know a great deal about the obligations adult children will feel for elderly infirm step-parents, or for the natural parents with whom they lived for only part of their childhood. If these obligations are weaker than those they experience towards natural parents with whom they lived continuously as children, then older men and women will be more, rather than less, dependent upon spouse care in old age.

How are men and women responding to these changes and how are they likely to respond in the future? What kind of social policies would enable men to care more willingly and effectively and in ways which would not damage women's self-esteem? It is clear that preparation for retirement ought to include some discussion about the possibility that men as well as women may find themselves with considerable caring responsibilities. This will mean changing attitudes from those contained, for example, in an article on early retirement which urged consideration of the question: 'How am I going to fill my 2,500 hours of new found leisure enjoyably apart from intensive gardening, house decoration *and being a domestic nuisance*? (my emphasis).[34]

To date, very little research has looked at male carers. Martin Bulmer's recent book reviewing comminity care has 'women as carers' in the index, but not 'men as carers'.[35] An exception[36] is Clare Ungerson's recent study of carers which included a few men. Her findings confirm that for men the experience of caring is very different from the experience of women. They used different language to describe and explain why they cared: 'love' was the term men used, 'duty' the term women more often used. We need to understand far more about these differences if we are to develop social policies which are sensitive to the needs of *all* carers. After all, there are circumstances in which men *do* care. For example, the National Institute for Social Work Training's report on the case of the confused elderly found that women were just as likely to be being looked after by their husbands as men were by their wives. This contrasted with twice as many daughters as sons caring for the elderly person.[37]

However, the ideological structures which define women as dependants and carers and men as independent are very powerful and so far have proved resistant to change. To conclude as Martin Bulmer does in his study that 'Community care cannot be ridden on the backs of women relatives indefinitely, and certain social trends – geographical mobility, increases in married women's activities rates, the growth in divorce and reconstruction of families, are tending to reduce the availability of care from such informal services'[38] is to fly in the face of the evidence to date and to overlook the ideological pressure on women to care. As Hilary Graham has written:

> caring defines *both* the identity *and* the activity of women in Western Society. It defines what it feels like to be a woman in a male-dominated and capitalist social order. Men negotiate their social position through something recognised as 'doing', 'doing' based on 'knowledge'which enables them to 'think' and engage in 'skilled work'. Women's social position is negotiated through a different kind of activity called 'caring', a caring infomed not by knowledge but by 'intuition' through which women find their way into 'unskilled' jobs.[39]

Nevertheless, as Clare Ungerson's study demonstrates, it would be a mistake both to ignore the material pressures on women to care and to assume they will not change. So far there is no evidence that women are caring less than their mothers and grandmothers did. Indeed, they have continued to care in spite of the trends listed above by Martin Bulmer. Many do so, however, at great cost to themselves; poverty too often remains the price they pay, and if we continue to go down the road mapped out by John Moore and his colleagues that poverty will be deeper and more extensive. What lessons will our daughters *and* sons learn from an ever stronger link between caring and dependence and poverty? Rather than wait to find out, the assumptions about men and women and caring and dependency must be challenged. The dichotomy between dependence and independence is a false one, but to recognize that is to begin to change the way in which we define and construct gender differences.

Notes

1 'An independent approach to the welfare state', the *Guardian*, 2 October 1987. See also 'The social security reforms', *Politics Today*, Conservative Research Department 16, 12 November 1987.
2 See, for example, P. Townsend, 'The structured dependency of the elderly: a creation of social policy in the twentieth century', *Ageing and Society*, 1, 1981; A. Walker, 'The social creation of poverty and dependency in old age', *Journal of Social Policy*, 9, 1980.
3 P. Johnson, *The Structured Dependency of the Elderly: a Critical Note*, Discussion Paper 202, CEPR, 1987, p. 8.

4 Ibid, p. 10.
5 In the same way the experience of heat is relative – nearly every schoolchild does the experiment of putting one hand in hot water, the other in cold and then putting both in a bowl of lukewarm water, to discover one hand feels hot, and the other cold, although objectively it is the same water.
6 'An independent approach to the welfare state', the *Guardian*, 2 October 1987.
7 Department of Employment *Gazette*, November 1987.
8 R. M. Titmuss, *Essays on the Welfare State* (London: Allen & Unwin, 1957), p. 74.
9 The *Guardian* op. cit.
10 For example, see H. Land, 'Social policies and women in the labour market', in F. Ashton, and G. Whitting, *Feminist Theory and Practical Policies*, (Bristol: University of Bristol School of Advanced Urban Studies, 1987).
11 R. H. Tawney, *The Attack and Other Papers* (London: Allen & Unwin, 1981), p. 84.
12 R. M. Titmuss, *Social Policy* (London: Allen & Unwin, 1976), p. 66.
13 *Monthly Digest of Statistics*, June 1987, Table 13.4.
14 S. Plowden and M. Hillman, *Danger on the Road: the Needless Scourge* (London: P S I, 1984), p. 36.
15 Ibid. p. 37.
16 National Consumer Council, *What's Wrong with Walking?* (London: HMSO, 1987), p. 23.
17 S. Plowden and M. Hillman, op. cit. p. 37.
18 National Consumer Council, op cit. p. 143.
19 H. Hernes, 'Women and the welfare state: the transition from private to public dependence' in H. Holter, (ed.) *Patriarchy in a Welfare Society* (Oslo: Norwegian University Press, 1984), p. 36.
20 National Consumer Council, op. cit. p. 142.
21 Ibid.
22 S. Plowden, and M. Hillman, op. cit., p. 17.
23 B. Davis, 'An end to road deaths?' *New Society*, 84, 22 April 1988, p. 23.
24 J. Gershuny, 'Time use, technology and the future of work', *Market Research Society* 1986, 28, p. 352.
25 Ibid., p. 355.
26 H. Graham, 'Caring: a labour of love', in J. Finch, and D. Groves, *A Labour of Love, Women, Work and Caring* (London: RKP, 1983), p. 24.
27 Social Security Advisory Committee.
28 F. Wright, 'Single Carers, employment, housework and caring', in J. Finch and D. Groves, op. cit.
29 H. Graham, op. cit., p.24.
30 OPCS, *General Household Survey 1984*, 1986
31 C. Ungerson, 'Paid work and unpaid caring', in P. Close and R. Collins, (eds) *Family and Economy in Modern Society* (London: Macmillan, 1985), p. 158.

32 OPCS, *General Household Survey 1984*, op. cit., p. 127.
33 Ibid., p. 129
34 'Pension management' *Financial Times*, November 1987, p. 24.
35 M. Bulmer. *The Social Basis of Community Care* (London: Allen & Unwin, 1987).
36 C. Ungerson, *Policy is Personal: Sex, Gender and Informal Care* (London: Tavistock, 1987).
37 National Institute for Social Work Training, Research Unit, *The Supporters of Confused Elderly Persons at Home*, 1, 1986, p. 20.
38 M. Bulmer, op. cit., p. 212.
39 H. Graham., op. cit., p. 30.

8 Social policy, social engineering and the family in the 1990s

JANET FINCH

The relationship between social policy and family life has achieved much greater prominence in the 1980s than for many years, in two senses. Government policy thinking *about* 'the family' has become more explicit, and the impact of a range of public policies *upon* family relationships has been recognized increasingly as significant – in social security, housing, education, health care and the organization of welfare services. I do not propose to review these developments but rather look forward a little way into the 1990s and to consider where we are heading in the relationship between social policy and the family. In thinking about this, I find it useful to pull out and make explicit a theme which is often implicit in writing on this topic (including Hilary Land's chapter, in this volume, Chapter 7): the concept of social engineering.

How does this apply to the changing relationships between social policy and the family? In this context I would define social engineering as explicit attempts on the part of governments to change the nature of society on two levels: the social and economic relationships between individuals, and also the ideas and values which underpin those relationships. In this chapter I shall be concerned particularly with the second of these. Although traditionally within Conservative politics, the term 'social engineering' has been used as a term of abuse by right-wing critics of socialist social policies (Cox and Boyson, 1979), Conservative governments in the 1980s quite clearly have been engaging in a number of attempts not only to change our social and economic relationships, but also to alter radically the way in which citizens think about British society: what we should expect from the state, what we can expect from each other, what we should do for each other. But how successful have these endeavours been? Will they be bearing fruit in the 1990s? The answers to these questions are of profound significance for any discussion of social policy and the family in the future, because a major area where the government has tried to engage in social engineering concerns their entirely open and stoutly defended attempts to shift the boundaries between the state, the family and the market in the provision of social welfare.

Looking at current changes from this perspective gives rise to some interesting questions. In practice, can governments successfully manipulate what we think as well as what we do? If not, does that place limits upon what governments themselves can do? These are the questions upon which I shall focus in this chapter. I make no claims to provide definitive answers, but I shall explore some possible lines of analysis which may serve to clarify some issues which those who study social policy could address usefully, as we look forward to the end of the century.

Two illustrations should serve to highlight the distinction which I am making between changing what we think and changing what we do, in the context of social policies oriented to the family. My first illustration concerns the way in which women are locked into unhappy and even violent marriages by a range of social and economic policies – an analysis which Hilary Land sets out in her chapter. It is one thing to make it very difficult financially for women to leave such marriages, but quite a different matter to create or recreate the conditions under which women accept that life-long dependence upon a man is the proper state of affairs, whatever the personal cost. Similarly, it is one thing to oblige daughters to take on substantial amounts of nursing care for their parents through lack of available alternatives, but that does not necessarily mean that either those daughters or their parents believe that this is the best way to care for elderly people in a civilized society. Clearly it is important to distinguish between the effects of government policies upon people's lives in practice, and the extent to which such policies can and do shape the political, intellectual and moral climate in relation to beliefs and values about welfare. Governments may well be in danger of assuming too simple a relationship between these two, but so also do many academic commentators upon social policy, both those who approve of the intended changes and those who do not.

As we move into the 1990s, how safe is it to assume that the policies pursued in the 1980s have succeeded in changing citizens' ideas about welfare, so that most people have come to accept a reduced role for the state and an enhanced role for the family and the market? On the face of it, the chances of success are quite good. The generation moving into full adult life in the 1990s will have grown through their formative years knowing no other government than the present one. People who will be aged 20 in 1990 were just 9 years old when the first Thatcher government came to power and were just entering primary schools in the mid–1970s, when many of the significant shifts in social policy in fact were beginning – under the previous Labour administration. Among other things, this means that they have been reared upon assumptions which are radically different from those of the generation born during and immediately after the Second World War – that is, of their own parents in demographically typical cases. Some brief examples should serve to highlight the importance of this. They will presumably regard home ownership as the norm to which everyone can aspire and which most people realistically can expect to achieve, since by the late 1980s 62 per cent of housing stock was owner-occupied (*Social Trends* 1987, Table 8.1). This, in turn, will inevitably affect – in ways which, as yet, we know little about – expectations about inheritance and the flows· of resources between generations in families. In relation to the education of their children, they will have been reared upon the assumption that this is the business of parents rather than professionals or indeed the state, following the changes introduced in the last decade (beginning with the Education (No. 2) Act 1980) designed to increase control of parents over schools and to diminish that of teachers and local authorities. And, of course, they will be very used to the idea that the family and not the state should be seen as the first – and indeed the morally preferable – line of social support for dependent individuals, especially for those unable to purchase care on the commercial market.

For some commentators, this simply amounts to a return to a normal state of affairs. For example, publications from the Social Affairs Unit commonly argue that the post–war period has seen the idea of a welfare state replacing inappropriately the structures of support which naturally reside in the family, and that in re-drawing the boundaries to place more responsibility within the orbit of the family, the Thatcher governments have simply begun the task of restoring the natural balance:

> the expansion of the modern state has led to the responsibility of the family for children and young people being subverted by the state itself . . . There is no possibility that the state can ever do what, in particular, the family does in bringing up children, teaching, keeping them and its adult members fed and healthy, in looking after its elderly (Anderson and Dawson, 1986, pp. 11–12).

Whilst of itself this view clearly is ideologically partisan, it does contain an implied analysis which would be accepted much more widely; namely that if we take the long view and look at the history of social policy in Britain over the last two centuries, the shift of emphasis in the 1980s begins to look less like a radical departure and more like a return to the kind of thinking which has prevailed in Britain since industrialization, if not before. Rather than taking the welfare state established in the 1940s as the norm against which future changes are judged, it is precisely those post–war reforms (and the generation reared on the ideas which supported them) which are out of line. That analysis would further support the view that the prospects for successfully re-drawing the boundaries between the state and the family in the provision of welfare are quite rosy, since the change in beliefs and values which needs to be engineered is merely a re-assertion of values and ideas which have strong historical roots in British cultural life, even if they have been somewhat obscured and overlaid by naive socialist ideas prevalent in the post–war period.

The analysis so far suggests that there are good grounds for expecting that these attempts at social engineering will bear fruit in the 1990s. Clearly that view is entirely plausible and may prove to be correct in the event. However, looking forward from the perspective of the late 1980s, it seems to me that there are a number of reasons to doubt that conclusion, of which I shall mention four. First, that same generation who have been reared on a different vision of welfare have also grown up at a time when certain other changes have been occurring which at the very least cast some doubt upon the idea that marriage and family life can be relied upon to provide a stable source of support for individuals. These same young people have been growing up at a time when one-third of newly-contracted marriages will end in divorce and when one out of five children currently being born will see their own parents divorce before their sixteenth birthday (Henwood, 1987). The concept of the stable family unit providing the basic structures of support for its members looks a bit thin when its members keep changing. In addition, there is the question of the availability of women's labour to provide support and care for children, infirm adults and elderly people in the context of the family, which is inevitably called into question by evidence about the rising number of women in employment, albeit often in part-time jobs. Whilst it is almost certainly true, as I have argued elsewhere (Finch, 1986), that most women will go to great lengths to fulfil family responsibilities, even if they are also in employment, limits of some kind on women's availability must be set by their increased participation in the labour market, especially in younger generations. Young women growing into adulthood in the 1990s will have been reared on the clear expectations of participation in paid work and – on the authoritative projections of the Women and Employment Survey – can expect to spend at least two-thirds of their adult lives in the labour market (Martin and Roberts, 1984, p. 136).

Second, the results of public opinion surveys in the 1980s continue to show high levels of support for state-provided services, especially for those categories of people who are conventionally regarded as deserving, such as people who are sick or elderly (West, *et al.*, 1984; Taylor-Gooby, 1985). The Annual *British Social Attitudes* surveys have asked the question:

Suppose the government had to choose between these three options, which do you think it should choose?
(a) Reduce taxes and spend less on health, education and social benefits;
(b) Keep tax and spending on these benefits at the same level as now;
(c) Increase taxes and spend more on health, education and social benefits.

There have been consistently low proportions of people on this national survey opting for reduced taxes and benefits: 9 per cent in

1983, falling to 6 per cent in 1984 and 1985. Conversely, about one-third of respondents chose to increase both taxes and benefits (Jowell and Airey, 1984; Jowell and Witherspoon, 1985; Jowell, Witherspoon and Brook, 1986). We used exactly the same question in a study in which I have been engaged in the Greater Manchester area, and found the same very small proportions opting for reducing taxes and spending, but even higher proportions saying that the government should increase both taxes and social spending – exactly half of our sample of 978.[1] The point of citing this work in the context of this chapter is to argue that support for state-funded social and welfare services remains strong in British society. If the government has been achieving success in its attempts to change what we think as well as what we do, there were no signs of this being reflected in the evidence available in the late 1980s.

Third, in British society increasing legitimacy is being accorded to the claim that women's dependent status in the marriage relationship is out-dated, and that more generally women do have the right to equal status and equal opportunities with men in all areas of social and economic life. I do not believe by any means that we have witnessed a revolution in the role and status of women; at the level of publicly acknowledged beliefs and values, however, there certainly have been some changes, some of them encouraged by successive governments. Examples would include the change in terminology within the social security system to the concept of the 'main breadwinner' as the person with the right to claim state support rather than the explicitly sexist concept of the male head of household; or the active official encouragement for more girls to be educated in science and technology. In some cases the concept that women should not be the life-long dependants of men has gone beyond rhetoric and being incorporated into the law, most obviously in the Matrimonial and Family Proceedings Act 1984, the explicit aim of which was to prevent marriage from becoming a 'meal ticket' for women, by removing the right to life-long maintenance after divorce except in specified circumstances (Hamilton and Meteyard, 1985). My purpose in mentioning these instances is not to hold them up as shining examples of a commitment to women's rights (which they certainly are not), but to contrast them with the many measures of the 1980s which have had the effect of increasing women's dependence upon men, many of which are documented in Chapter 7. In relation to the question of women's dependent status, there are mixed messages even from the government itself, and this must raise doubts about whether women in the 1990s will straight-forwardly accept as proper and desirable roles defined as nurturers and labourers within the family, however strongly in practice social policies push them in that direction.

Fourth and finally, there are some important questions about relationships between generations. Existing evidence from studies of kin relationships in Britain conducted in the post–war period demonstrates that the dependence of one adult generation upon another contravenes deeply held normative beliefs and expectations about family relationships. Support between generations is tradi-tionally built upon reciprocal relationships in British society, and it is possible to disturb the acceptable balance by one party becoming too dependent (Firth, Hubert and Forge, 1969; Anderson, 1977). Currently we lack broadly-based contemporary data about these issues,[2] but the evidence from smaller scale studies in the 1980s confirms that older people expect to be givers as well as receivers in their personal and family relationships (Wenger, 1984; Qureshi and Simons, 1987). Despite the fact that the importance of reciprocity in family relationships has been recognized by some academic com-mentators in social policy (for example, Pinker, 1971, 1979; Bulmer, 1987) this appears to be entirely overlooked in the current drift of public policies in which families are to take more responsi-bility for their members. This seems to cut across what we know about the delicate balance between dependence and independence for which people apparently aim in their family relationships, not to mention completely disregarding the fact that Britain now is a multi-racial society in which we have a variety of different cultural traditions, each of which has its own distinctive conceptions of what constitute proper forms of dependency in family life.

It seems to me, therefore, that it is at least as plausible as the opposite view, to argue that social engineering has been – and will continue to be – less successful than is assumed both by supporters and critics of the Thatcher government. Government policies may well be pushing women and men, and parents and children, into particular patterns of dependence upon each other, but they are not necessarily altering ideas, beliefs and values about family relation-ships in a way which supports these changes. If that analysis is correct, we may well be heading for a situation in the 1990s in which people are increasingly constrained into patterns of family relationships which they themselves do not regard as desirable or proper.

What will happen then? The argument becomes even more speculative at this point, and one can simply look for pointers about likely outcomes without knowing the full range of social and economic factors which will be relevant in the next decade. We know that human beings can never be regarded as passive victims of the social system, simply falling into line with what government requires of them; but what actions people might take in such circumstances cannot be predicted easily. My own view is that one should look for clues in our history, and in this context I find especially instructive Michael Anderson's (1977) work on the impact of pressure brought by the nineteenth-century Boards of Guardians upon relatives of elderly people, whom they expected to house and maintain the elderly person in order to keep her or him off poor relief. Anderson argues that this was a situation in which the law of those who implemented it were trying to enforce a one-sided model of obligation, in a situation where people's relationships with their kin depended upon a balance of mutual support. The effect was to create an incentive for younger generations to 'lose touch' with their elderly relatives, so that they would not be targets for pressure to provide support beyond that which they regarded as appropriate. I think that one can find other historical examples which parallel this, and elsewhere I have developed more generally the argument that people tend to develop 'avoidance strategies' in situations where government policies are attempting to alter personal behaviour or relationships in a direction not consistent with their own values and beliefs (Finch, forthcoming).

It is inevitable that I finish this discussion in an inconclusive way. I do not know for certain – nor can anyone – whether the government will succeed in changing what we think as well as what we do in these aspects of family life which are so central to current attempts to re-draw the boundaries between the state, the family and the market. Much probably depends upon what the ideals of the post–war reconstruction – in which family support for individuals was de-emphasized (although by no means removed) – look like at the end of the century. Will they turn out to have been a passing phenomenon, rather out of step with long-standing beliefs in Britain about where one should turn for assistance in times of need? Or will it seem – as some historical evidence tends to suggest – that those ideals actually picked upon and expressed a long-standing resistance to the idea that families should provide the safety-net for individuals in all circumstances? If the latter is true, then attempts at social engineering may indeed meet with, if not direct resistance, then strategic avoidance. In the long run that must also place limits upon what governments can accomplish in practice if they have aspirations to make families responsible for their members, and to keep women in a dependent relationship with men in order to facilitate this.

Notes

1 The survey referred to here was conducted in late 1985, as part of the Family Obligations project based at Lancaster University and directed by myself. I should like to acknowledge the financial support of the Economic and Social Research Council who have funded this project between 1985 and 1989. The survey population was a random sample of adults drawn from the electoral register, in which we achieved a response rate of 72 per cent.
2 The Family Obligations project, *inter alia*, will provide such data drawing upon both the large-scale survey referred to above, and upon the second stage of the study in which we have conducted semi-structured interviews with a sub-sample of the survey population and, in some cases, their relatives.

References

D. Anderson, and G. Dawson, 'Popular but not unrepresented: the curious case of the normal family', in D. Anderson and G. Dawson (eds), *Family Portraits* (London: Social Affairs Unit, 1986).

M. Anderson, 'The impact on the family relationships of elderly people of changes since Victorian times in governmental income-maintenance provision', in E. Shanas and M. B. Sussman (eds), *Family Bureaucracy and the Elderly* (Durham, N.C.: Duke University Press, 1977).

M. Bulmer, (1987), *The Social Basis of Community Care* (London: Allen & Unwin, 1987).

C. B. Cox, and R. Boyson, (eds) *Fight for Education: Black Papers 1975* (London: J. M. Dent, 1979).

J. Finch, 'Whose responsibility? Women and the future of family care', in I. Allen, M. Wicks, J. Finch and D. Leat, *Informal Care Tomorrow* (London: Policy Studies Institute, 1986).

J. Finch, *Duty Bound? Family Relations and Social Change* (Cambridge: Polity Press, forthcoming).

R. Firth, A. Hubert, and J. Forge, *Families and Their Relatives* (London: Routledge & Kegan Paul 1969).

J. Hamilton, and B. Meteyard, 'The Matrimonial and Family Proceedings Act 1984: maintenance provision', *Family Law*, 15, 1985.

Henwood, M. 'Marriage in focus', *Family Policy*, 4. p. 4, 1987.

R. Jowell, and C. Airey (eds), *British Social Attitudes: the 1984 Report* (Aldershot: Gower, 1984).

R. Jowell, and S. Witherspoon (eds), *British Social Attitudes: the 1985 Survey* (Aldershot: Gower, 1985).

R. Jowell, S. Witherspoon, and L. Brook (eds), *British Social Attitudes: the 1986 Report* (Aldershot: Gower, 1986).

J. Martin, and C. Roberts, *Women and Employment: a lifetime perspective* (London: HMSO, 1984).

R. Pinker, *Social Theory and Social Policy* (London: Heinemann, 1971).

R. Pinker, *The Idea of Welfare* (London: Heinemann, 1979).

H. Qureshi, and Q. Simons, 'Resources within families: caring for elderly people', in J. Brannen and G. Wilson (eds), *Give and Take in Families* (London: Allen & Unwin, 1987).

P. Taylor-Gooby, *Public Opinion, Ideology and State Welfare* (London: Routledge & Kegan Paul, 1985).

G. C. Wenger, *The Supportive Network: Coping With Old Age* (London: Allen & Unwin, 1984).

P. West, R. Illsley, and H. Kelman, 'Public prefences for the care of dependency groups', *Social Science and Medicine*, 18, (4), 1984, pp. 287–95.

9 Dependency in the welfare state

KARI WÆRNESS

Dependency is part of the human condition and the need for welfare state services and provisions is related to that fact. To discuss the principles which should guide the formation of social policy in terms of independence versus dependence is therefore misleading. As Hilary Land (Chapter 7) points out, the question is rather what kinds of dependencies will be created by different social policies and what consequences these will have for different groups of people.

In 1971 I did a study on a small group of Norwegian divorced working-class mothers (Wærness, 1972) and I learned an important lesson about these differences. As an academic middle-class feminist I had great difficulties in understanding why my informants *neither* expressed strong wishes to get employment *nor* to remarry. They tried as best they could not to let other people know they were living on social assistance. To some extent they also tried to conceal that they were divorced. Lack of money was a constant problem, more so than earlier when they were married and provided for by their husbands. They appreciated the kind of *independence* they experienced as recipients of social assistance, an independence they did not have as married housewives. This experience of independence was an important reason for not wanting to remarry. Employment, on the other hand, would have meant that they could not have fulfilled their obligations as mothers in a satisfactory manner. They defined childcare and housework as their primary obligations, which they worked hard to fulfil on a small household budget. Because of these obligations they considered they had a right to public provision. As they saw it, divorce was a result of bad luck, not a result of their wants or initiatives. Their husbands had deserted them, and most of them felt that their former husbands could not afford to provide for them and their children. In this situation there was no other solution than public provision. Their main reference group was married working-class mothers, the majority of whom at that time were full-time housewives. As their children were social deviants due to their parents' divorce they should not, according to their mothers' judgement, become deviants in still another way, namely by having an employed mother.

Over the past fifteen years both the employment rate for mothers and the divorce rate have increased rapidly in Norway.[1] The norms affecting the ways in which women combine their roles as employees and mothers have changed accordingly. The situation is still, however, much the same as in England. As Hilary Land points out: for many women, being dependent on either familial or public provision is not synonymous with receiving care, but with giving it.

Yet we should take care not to infer that different groups of clients, especially 'working mothers', define their relation to the welfare system as one of unilateral exchange, even when they feel stigmatized and humiliated by the conditions under which the help is given. Some years ago, Pinker (1971) reminded us that we know more about philosophers' and social scientists' sentiments about the welfare system than about the sentiments of ordinary people in everyday life. Our understanding of these sentiments is not that much better today. I assume that one reason for this is that most social policy research does not treat gender as a *sociological* variable, only as a statistical one. The same holds for mainstream sociology in general. Most social science research has, for instance, not taken seriously what Durkheim discovered in 1897 and Jessie Bernard has argued much later, (in 1972) namely, that there are two marriages 'his' and 'hers', and that his marriage is far better than hers. Newer Scandinavian research on divorce and measures on health and welfare indicates that Durkheim and Bernard's conclusions are still relevant in societies with a relatively high standing on indicators of gender equality.[2]

In order to improve social policy research on ordinary people's sentiments about the welfare system the evidence of the two types of marriages should be taken into consideration. More importantly we must pay attention to the general fact that men and women have different and changing roles and statuses throughout the life-cycle. This means that all analyses of problems of dependency and consequences of changes in social policy should not be based on the assumption of gender neutrality and consequently should account for gender differences.

Studies from Scandinavia indicate that the preference for public rather than family care has increased rapidly during the last ten to fifteen years, especially among elderly women.[3] To an increasing extent, public care services seem to be defined as *social rights* that should be met when old people no longer can manage on their own in everyday life. So far, there is no reason to believe that the public care system has decreased older women's efforts to manage on their own for as long as possible. Neither does it seem to have weakened the quality of their family relations. Instead the growth of the public home help services in particular has reduced the total dependency of many elderly on practical aid and support from their family.[4] Thereby they are to some extent able to realize the norm which Rosenmayr and Köckeis (1965) named 'intimacy, but at a distance' in relation to their children.

The greater preference of elderly men for family care may be explained in the following way: men's lack of knowledge about and experience of housework and family care at an earlier age has the effect that when they become dependent on a lot of help and care in everyday life, they are not conscious as to the strain this situation may impose on close family members. Therefore, they may take family care for granted to an extent that is not likely in the case of women. The use of public care services, on the other hand, would result in their status as dependants becoming visible and clear.

The consequences of the rise of the multigenerational family in Western society should be an important field for social policy research. Due to the multigenerational family the middle generation of women often may find itself in a stressful position, experiencing at least two generations making claims on their attention, help and care. Especially for 'the women in the middle', kin-keeping may prove a heavy burden. As Hilary Land points out, we do not know very much about how the weakening of the conjugal bond will affect the vertical bonds between the generations in the family. Some researchers assume that modern society will become increasingly matrilinear in its intergenerational continuities, and that blended families will increase the possibilities of tensions in the definition of loyalties and in the distribution of time and material resources. As for long-term parent care, it can overlay many different ages and stages in the life course of different individuals and families. This means that it may compete for time and attention with many other different obligations and that there can thus be no set of uniform behavioural norms for parental care on which old age policy in the modern welfare state can be based.

As for the importance of spouse care in old age, it probably will continue to be most important for men. This is not only a result of the difference in the remarriage rate between men and women, but is also due more to the usual age difference between spouses, and the longer life expectancy of women. Even if marriage roles should become more symmetrical, this would not solve the problems of women's need for care in old age, because most married women become widows *before* they are unable to manage on their own in everyday life. Unless women start to marry younger men, and unless the difference in life expectancy between the sexes become smaller, this situation will not change.

In Scandinavia today, elderly as well as young handicapped people seem to want less dependency on family care. Not only have norms claiming that young people in general have the right to be financially independent of their parents become stronger. In addition, the organizations of younger handicapped people have claimed their members' right to live as adults, which means having the right to set up their own households. Accordingly they demand both sufficient public provision and adequate public care services to realize this goal.

On the other hand, the Norwegian Housewives' Association struggles hard to have taxation and social security laws changed in such a way as to ensure that women receive better economic compensation for all kinds of family care for dependants. For women and young people the struggle for independence today seems therefore first and foremost to be a struggle for greater independence in relation to the family, not in relation to the welfare state. At the same time the governmental authorities and a great part of the male intellectual elite want to reduce or at least not to increase state intervention. Instead they stress the importance of strengthening the so-called 'informal care network' and the positive aspects of 'privatization'.

In face of the many complex changes, both in worklife and family life going on nowadays a very reasonable reform seems to me to detach more of the income guarantees of the welfare state from the individual's position in the labour market and make them individual citizenship rights. At least this would be a social policy in the interest of the majority of women and other vulnerable groups in the labour market.

As for the many critiques of the social control aspects of the welfare bureaucracies, I agree with Hilary Land and Tawney that to leave more to the market (and, I would add, to the family) is not in the interest of most people. In wrestling with welfare bureaucracies many of the people most in need of help often do not get what they really want, rather, another interpretation of their needs. At the same time the most controlling services often are the only means of protecting victims of family violence, most often children and women, or individuals of both sexes from self-destructive behaviour. There is a tension between the welfare-enhancing and controlling aspects of many welfare state services, a tension that never can be completely erased, but can be made weaker or stronger. For social policy research it always will be an important task to provide good analyses of what conditions contribute to weakening rather than strengthening this tension.

Notes

1 Indicators of the change in women's employment: The employment rate for married women in the age group 35–44 increased from 45 per cent in 1972 to 74 per cent in 1981, and among women who had their first child in 1976–78 46 per cent had had a stable labour market involvement until 1981, against only 27 per cent of the women who had their first child in 1970–72. Indicator of change in divorce propensity: In 1970 there were 3.8 divorces per 1,000 marriages; in 1981 7.8 (*Social Survey*, 1983, SA 51. *Central Bureau of Statistics*, Oslo.)

2 Indicators of this difference: Both Ødegård (1984) and Koch Nielsen (1983) find a negative correlation between marriage and mental health for women, against a positive correlation for men. Dalgard (1980) operationalizing mental health in a different way, finds a negative correlation between divorce and mental health for both sexes, but finds the relative difference between divorced and married persons greater for men than for women. Research on divorce and death rates shows that the relative negative difference between divorced and married are much greater for men than for women (*Social Survey*, 1983, Mellstrøm, 1983).

3 This conclusion is based on more different qualitative studies and two surveys among the elderly in a Norwegian town in 1969 and 1981 (see Wærness, 1987).

4 In 1970 about 11 per cent of the elderly (aged 65 and over) in Norway got help from the public home-help service, in 1980 the proportion had

increased to about 22 per cent. Most clients get only a few hours help per week, the mean is about three to four hours (Daatland and Sundstrøm, 1985).

References

Jessie Bernard, *The Future of Marriage* (New York: Bantam Books, 1972).
Svein Olav Daatland, and Gerdt Sundstrøm, *Gammel i Norden* (Stockholm: Nord, 1985).
Odd Steffen Dalgard, *Bomiljø on psykisk helse* (Oslo: University Press, 1980).
Emile Durkheim, *Suicide* (London: Routledge & Kegan Paul, 1952).
Inger Koch-Nielsen, *Skilsmisser*, Publication no. 118, The Danish Institute of Social Research, Copenhagen, 1983.
Dan Mellström, 'Medicinsk demografi og livsstilar hos eldre i Sverige', in Brigitta Oden *et.al.* (eds) *Äldre i samhället, – för, nu och i framtiden* (Stockholm: Liber, 1983).
Robert Pinker, *Social Theory and Social Policy* (London: Heinemann Educational, 1971).
Leopold Rosenmayr, and Eva Köckeis, 'Propositions for a sociological theory of aging and the family' in *International Social Science Journal* 15, 1965, pp. 410–26.
Kari Wærness, *Verdikonflikter ved realisering av sosiale hjelpetiltak for enslige mødre*, Social Policy Report no. 6, Department of Sociology, University of Bergen, 1972.
Kari Wærness, 'A feminist perspective on the new ideology of community care for the elderly', in *Acta Sociologica* (30), 2, 1987, pp. 133–50.
Tone Ødegård, 'Konflikter i kvinners livssammenheng: Lammelse eller vekst?', in Trine Anstorp, *et. al. Kvinne(p)syke* (Oslo: University Press, 1984).

10 The social construction of dependency: comments from a Third World perspective

CAROLINE O. N. MOSER

Introduction

The essential difference between the British welfare state, with its institutionalization of welfare provision, and developing countries with their residual or at best incremental social welfare policies, would appear *a priori* to limit the relevance of commenting on Hilary Land's Chapter 7 from a Third World perspective.[1] For the specific legislation to which she refers has never existed to assist low-income women in the majority of Third World countries. At a more general level, however, her paper is concerned with the way policy changes designed to decrease the dependence of people on the state, result for women in increased dependence on men. This issue is not specific to Great Britain. The critical debate as to whether for women the issue is dependence on the state or dependence on men, rather than dependence on the state or independence, is a global concern, and therefore of importance in the formulation of future social policy.

This comment contributes to this debate by briefly examining the meaning of dependence and independence for Third World women from one particular perspective. This concerns the manner in which dependency has been socially constructed, not only by policy formulated internally at the *national* level as in Great Britain but also externally at the *international* level. A very brief description of two policies 'imposed' on many Third World countries at different historical periods follows. First, colonial social policy introduced prior to this century, and secondly current structural adjustment policy, as formulated by the International Monetary Fund and the World Bank, are used to show that in a Third World context the debate for women about dependency does not stop at the level of the state – as in the UK – but must also encompass an international dimension.

Colonial dependency and the status of women

The neo-Marxist dependency debates which dominated Third World development theory in the 1970s highlighted the limitations of modernization approaches to development, with their rationale that through accelerated growth developing countries would 'catch up' with advanced economies. Implicit in this was also a critique of incremental social policy and its assumption that developing countries would increase their social welfare provision as and when they were able to afford it.[2] Despite the failure of dependency theory adequately to explain the historical specificities of peripheral capitalist development in terms of such factors as capital accumulation, class struggle and the role of the state, it nevertheless shifted the terms of the debate to include the 'development of underdevelopment'.[3] Only recently, however, has attention focused on the internal structures of dependency which were recreated *within* society in relation particularly to ethnicity and, above all, gender. It is now recognized that many of the stereotype assumptions about the role of women in developing societies have been influenced, if not determined, by the imposition of colonial administrative policy, the teachings of missionaries and, more recently, multinational labour legislation.

An example of this is provided by MacEwen Scott in her study of the convergent trends in patterns of gender segregation at the global level. She argues that the gender roles which underlie gender segregation are cultural products, forged by political and ideological processes as well as economic ones, and illustrates this with reference to the UK, Peru, Egypt and Ghana.[4] In the case of Peru, for instance, she examines why the patterns of gender segregation in Lima are so similar to those of the UK, despite the fact that Peru is a much less industrialized country with a different indigenous culture, in which the peasantry had a relatively egalitarian structure of

gender relations. She argues that modern enterprise gender segregation in Lima replicates European and North American patterns,
and that this compatability is the product of a common European
heritage, transported to Peru in Spanish colonial times, persisting in
post-independence institutions until it formed part of the ruling
class culture, and 'imposed on indigenous groups through colonization, proselytism, education, miscegenation, and status order'.[5]
Today, because of the predominance of foreign companies in
contemporary Peru, and the gender assumptions implicit in their
technology and management practices, the current gender preferences of employers relate not only to Peruvian domestic ideology
but also to that of the USA and Europe, and are also reinforced in
national companies and state bureaucracies whose managers and
technicians have been trained abroad and who use foreign technology.

Although in Peru, as in Britain, women's roles were already some
what oriented towards dependence and domesticity at the onset of
industrialization, in Ghana, by contrast, this was relatively
unknown. Prior to colonization women experienced considerable
autonomy within the family and the economy, as well as having
independent sources of prestige and political authority. The fact that
today the pattern of female employment in the modern enterprises
of Ghana replicates that of the West has occurred not only through
economic changes but also through the imposition of Western
values on Ghanaian society by the colonial state, foreign traders,
missionaries and the status system implanted by the colonial
elite. The colonial administration, for instance, from 1874–1957
created a selective process of training and recruitment for administrative jobs which reflected the sex roles of Victorian Britain rather
than Ghana, assuming that only men were suitable for positions of
responsibility and that female employment should be tied to marital
status.

Equally, the education system replicated that of late Victorian
Britain, both structurally and ideologically, assuming that girls'
education should be oriented towards domestic skills and social
graces. Thus the early schools run by Christian missionaries dis-
seminated an alien ideology about family structure and sexual
morality, while sustaining a continuous onslaught on indigenous
kinship systems. Finally women were deprived of two important
sources of economic status and political power in traditional society

by the colonial administration and the Christian missions' refusal to recognize their political office or religious role. Although post-colonial governments have removed some of the more blatant forms of sex discrimination, the structural and ideological influences of the colonial period have been perpetuated through the incipient class system. Both the examples of Peru and Ghana cited by McEwen Scott show only too clearly the manner and extent to which social policy imposed by colonial powers increased the dependency of women on men in their colonies. Although it might be expected that such practices ceased with the end of colonialism, this has not necessarily been the case – with recently implemented economic structural adjustment policies designed by the IMF and the World Bank providing another example, this time from the 1980s.

Structural adjustment policies and the dependency of women

During the past two decades the important contribution of women to Third World development processes has been increasingly recognized by national governments and international agencies alike.[6] This has been reflected in significant shifts in policy approaches to women.[7] Early policy directed specifically towards women in developing countries, first widely initiated by international aid relief agencies soon after the Second World War, was based on a *welfarist* concern to bring women into the development process as better mothers and wives. It identified the importance of women only in their reproductive roles, and saw them as dependent beneficiaries of development. In marked contrast to this is the *anti-poverty* approach, first introduced in the 1970s when it was linked with basic needs policies, but still widely popular. This identifies poverty as the problem of underdevelopment and seeks to increase the economic productivity of low-income women, thereby recognizing their independent productive contribution to development, although it tends not to refer to their reproductive role. (In parenthesis it is also perhaps significant to mention the fact that the *equity/autonomy* approach, introduced particularly during the 1975–85 UN Decade for Women, has been far less successful. Because it challenges the subordinate position of women by seeking to reduce inequality between men and women, especially in the sexual division of labour, and give women 'real autonomy' this approach is considered particularly threatening and consequently not widely implemented.)

Shifts in attitudes towards the contribution of women to development processes have occurred alongside a marked deterioration in the world economy. Ironically, this has meant that recent international economic policy appears once again to be reinforcing not only the dependency status of Third World countries, but within them the dependent status of low-income women. I am referring here to those policies designed by the International Monetary Fund and the World Bank to effect economic stabilization and adjustment, and increasingly implemented by national governments particularly in Latin America and Africa where the problems of recession have been compounded by falling export prices, protectionism and the mounting burden of debt. Structural adjustment policies are designed, through both demand management and supply expansion, to reallocate resources so as to restore balance of payments equilibrium, increase exports and restore growth rates.[8] However the residualist approach employed by the IMF and the World Bank in their lending and 'conditionality' policies, designed to reduce the dependency of people on the state, has resulted amongst other measures in reductions in food subsidies, and severe social expenditure cuts in countries receiving international credit.[9]

Policies such as these have particular gender implications. Although, as Elson has argued, these macroeconomic policies are presented in a language which is perceived as being gender neutral, this in fact masks a gender bias concerning the process of the reproduction and maintenance of human resources.[10] The fact that the economy is defined in terms of marketed goods and services and subsistence cash production means that it excludes such reproductive work undertaken by women as caring for children, gathering fuel, processing food, preparing meals, nursing the sick. This built-in conceptual bias against women means that macroeconomic policies to reallocate resources implicitly assume that women's unpaid labour is elastic, able to stretch and to make up any shortfall in other resources available for reproduction and maintenance of the labour force.

This suggests that the success of macroeconomic policies relies on the invisible cost of women's unpaid time, through the extension of their working day. Disinvestment in human resources, represented in the decline in income levels, cuts in government health and education expenditure and in food subsidies is cushioned by the elasticity of women's labour in increasing self-production of food, changes in purchasing habits and consumption patterns. Given the complex ways in which caring and dependency are linked, with, as Hilary Graham has argued, dependency for women synonomous with giving rather than receiving care, it is clear that policies such as these increase women's dependency, for it is they rather than men who bear the main burden of devising the survival strategies necessary to compensate for reductions in purchased resources.[11]

Until recently, structural adjustment has been seen as an economic issue, evaluated in economic terms.[12] Although evidence as to its 'social costs' is still very unsystematic, it does show that deterioration in living conditions has gender differentiated impact on intra-household resource distribution.[13] Within the household, declines in consumption are not always the same for men and women, boys and girls; charges for education and healthcare can reduce access more severely for girls rather than for boys. Further evidence suggests that the capacity of the 'family' to shoulder the burden of adjustment has detrimental effects in terms of human relationships, expressed in increased domestic violence, mental health disorders and increasing numbers of women-headed households from the breakdown in family structures.[14]

The effects of structural adjustment policies on women's employment has varied, although the lowering of incomes has resulted in increased participation in productive work, whether it be through the feminization of rural agriculture (as men increasingly migrate), or through the growth of the urban informal sector.[15] It could be argued that the increasing dependence of the household on their income has increased women's independence but this has only been the case when it has been accompanied by relevant support services. While Hilary Land identified the necessity of mothers taking their children to school as limiting their availability for paid work and hence their ability to acquire a measure of independence (Chapter 7), in a Third World context lack of adequate access to such basic public services as water, electricity and public transport all structure women's activities and their capacity to acquire economic independence through paid work. As Elson has so aptly commented, 'For all but very well off women there is a complementarity between provision of services required for human resource development and the ability for women to gain from participation in the market'.[16]

The fact that the *efficiency* approach, is the policy approach towards women, currently gaining popularity by both international aid agencies and national governments alike is no coincidence.[17] For increased efficiency and productivity, two of the main objectives of structural adjustment policies in reality often simply mean a shifting of costs from the paid to the unpaid economy, particularly through the use of women's unpaid time. These rely on women in any one of their triple roles – their reproductive role within the household, their productive income earning role, and also increasingly on their community managing role. For in their gender ascribed roles as wives and mothers, women struggle to manage their neighbour-hoods, organizing at the community level in relation to the pro-vision of items of collective consumption.[18] A sectoral example of current policy is provided by housing projects with self-help components, which now regularly include women at the implementation phase. This is done not only because of their greater reliability in their reproductive role in repaying loans, or because of recognition that women in their productive role are equally capable of self-building alongside men, but also because women in their community managing roles have shown far greater ability to ensure that services are maintained.[19]

Current preoccupation with the 'social costs' of economic adjust-ment policy are the consequence of increasing evidence as to their disastrous effects on the income levels of low-income populations, with particularly detrimental effects identified on the lives of children and women.[20] UNICEF's widely publicized plea to devise adjust-ment policies 'with the human face' now challenges IMF and World Bank policy on the basis that economic policy can no longer ignore social policy. It argues that women's concerns, both in the household and in the workplace, need consciously to be made part of the analy-sis and formulation of adjustment policies, which, in turn, will mean that women need to be involved directly in both the definition of development and adjustment and in their management.[21] On paper, UNICEF's current policy proposals for women, which include such measures as increased access to credit and the recommendation that policies for restructuring within the productive sectors should be an important focus for women's concerns, both in the formal and in the informal sector would appear highly laudable.

Yet optimism that an international agency such as UNICEF has the capacity to effect policy measures designed to increase the independence of women must be treated with caution. One glance at some of the recent compensatory policies (to protect basic health and nutrition of the low-incomed during adjustment before growth resumption enables them to meet their minimum needs independently) endorsed by UNICEF, shows that in many respects they rely yet again on the invisible costs of women's unpaid time. In many nutrition interventions such as targeted food subsidies and direct feeding for the most vulnerable, it is assumed that women in their community-managing role will take responsibility for the efficient delivery of such services.[22]

Conclusion

The evidence suggests that at international, as much as at national, level the ideological structures which define women as dependants and carers and men as independent and powerful remain resistant to change. The fundamental difference between the UK and many Third World countries, however, lies in the level of statutory intervention in welfare matters on the part of government. In most Third World countries, where dependence on the state is much less, the emergence of informal sector solutions is now taken for granted, with an informal sector of employment, of childcare provision, very often of health and certainly of housing often the only means by which low-income families survive.[23] Most ordinary Third World women, therefore, have had to rely far less on the state and its capacity to deliver welfare and services than has been the case in the UK.

One consequence of this has been the increasing independence women have achieved through their own self-help solutions, in which they have shown themselves dependent neither on the state nor on men. The differences between British and Third World Women was aptly illustrated in a recent Women and Housing Conference, 'Our Homes Our Selves', organized during 1987, the International Year of Shelter for the Homeless, with 600 women attending both from Britain and the Third World. For the UK women the most important debate related to the definitions of the state's responsibility for the provision of working-class housing, the effects the new Housing Bill would have on their lives, and identification of the most appropriate methods to challenge the current cuts in the British government's budget for housing provision. For Third World women, such as an activist from a community-level organization in Santiago, Chile, an organizer from the Women Pavement Dwellers Association in Bombay, an engineer from a low-cost housing association in El Salvador and a social worker from a war-torn area of Southern Sudan, the debate was a very different one. In countries such as these where the state has never provided housing for large numbers of people, the debate related to the rights of women to own land and its implications in terms of government support and collaboration in self-help housing solutions. Their concern, therefore, was more with such issues as the identification of the most successful mechanisms for low-income women to push the limits of upgrading or site and service programmes through confronting outdated zoning legislation, resisting inappropriate squatter land resettlement policies or clarifying the conditions under which land invasions are less likely to be brutally broken up by the police.

It is critically important neither to romanticize the informal sector, nor to see community-level self-help solutions as the panacea for development. Nevertheless, as Hilary Land highlights, (Chapter 7) given the current preoccupation in the UK that withdrawal of state provision for women will result in increasing dependence on men, it may be that women in the UK can learn much from their better organized sisters in the Third World, who long ago learnt the limitations of relying on the state to reduce their dependence on men.

Notes

1 For a description of the institutionalization of welfare in the UK, see R. Mishra, *Society and Social Policy* (London: Macmillan, 1977).

2 For a discussion of the residual and incremental approaches to social welfare in the Third World, see M. Hardiman, and J. Midgley, *The Social Dimensions of Development* (London: Wiley, 1982).

3 A recent critique of the limitations of the dependency debates is provided by D. Booth, 'Marxism and development sociology: interpreting the impasse', *World Development*, 13 (7) July 1985. The chief proponent of the thesis of the 'development of underdevelopment' was provided by A. Gunder Frank, *Capitalism and Underdevelopment in Latin America*, Monthly Review Press, 1969.

4   A. MacEwen Scott, 'Industrialization, gender segregation and stratification theory', in R. Crompton, and M. Mann, (eds) *Gender and Stratification*, Polity Press, 1986, p. 169.

5   Ibid., p. 177.

6   One of the earliest contributions to this debate was E. Boserup, *Women's Role in Economic Development* (New York: St Martins Press, 1970). A recent review of the issues in the context of the Women's Decade is provided by I. Tinker, and J. Jaquette, 'UN decade for women: its impact and legacy', *World Development*, 15 (3), 1987.

7   For reviews of policy approaches to Third World women, see M. Buvinic, 'Projects for women in the Third World: explaining their misbehaviour', *World Development*, 14 (5); and C. O. N. Moser, 'Gender planning in the Third World: meeting women's practical and strategic needs', mimeo, 1988.

8   A succinct description of the social effects of structural adjustment policy is provided by A. Cornia, R. Jolly, and R. Stewart, *Adjustment with a Human Face*, Vol. 1 (London: Oxford University Press, 1987).

9   See S. MacPherson, and J. Midgley, *Comparative Social Policy and the Third World* (Sussex: Wheatsheaf Books, 1987).

10 See D. Elson, 'The impact of structural adjustment on women: concepts and issues', paper presented at Institute for Africa Alternatives conference, City University, September 1987.

11 H. Graham, 'Caring a labour of love', in J. Finch and D. A. Groves, *Labour of Love, Women, Work and Caring* (London: RKP, 1983), p. 24.

12 See R. Jolly, 'Women's needs and adjustment policies in developing countries', address given to Women's Development Group, OECD, Paris 1987.

13 See D. Elson, op. cit., p. 16; A. Cornia *et. al.*, op. cit.

14 See UNICEF Americas and the Caribbean Regional Office, *The Invisible Adjustment, Poor Women and the Economic Crisis*, p. 19–23.

15 Ibid., p. 18.

16 D. Elson, op. cit., p. 14.

17 C. O. N. Moser, 'A theory of gender planning: meeting women's practical and strategic needs', mimeo, 1988.

18 Ibid., p. 6–7.

19 For examples of women's participation in housing projects, see C. O. N. Moser, and L. Peake, (eds) *Women, Human Settlements and Housing* (London: Tavistock, 1987).

20 See A. Cornia *et. al.*, op. cit., A. Cornia, R. Jolly, and F. Stewart, *Adjustment with a Human Face Vol II* (London: Oxford University Press, 1988).

21 R. Jolly, op. cit., pp. 5–6.

22 In Lima, Peru, for instance, both the *Vaso de Leche*, a direct feeding programme which provided a free glass of milk daily to young children in the low-income areas of the city, was managed by women in their unpaid time. Similarly, the much-acclaimed communal kitchen in which women receive targeted food subsidies, depends on their organizational and cooking ability to ensure that the cooked food

reached families in the community. For a detailed account of communal kitchens see V. Sara-Lafosse, *Comedores Communales: La Mujer Frente a la Crisis*, Grupo de Trabajo, Servicios Urbanos y Mujeres de Bajos Ingressos, Lima, Peru, 1986.

23 For a review of the Informal Sector debate see C. O. N. Moser, 'Informal sector or petty commodity production: dualism or dependence in urban development', *World Development*, 6 (9/10), 1978.

PART IV

Social Policy and the Community

11 *Introduction*

MARTIN BULMER

The boundaries of social policy and 'the community' are less clear-cut than those of the preceding and following sections on social policy and the family and social policy and the economy. 'Community' is a notoriously slippery term in social science, and though the term resonates powerfully in public discourse, for example, in talk of 'community policing' and 'community care', pinning down its meaning and reference is far from easy. A recent review identified eighteen different contexts in social policy in which 'community' is used.[1] In the setting of the conference, the aim was to capture some aspects of social policy which shared three characteristics – they are public, social structural and have some basis in locality.

The concern with social policy in this section is public by contrast to the private worlds of the family treated in the previous section. Issues of political mobilization, social control and race relations are issues of a public kind, concerned with process taking place in the public arena, for which public remedies are sought. To give an example, two issues arouse strong passions and both are matters of legitimate public interest and policy discussion. But they relate to different spheres. The issue of racial attacks is a social policy issue in the public realm, while child sexual abuse within the family pertains to the private realm. To be sure, the line between public and private cannot be drawn with total precision, and the whole issue of community care forms a bridge between the two, but the distinction is clear enough.

The issues addressed in this section of the book are social structural, by contrast to the economic issues focused on in the following section. The papers in this section address the impli-cations of class, racial and geographic variation for social policy, rather than issues in resource allocation or public expenditure or the allocation of scarce resources between competing ends. The contribution of an analysis slanted toward sociology and political science is to emphasize the wider context within which social policy develops and seeks to be effective, including, in Chapter 12 by David Donnison, the question of how change can be effected.

Such an approach has much in common with social policy and the family, for gender differences are another important social variable, in the present context sufficiently important to be the subject of a separate group of papers with a distinctly sociological emphasis. There are, moreover, issues – poverty is a prime example, unemployment another – which are both social and economic, and for which the distinction between this and the following section is artificial (though sociological and economic approaches to phenomena such as inequality and poverty may be distinctively different).[2] Nevertheless, the sociological concerns of this section are clear enough.

They are given a degree of focus by their local geographical reference. Issues of social policy in the family or in the economy tend to be concerned either with the individual or with the region or nation, and with the relationship between nationally-framed policies and the life chances of individuals and families. Here we are concerned with policies which are played out at the local level and are dealing with various aspects of uneven spatial distribution. This has been a longstanding concern of criminologists, but more recently has become of much greater interest in other fields, for example, housing and health.[3] Such an emphasis is not inappropriate in a department in which the concept of 'territorial justice' originated.[4] There are considerable problems of explanation involved in dealing with geographical aggregates,[5] but the local focus remains highly appropriate for certain social policy issues.

The issues treated in this section, then, are public, social and local in their reference. Five issues are paid particular attention: the potential for community mobilization, the sclerotic features of large bureaucracies, tendencies to increasing social polarization and the possible creation of an 'underclass', contemporary urban race relations and urban crime. The first two are the focus of David Donnison's wide-ranging Chapter 12, which addresses the potential for mobilizing community action, but is equally telling in its asides about social tendencies – such as the failings of large bureaucracies – which make such an emphasis necessary. S. M. Miller addresses these issues of community participation and links them to the 'underclass' debate in Chapter 13, while A. H. Halsey in Chapter 14 takes up the issues of social polarization in the inner city. David Downes in Chapter 15 considers the evidence about the spatial distribution of crime, analyses the concept of the 'underclass' and considers their implications for future research.

The topics covered are selective, and represent only some of the salient issues to do with social policy and the community today. One major social variable not much discussed here, which might also fall under the family, is age. Gerontology is an area of growing importance in social policy. Two major substantive omissions, well covered in the mainstream literature, are poverty and housing. Other more specific social policy issues with a community focus, not discussed in detail here, include relations between lower level bureaucrats and members of the public, the deinstitutionalization of mentally-ill and mentally-handicapped people, substance abuse, homelessness, and urban racial disturbances.

This section of the book does not claim to provide a comprehensive agenda for future research in this area. It does, however, seek to suggest the significance of certain themes for future consideration, two in particular which underlie a range of social policy issues, some touched on in this section and some not. These two themes are empowerment and social polarization. Empowerment, an issue addressed by David Donnison, is the extent to which people can be involved in decisions about themselves, their community and the various groups to which they belong. Past over-optimism about the part which government could play has given way to the market orientation of British and American social policy of the last decade. This has sought in various ways to return to the individual the power to choose between alternative ends and means in social policy. Such choice is exercised, by and large, through market decisions made by the individual as a consumer. Indeed, in certain services the debate is now all about how consumer preferences can more effectively be taken into account – health is a prime example. Much less attention, however, has been given to how people can be involved in levels of decision-making intermediate between the family and the nation. There are many types of social choice and decision which are made at this level. The locality is one setting in which issues of empowerment may be addressed, as David Donnison's paper shows.

Social polarization refers to the apparent widening of the gap between the more prosperous and less prosperous members of society, at least in Britain and the United States, in the last decade. The issue is most commonly discussed in Britain in relation to the erosion of state income support, cuts in resources devoted to state cash benefits, and widening income and wealth differentials between the better-off and poorer sections of the population. In the United States this is also a theme, linked also to the funding of Medicare and Medicaid. These have been conventional concerns of academic social policy, indeed the 'crisis of the welfare state' is often discussed partly in these terms.

Another manifestation of the widening gap in access to resources and opportunities are regional differences in prosperity between different parts of a country, whether sunbelt and snowbelt in the United States, north and south in Britain, or north and south in West Germany. Coming down to the local level, in the United States a further dimension of polarization is apparent. Greater income and wealth inequality than in many European countries is reinforced by geographical segregation along social and particularly racial lines.

In recent years in both Britain and America concern has focused upon social conditions in the inner city, where deprivation has become concentrated in particular areas. How far that dislocation may go is illustrated by conditions in some of America's inner city areas. These have been graphically portrayed in a number of recent articles, which emphasize the concentration of disadvantage and the occurrence together of several forms of deprivation.[6] One example will suffice here for brevity. The Robert Taylor Homes on the South Side of Chicago is the largest public housing project in the city, consisting of twenty-eight sixteen-storey buildings, covering ninety-two acres. In 1980 the official population was 20,000 but another 7,000 unregistered residents were estimated to live there. In 1983 the entire population of the Homes was black, and over two-thirds were under the age of 18. Median family income was $5,470. Of families with children, 93 per cent were headed by a single parent. Of families with children, over four-fifths received AFDC, the American income support for low income families with children. Unemployment was estimated to be 47 per cent in 1980. Although in 1980 only 0.3 per cent of the city's population lived there, 11 per cent of the city's murders, 9 per cent of its rapes and 10 per cent of its aggravated assaults were committed in the project.[7]

How is one to interpret such an extreme concentration of the ills of modern industrial society? American cities are racially more highly segregated residentially than British urban areas. American public housing draws its tenants from a more restricted group than British council housing, and constitutes a much smaller proportion of the total housing stock. There may nevertheless be something to be learned from the American debate. It can not be maintained confidently that European cities will not display some of these characteristics in the future. For example, increasing interest is being paid to tendencies toward social polarization inherent in the British housing market, particularly as a result of changes in the public housing sector.[8]

There is also increasing concern about the growth of crime in certain areas and the breakdown of social control, linked to what is perceived as 'the decline of community'. Though traditional working class areas had equivocal relations with the police, and there were always 'rough' areas where the rule of law was minimal, for a long period until at least the 1960s there was a system of formal and informal regulation, and a degree of respect for the police as an institution, which kept crime down to tolerable levels, ensured a reasonable level of support for the law, and did not induce fear or damage communities.[9] This situation is now changing. Coupled with wider social changes, many of the informal institutions and networks which acted to discourage offending have gone, in many areas the local population is much more heterogeneous; there is a heightened perception of crime as a problem among local residents; and especially among young people and ethnic minorities there is considerable dissatisfaction with the way in which the police operate.[10] Indeed, recent urban unrest in British cities in 1981 and 1985 have been described not so much as inter-racial disturbances as clashes between young black people and the police. American cities are still more crime-prone than British cities, but the parallels can not be dismissed as irrelevant, just as the common link with economic deprivation is pertinent to the explanation of the phenomenon.

Some of the more incisive comment upon contemporary urban trends is currently coming from outside the academic social policy community. The Archbishop of Canterbury's Commission on

Urban Priority Areas, *Faith in the City*, in effect an unofficial royal commission, unequivocally pointed to a process of social polarization.

> Though the quality of life in the inner city improved relatively in the period from the Second World War up to the mid–1970s, the more recent history has been one of growing inequality – in life chances, income, housing, education, public services and the general level of civic amenity. Moreover, and more alarming, the migration of people and the movement of capital, employment opportunities, private enterprise and voluntary effort is increasingly away from the urban priority area districts to the more sylvan and salubrious areas of the South and East . . . The process is one of deprived people being left (in the inner city) as the successful move out to middle Britain. The former have decreasing wealth, health, services, income, investment and amenity; the latter have rising affluence, opportunity, power and advantage: in one ugly word – polarisation. The process of polarisation is a general one in Britain today.[11]

The Audit Commission has gone further. In a report on *The Management of London's Local Authorities: preventing the breakdown of services*, they observe:

> There are very disturbing parallels between the situation in parts of London and that in parts of New York and Chicago. The South Bronx and the South Side of Chicago represent a future to be avoided at almost any cost. There, a combination of poor housing and education, high crime rates much of it drug-related, large scale immigration and associated racial tensions, an exodus of jobs and the more well-off to the suburbs, high youth unemployment and welfare dependency and the break-up of traditional family structures (with a very high proportion of single parent families), have served to create what some commentators in the United States have described as an urban 'underclass' . . . Once such a situation develops, it is extraordinarily difficult to retrieve.[12]

This has led some social scientists to describe those at the bottom of the social scale as an 'underclass' who suffer multiple and cumulative deprivations and whose situation, socially, economically and spatially, is deteriorating. The term is in most widespread current use in the United States, and used to refer to conditions in inner areas of large conurbations such as New York, Detroit, Chicago and Washington DC.[13]

William J. Wilson has identified some of the particular features of this social group.

> Today's (US) ghetto neighbourhoods are populated almost exclusively by the most disadvantaged segments of the black urban community, that heterogeneous grouping of families and individuals who are outside the mainstream of the American occupational system. Included in this group are individuals who lack training and skills and either experience long-term employment or are not members of the labour force, individuals who are engaged in street crime and other forms of aberrant behaviour, and families that experience long-term spells of poverty and/or welfare dependency. These are the populations to which I refer when I speak of the *underclass*. I use this term to depict a reality not captured in the more standard designation *lower class*.[14]

It is not sufficient, Wilson suggests, to debate whether or not the concept should be used, rather use it to study the increasing social dislocation and polarization of the inner city. He does not see the underclass primarily as a racial issue, despite the high concentration of black people in the most disadvantaged areas.

The applicability of the concept is by no means confined to one country. Peter Hall has suggested that an 'underclass' is beginning to develop in Britain.[15] In *The Underclass and the Future of Britain*, Ralf Dahrendorf has presented the issue in almost apocalyptic terms, describing the underclass as 'a cancer on society'. 'If some have no stake in society, a society puts itself at risk. It becomes defensive – there is such a thing as social protectionism as well as protectionism in trade – and in the end, closed. Extending full citizenship rights to all is therefore the main task of social policy'.[16] His formulation of the issue contains echoes of T. H. Marshall's discussion of citizenship.

Whether or not an 'underclass' exists or is being brought into being is an issue addressed by A. H. Halsey (Chapter 14), S. M. Miller (Chapter 13) and David Downes (Chapter 15) in this section of the book and returned to in Chapter 16 written by myself.

Whatever the answer, the coexistence of various forms of depri- vation – low incomes, poor housing, inadequate education, lack of jobs, and a greater chance of criminal victimization – within particular urban settings is a major policy issue for the final decade of the second millennium.

Social polarization is also receiving more attention because of interest in the extent and causes of welfare dependency. S. M. Miller refers to the attention given to Charles Murray's *Losing Ground*, but this is only one of a number of serious analytic studies which has put forward accounts at odds with the assumptions underlying social- democratic welfare interventionism.[17] The wrath of liberals was aroused by the suggestions of Murray and Lawrence Mead that government intervention in the 1970s had the effect of increasing dependency rather than reducing poverty, but to some extent their fire was misdirected at the author's value premises. Though much of the debate turned on the evidence, insufficient attention has been paid to the underlying explanatory models being used, by the critics as much as of the revisionists. There is now greater diversity apparent in explanations of the condition of less fortunate members of society.

The issues of empowerment and social polarization come together in the question of the political representation and involve- ment of disadvantaged groups at the local level. This is the subject of David Donnison's paper in Chapter 12.

Notes

1 P. Willmott, *Community as Social Policy* (London: Policy Studies Institute, 1984).
2 cf. W. G. Runciman, *Relative Deprivation and Social Justice* (London: Routledge & Kegan Paul, 1966) and A. K. Sen, *Poverty and Famines* (Oxford: Oxford University Press, 1983).
3 cf. P. Townsend *et al.*, *Inequalities of Health: The Black Report* and *The Health Divide* (Harmondsworth: Penguin, 1988 – Black Report first published 1980); P. Townsend, P. Phillimore and A. Beattie *Health and Deprivation: Inequality and the North* (London: Croom Helm, 1988).
4 cf. B. Davies, *Social Needs and Resources in Local Services* (London: Michael Joseph, 1968).
5 M. Bulmer *et al.* *Social Science and Social Policy* (London: Allen & Unwin, 1986) pp. 123–46.
6 cf. N. Lemann, 'The origins of the underclass', *The Atlantic Monthly*, June 1986, pp. 31–55 and July 1986, pp. 54–68; R. P. Nathan, 'Will the

underclass always be with us?', *Society/Transaction* 24 (3), March–April 1987, pp. 57–62; A. Hacker, 'American apartheid' and 'Black crime, white racism', *New York Review of Books*, 3 December, 1987, pp. 26–33 and 3 March, 1988, pp. 36–41. The modern origin of the term is sometimes credited to Ken Auletta's book *The Underclass* (New York: Random House, 1982), but in fact the term was in use by social scientists before then, as in D. G. Glasgow, *The Black Underclass: poverty, unemployment and the entrapment of ghetto youth* (San Francisco: Jossey Bass, 1980).

7   W. J. Wilson *The Truly Disadvantaged: The Inner City, The Underclass and Public Policy* (Chicago: University of Chicago Press, 1987), p. 25. For a description of the housing project, see Devereux Bowly Jr., *The Poorhouse: subsidized housing in Chicago 1895–1976* (Carbondale, Illinois: Southern Illinois University Press, 1978); and for an account of post–war housing policies which created these conditions see A. R. Hirsch, *Making the Second Ghetto: race and housing in Chicago 1940–1960* (Cambridge: Cambridge University Press, 1983).

8   cf. A. Power, *Council Housing: Conflict, Change, Decision-Making* (London: London School of Economics, ST/ICERD Welfare State Programme Paper no. WSP/27, 1988); P. Willmott and A. Murie, *Polarisation and Social Housing: The British and French experience* (London: Policy Studies Institute Research Report 676, 1988), especially Chapters 3 and 4.

9   cf. M. J. Clarke, 'Citizenship, community and the management of crime', *British Journal of Criminology*, 27 (4), autumn 1987, pp. 384–400.

10 cf. T. Hope and M. Shaw (eds), *Communities and Crime Reduction* (London: HMSO, 1988), especially pp. 2–15; see also P. Cohen, 'Subcultural conflict and the working class community', *Working Papers in Cultural Studies* (Centre for Contemporary Cultural Studies, University of Birmingham), 2, 1972, pp. 5–51.

11 Archbishop of Canterbury's Commission on Urban Priority Areas, *Faith in the City: a call for action by church and nation* (London: Church House Publishing, 1985), pp. 22–3. See also A. H. Halsey, 'Social Trends since the Second World War', *Social Trends*, 17 (London: HMSO, 1987), pp. 11–19.

12 Audit Commission, *The Management of London's Authorities: preventing the breakdown of services* (London: Audit Commission Occasional Papers no. 2, January 1987) p. 2.

13 For a review, see M. A. Gephart and R. W. Pearson, 'Contemporary research on the urban underclass', *Items* (SSRC New York), 42, (1/2), June 1988, pp. 1–10.

14 Wilson, *The Truly Disadvantaged*, pp. 7–8.

15 P. Hall, 'Britain 2013', *New Society*, 18 December 1987, pp. 39–41.

16 R. Dahrendorf, *The Underclass and the Future of Britain* (Windsor, Berkshire: St George's House Tenth Annual Lecture, 1987), p. 7 and R. Dahrendorf, *The Modern Social Conflict* (London: Weidenfeld & Nicolson, 1988), Chapter 7, 'Conflict after class'.

17 C. Murray, *Losing Ground: American Social Policy 1950–1980* (New

York: Basic Books, 1984); Lawrence Mead, *Beyond Entitlement: The Social Obligations of Citizenship* (New York: Free Press, 1986); R. E. Morgan, *Disabling America: the 'rights industry' in our time* (New York: Basic Books, 1984). The vigour of current American debate is exemplified in A. Gutmann (ed.), *Democracy and the Welfare State* (Princeton, NJ: Princeton University Press, 1988).

12 Social policy: the community-based approach

DAVID DONNISON

Introduction

The issues I want to explore in this chapter can be posed in several different ways. They can be described as new forms of collective action and collective consumption; or as new patterns of authority which are changing the character of government and professional practice; or as new relationships between citizens and the state. These are different aspects of a pattern of changes now to be seen in Britain and other countries. If this description of my subject sounds a bit vague, that reflects the groping response we are making to our problems. The problems themselves can be more plainly described. Authority is power, and people do not part with power willingly; so new styles of authority begin to emerge when the old styles prove unworkable and are discredited. The old styles are indeed breaking down. So what must we do? This chapter is about some of the answers now being given to that question in Britain and Ireland.

After briefly exploring the reasons for these changes, I shall describe some of the new patterns which are taking shape and note their strengths and weaknesses. Next I consider the common features of the more successful projects; finally I offer some practical conclusions.

This paper is drawn from discussions which I have had with the leading spirits in about twenty community-based projects in Britain and in Ireland, north and south. The range of projects one might have studied is so large and varied that it would have been

impossible to visit a representative selection of them unless con-
fining one's attention to a small part of this field. Since I wanted to
make a broader review of the issues I used my contacts with some
of the more successful, thoughtful and approachable people
working in the field. I am writing to tell these people what was
learnt from their collective experience, in the hope that this may be
a way of thanking them for their help and of seeking further help in
getting this account of their work right.

Definitions

In what I describe as 'community-based' projects the users of a
service have some control over the resources required to provide
the service. Their control may be complete, or it may be no more
than a powerful influence; the project may be statutory or voluntary in form; and it may be funded from public, commercial or
charitable sources, or from some mixture of these. The projects I
have in mind include credit unions and food co-operatives; neighbourhood watch associations set up to protect their members'
property and deter intruders; associations offering mutual support
to people who suffer from the same disease or handicap; housing
management co-operatives and housing associations, if they are
run by the tenants of the houses concerned; adult education and
arts groups in which the participants choose the work they do and
decide for themselves how to do it; and more broadly based community associations which organize a wider range of activities
which may include business enterprises, a newspaper, social clubs
and youth projects, a creche, welfare rights and pressure group
work, sports and drama groups, and so on.

This is not a precise definition. It excludes decentralization of
public services which only involves the dispersal of work from
central offices to numerous small neighbourhood offices ('decon-
centration' this might be called); and it excludes procedures for
consulting the public which do not give away any real power over
the services concerned. It also excludes trade unions, most of
which have become nationwide organizations with bureaucracies
of their own which are not directly accountable to local, small-
scale communities. Less justifiably, perhaps, even the more democratic, locally based churches have been excluded; although they

may give practical help to their members, that is not their main task.

But while those frontiers are fairly clearly marked, there is no clear boundary distinguishing the community-based projects I shall be discussing from community businesses and producer co-operatives, owned by those who work in them, which trade with a wider public. These enterprises have been included if they are accountable to a community closely associated with them, and are primarily designed to benefit that community by selling them goods and services or by earning surpluses which are spent on projects chosen by the community. But enterprises which operate much like any other profit-making business have been excluded, even if they have a co-operative constitution.

Why are community-based approaches developing?

Advocates of the community-based approach tend to explain its growth by saying how well it works. But that does not explain why it is developing *now*. And to cynics their enthusiasm may suggest that this is no more than a flavour of the month – a fashionable fad which will be replaced by some other before long.

There are in fact more compelling reasons for this development than the enthusiasm of its advocates. The distribution of power shifts only when it has to. How strong the compulsions for change must be is made clear by the fact that it is often in the most centralized, authoritarian services that the new styles are to be seen – the services which are, in the old fashioned sense, most 'professional' (meaning that their professionals have conceded least power to their clients).

The army were among the first to recognize that in guerilla warfare and the 'low intensity operations' which in a nuclear age have become the main field of military action, the winning of the hearts and minds of the civilian population is more important than the winning of battles.[1]

The police, investigated by Lord Scarman after disturbances which drove them off the Brixton streets, are adopting his proposals[2] for liaison groups and other projects which are designed to elicit support from the public. Crime prevention, which used to be all about burglar alarms and similar hardware, is now all about 'community policing'.

Medical services have increasingly come to accept the view, eloquently expressed by the World Health Organisation,[3] that their most important task is not to cure disease but to help citizens take more effective care of their own health. AIDS will reinforce this trend; confronted with this disaster, medical authorities,unable to offer any remedies, can only appeal to the most vulnerable groups to get together and collectively adopt safer living patterns.

The Manpower Services Commission, unable to find jobs for large numbers of unemployed people, and unable in the worst areas to induce commercial employers to provide temporary work or training opportunities on anything like the scale required, have increasingly turned to community projects of various kinds to fill the gap.

Meanwhile the local housing authorities in some of Britain's oldest cities, having completed the biggest slum clearance and rehousing programmes the world has ever seen, find that people refuse to live in some of the houses built for them only a few years ago. As vacancies increase, so do vandalism, lost rents and the turnover of tenants. Already, some years before, when they tried to improve older housing, many of these authorities found that their procedures, which worked reasonably well when they were bull-dozing large areas, provoked fierce opposition among the people whose homes were to be modernized. Housing authorities have therefore turned increasingly to housing management co-operatives, housing associations and community ownership schemes to tackle all these problems.

This list could be extended, but already it makes the point clear enough. The community-based approach is not an invention of starry eyed enthusiasts. It has been developed, sometimes as an act of desperation, in order to solve problems which defeated conventional services operating in conventional ways. Something like this would have happened – and often has happened – without any help from community workers or others professionally engaged in their kind of work.

A pervasive factor, among others which explain why similar changes appeared in so many different services (and countries) at this time, is the new political climate which developed as a post–war generation came to maturity in the 1970s. The previous generation, which played major parts in building the modern state and its public service professions, gained its formative political experiences

before, during and just after the Second World War. Each generation creates, during its early formative years, its own political
drama to interpret the political issues of its day – a drama with a
familiar cast of actors who serve as characters in political cartoons
and popular debate thereafter. For that generation, emerging from
the depression and the brutal political experiences it generated, a
'monopoly' was, typically, a commercial enterprise which domi-
nates its market and exploits its customers; a 'trade union' meant the
organized workers fighting rich bosses; a 'landlord' was a fat man in
a black suit holding money bags ... and so on. There were also
more conservative ways of describing the same cast of actors. But
even among Conservatives, many saw the democratic state as the
main instrument of social progress – as the stage on which the heroes
of the drama acted their parts.

As reality moves on, however, it parts company with the old
drama, and a new generation, gaining different formative experiences, writes a new script for itself. In many parts of Britain today
the monopolies which make the biggest impact on people's lives are
the social security office, which is the only or main source of their
incomes, and the housing department which owns all the houses
they might want to live in. That department, not the cartoon figure
of the man with money bags, has in many places become the only
landlord that counts. And the trade unions which impinge most
directly on the most vulnerable people are the public service unions
representing local government officers, maintenance men, social
security clerks, teachers and others; organized producers of the
social services whose interests may conflict with those of their
poorer and less well-organized customers.[4] For Catholics in
Northern Ireland, for blacks in Britain, and for many others who
feel themselves to be excluded from power of any kind, the state
looks more like a stage for their oppressors than for heroes of any
sort.

In the new political drama which began to take shape around the
1970s the state and the public service professions were less likely to
be seen as the natural instruments of social progress – and hence the
Labour Party, which cast itself as hero of the old drama, lost control
of Merseyside, Islington, Bermondsey and other inner city territories which it had regarded as its own fiefdoms. To give the
'welfare state' a more attractive and humane face became an urgent
political priority for many local councils.[5]

The end of the long post-war boom, which came at roughly the same time, pushed these changes forward. Hitherto, defenders and critics of the state both tended to assume when things went wrong that, with more resources, all would be well. Economic, demographic and urban growth seemed between them to guarantee that in time there would be enough money, enough staff, enough houses, schools and hospitals, to meet the needs of the poor without average voters having to pay a price for that in the form of reductions in their own real standard of living. As this positive sum game turned to a zero sum game or worse – a contest for resources in which every winner's gains had to be paid for by someone else's losses – it became clear that the old institutions were never going to solve all the problems: the voters would never give them the resources to try.

Thus new strategies had to be developed. The community-based approach was only one of the responses which followed. 'Privatization' was another.[6] Community-based policing was paralleled by growing reliance on organizations such as Securicor; community-based forms of alternative health care by a revival of private medicine; housing co-operatives by the drive to sell council houses. Sometimes the distinctions between these strategies became blurred: Glasgow's community ownership scheme which transferred council houses en bloc to their tenants seems to have been 'sold' simultaneously to a Labour council as a return to socialist principles, and to Conservative ministers as a form of privatization.[7]

There is now a real danger that the old romanticism about the state will be succeeded by new romanticisms about communities and markets. Attempts like the one made in this chapter to gain a more realistic understanding of the former should be matched by similar realism about the latter. If I point out some of the weaknesses of community-based action, that should not be interpreted as a preference for privatization.

Meanwhile other, harsher solutions are also being prepared. In parts of Northern Ireland, where many people never had much faith in the state, the old bureaucratic and professional patterns of authority have most obviously failed. There, brutal movements rule the streets, and governments have responded by creating an armed police force, backed by the army, and going a long way towards abolishing trial by jury and democratic local government – a pattern which could readily be developed in fascist directions and applied in

Britain if the opportunity were given. When turbulent times come, we shall only be saved from that fate if other, better solutions are available and widely understood. The people whose projects I now turn to are trying to formulate those better solutions.

Communtiy-based approaches

Most community-based projects are specialized or functional agencies performing a fairly clearly defined task, usually for a clearly defined population. The housing management co-operatives which Glasgow District Council has set up are an example of this type. They are given a budget by the council which is sufficient to employ a full-time person who serves a committee elected by all the tenants of the block of property involved. With its manager's help, the co-operative repairs and maintains the houses and carries out minor capital works. Within broad priorities agreed with the housing department, it also allocates vacant houses.

Credit unions, if they are managed not by employers for their workers but by their own members, are another example of this type. The Strathclyde Region has appointed a development officer to promote the formation of credit unions, particularly in deprived communities where banks, building societies and other conventional financial institutions are reluctant to set up branches.

Community businesses, producing a specific product or service under the management of a committee elected by the community they serve, sometimes illustrate the same pattern; one of the most striking examples in the UK is the Galliagh Co-operative, which built and successfully manages a supermarket in the largest housing estate in Derry. After providing support for local voluntary groups, its accumulated surplus amounts to about £100,000 which is now available for developing new projects.

There are many more examples of this sort: they include sports clubs, music and drama societies, wine buying societies, and all the other collective, non-profit enterprises to be found in well-established neighbourhoods. But our main interest lies in groups whose operations impinge more directly on the state and its social services.

Next, constituting a special and rapidly growing category of their own, there are the local branches of lay, self-help groups providing mutual support and care for members suffering from a particular disease, handicap or problem – cancers of various kinds, heart disease, eczema, asthma, drug additions, alcoholism, mental handicap, multiple sclerosis, and many others. There have recently been calculated to be 1,500 national organizations of this sort, with over 25,000 regional branches – more than 200 of them for eczema alone. Their members may be the sufferers, or the people responsible for caring for them; and their national headquarters may be a dominant influence or simply a back-up for local initiatives. Some have a fairly limited purpose such as campaigning for research funds and medical equipment. Others provide a much more extensive support service, coupled with a national role of public education and pressure.[8]

The self-help groups providing the most comprehensive array of services set an example which suggests the possibility of developing, for a fairly clearly defined population, a broader community association capable of tackling any task the members want to turn their hand to. An Irish group working with, and for, the travelling people who live in caravans illustrate a pattern of this sort. Along with legal advice and pressure group work, they have developed educational programmes for adults dealing with travellers' histories and traditions, as well as more basic skills of literacy, and have involved travellers themselves in planning and developing the project. A distinctive ethnic origin, culture and language have often been the basis for this kind of initiative. Asian communities in Britain would furnish other examples of this sort.

Where this kind of pattern develops on a more ambitious scale on behalf of a larger residential community it becomes a different kind of project for which there is no generally accepted name: a 'community action project', it might be called. The Craigmillar Festival Society in Edinburgh is such a project. So are the Pleck Community Council in Walsall, the Harlesden People's Community Council which set up the Stonebridge Bus Garage project in Brent, the Broadwater Farm Residents' Association and the nearby Youth Association, Dove House Community Resource Centre in Derry, the Falls Community Resource Centre, the Farsett Youth Project in Belfast, Dublin's North Central City Community Action Project and the Clare Resource Centre at Corofin in County Clare, along with others which we have visited in recent months.

Towards an appraisal of the specialized groups

What are the characteristic strengths and weaknesses of these projects? I will start with the more specialized, single-purpose groups which are much the most common of the types I have distinguished.

Community-based services of this kind can do some urgently needed things which statutory services are not empowered to do and private enterprise is unable or unwilling to do – like setting up credit unions in impoverished communities where people urgently need simple, reliable ways of saving and borrowing money. The alternatives are the illicit money lenders and the 'heavies' who police their territory, the grocery vans whose drivers take child benefit books in return for credit at high rates of interest, the exploitative clothing clubs – and unpaid rent and fuel bills. Other projects of this sort – like Glasgow's housing management co-operatives – do not create a new service but may well provide a better one, more accountable to its users, than the state was able to offer.

It could be argued that if the state or the private sector are failing, it would be wiser to make the conventional services more effective than to compel poor people to go to the trouble of creating community-based alternatives in the few neighbourhoods capable of doing so. But it would be difficult to make that argument altogether convincing. It is impossible for profit-making enterprise to provide an adequate range of services in impoverished areas. That has always been one of the arguments for intervention by the state. But the state has real limitations. There are reasons why an elected local authority, with its short-term political horizons, finds it particularly difficult to manage public housing both efficiently and fairly – reasons which explain why other countries normally rely on intermediary bodies of various kinds (co-operatives, non-profit municipal companies, and so on) to manage 'social rented housing'.

It must be recognized, however, that some community-based projects have been called into being by the present government's policies of switching resources from the public to the private sector. If improvement grants and capital expenditure are withdrawn from council housing while owner-occupiers continue to get grants and tax reliefs, the tenants of the worst council houses have a strong incentive to set up co-operatives which, being legally a form of private ownership, can secure benefits available to owner-occupiers.

That seems to have been the rather reluctant way in which some of Glasgow's community ownership schemes got started – although most of their members were soon convinced that these schemes were worth developing for their own sake.

Thus a sceptical question must always be asked about the reasons why community-based forms of service are needed. It should not be assumed too readily that they offer the only solution for defects in more conventional services, public or private. That would be to absolve too easily the public service professions and the entre-preneurs whose authoritarian or profit-motivated styles have some-times compelled people to do their own thing when they would have preferred to rely on conventional services if only they would operate in more responsive, 'user-friendly' ways.

Limitations

Meanwhile these single purpose projects have some fundamental limitations of their own. They usually stick to their clearly defined function and do not use that as a base and a training for other work. Although leading spirits in the credit union and housing association movements have called upon their comrades to extend their work into other kinds of enterprise for which they would be well prepared, this has rarely happened. That may be because the strength and unity of these groups depend on their capacity to focus on the original, unifying objective for which they mobilized, and their refusal to be distracted by other potentially divisive tasks.

Having argued and suffered together – sometimes for years – through the long meetings required to get their projects going, community groups create strong personal bonds and a power structure in which newcomers with new ideas may not be welcome. No matter how radical their original impetus, they can be pas-sionately conservative about the organization they have created. These organizations are not unchangeable; indeed, they evolve as time goes by – but often in somewhat conservative directions. The women who frequently played leading roles in the early, heroic years tend to be replaced by men experienced in committee pro-cedures. A new kind of bureaucracy, dominated by a new sort of mafia, may be created. The same tendencies and dilemmas have been noted by religious leaders in the 'woman church' and liberation theology movements who are well aware that, to survive, the radical group breaking away from the institutional church has to become institutionalized in its turn if it is to survive.[9]

Conservatism often extends beyond the services which the group provides to encompass the customers they serve. It is said that one of the more successful credit unions operating in a big council estate in Glasgow consists of 400 people drawn from twenty-five Irish families. Even if that is a caricature, it is one which illustrates the problem. It is clear that the selection procedures for tenants devised by housing management co-operatives in the same city would not recruit blacks, ex-prisoners, addicts or other stigmatized people unless they already had friends or relatives in the co-operative. It was the members of local community groups in deprived suburbs of Belfast and Dublin who mobilized with ugly threats of violence to drive travelling people out of their neighbourhoods.

We should not conclude that the community-based approach does not work. More conventional bureaucratic systems do not have a much better record when it comes to racist, sexist and other forms of discrimination, and recent research shows that these failings are deeply rooted and very difficult to correct.[10] Nevertheless the limitations of the single purpose community groups should be recognized. Coherence and discipline must somehow be maintained, without the help of conventional bureaucratic forms of authority. If the group has a clearly defined job to do for a clearly defined population, all of whom gain or lose from the success or failure of the enterprise, other kinds of discipline can be brought to bear. Their sanctions against rule breakers may be pretty formidable. Tenants on an impoverished estate who are run out of their credit union may lose a lot of friends and find themselves with no other legal source of credit to which they can turn.

These groups may be right to operate in this kind of way. Their strengths could easily be lost if they tried to extend their functions, their membership or their clientele. If so, however, we must recognize that although they undoubtedly make bits of the world into better places, they are not going to change the world in any fundamental way. They cannot debate economic and social priorities in any general sense because they have only one priority – the particular job they set out to do. They cannot take responsibility for bringing the outcast and deprived into the mainstream of society; indeed, they may reinforce their exclusion, and the problems of other neighbourhoods and institutions to which the excluded then have to resort. The state, which for better or worse does have these responsibilities, still has a central role, however extensive the community-based alternatives to its conventional services become. But the state's relations with the new system pose many problems.

Because they have a specialized function which they may perform very well, community-based groups are often valued by state agencies with a similar function which see them as useful instruments for their own purposes. That can form the basis for a benign partnership in which the state provides funds and advice, while leaving the group free to develop in its own way. The discreet support given to self-help health groups by the DHSS seems often to have worked like this. But objectives may not dovetail with each other so neatly. The youth groups and other projects funded by the Manpower Services Commission (and its counterparts in Ireland) on terms which seem mainly designed to reduce the unemployment figures and to keep the young docile (by eliminating broader educational and human development activities from the groups' programmes) often feel that they are being exploited rather than supported – exploited, moreover, in ways which reinforce, rather than correct, the defects of the traditional system.

Appraising community action

Realism about the limitations of the specialist, single purpose groups prompts us to ask whether the more ambitious community action projects offer hope of a bolder shift towards open, participative, accountable democracy. In parts of Northern Ireland it looked for a while as if that might be happening. In 1972, when disturbances in Belfast led to the temporary collapse of public services, and thousands of people were compelled by fear to move out of mixed areas into communities of their own faith, local groups took over many of the functions of government. They erected barriers at the entrances to their neighbourhoods and policed them for twenty-four hours a day. They allocated houses to the homeless, and provided relief for people who had lost all they possessed. They set up taxi services. If they had a bakery within their territory but no dairy, they bartered bread for milk with other community groups and distributed these things to the families in need of them. But those were heroic days and special circumstances. What has happened since, there and in the rest of the British isles?

Some community action groups operate on an impressive scale. The Pleck Community Council and its associated enterprises have set up projects which range from gardening to milk delivery to housing management to a boxing club, and more. The excellent play which was the Easterhouse Festival Society's (EFS) first major project was written, produced and acted by local people, and it was awarded a prize in the Edinburgh Festival Fringe. Later, EFS created the biggest outdoor mosaic in Europe – a beautiful and technically expert work of art. To take over the Stonebridge Bus Garage from London Transport and convert it into workshops, studios, a creche, a training centre, gynmasia, a theatre, a restaurant and more besides, the young Caribbeans of the Harlesden People's Community Council had to raise about £8 million from the Department of the Environment, the Greater London Council, the Borough of Brent, the Manpower Services Commission, charitable trusts and the EEC. They now employ about ninety people on the project – many of them part-time. Co-operative enterprises on the Broadwater Farm estate employ about twenty-five people. These achievements could be matched in many other places.

Sheer scale, however, is not the most impressive feature of these projects. They have taken initiatives which neither the public nor the private sector would have contemplated. Their capacity to mount political campaigns on behalf of their communities is well known, but there are many other places capable of successful pressure group activity. Celebration through drama, music and art have been a recurring theme in community action, producing performances of vivid quality which assert the identity and history of the neighbourhood, and create links for it with the outside world. In places where examples of excellence are scarce and people often feel isolated and forgotten those are important achievements.

Some groups – Pleck and the Corofin Centre, for example – have made a fairly sophisticated analysis of their community's expenditure and skills, and set about creating enterprises which will use these skills to substitute for services brought in from elsewhere. When raising funds to build community centres, youth clubs and other things, some groups – in Stonebridge and Broadwater Farm, for example – have successfully insisted that the jobs which those funds create come to their community. For black minorities in particular, that has been seen as an opportunity to gain skills and set up enterprises which will enable them to compete in the wider world. These groups are breaking out of the social isolation in which poor communities are often imprisoned. They are also bridging the gaps between economic and social policy, between physical and human development, and surmounting administrative barriers which cripple the state's services. Community action projects have often been more creative and adaptable than any bureaucracy could be.

Most important for the activists themselves has been the transforming experience and the personal growth these projects have given them. They have learnt capacities for leadership, gained the confidence to deal decisively with politicians, officials and professionals of all sorts, and demolished the myths of 'credentialism' – the idea that you cannot do things unless properly trained and qualified for the job.

But a heavy price has been paid for these achievements. Community action projects typically have a turbulent history: internal and external conflicts and betrayals, threatened bankruptcy, allegations of fraud are all commonplace. Friendships and families may break up. Leaders who stay the course may become unattractively hardened politicians. The characteristic styles of community action are spontaneous, emotionally direct, contentious, charismatic ... entirely different from the conventions of bureaucratic routine which help people to separate their personal from their professional lives, to argue without quarreling, to control the demands of their work with the help of the annual and monthly rhythms of budgets, committee meetings and holidays, and to get home at reasonably predictable times. It is not surprising that community activists tend to burn out fast.

The marks of success

Nevertheless, some of these groups succeed in the sense that they gain resources, involve a widening circle of people, provide a growing range of opportunities, and stay in business. How do they do it? These are the recurring patterns we found in the more successful community action projects.

(1)   They have *charismatic, committed leaders*. One will do, but often there will be several. Lacking the rituals which legitimize other kinds of leadership – appointment and promotion committees,

elections, chains of office, MBEs and OBEs . . . these people have to establish their claim to power by sheer force of personality. They must also be deeply committed to the communities in which they operate. Professional community workers, like others in the public services, gain promotion and move on. The indigenous activists stay, working for nothing or for a pittance, and declining the well-paid jobs which other places are apt to offer them as their achievements come to be recognized.

(2)   People are not born with the capacity for collective action – the conviction that they and their neighbours can get together, challenge established authority, and change things. It has to be learnt. Key members of the group usually have some *tradition of collective action* to draw on, but it may be derived from many different sources: from trade unionism, the revolutionary Labour movement or a father who fought in Spain (as we found in Craigmillar, Pleck, Broadwater Farm and in various parts of Belfast and Derry); from shared Caribbean or Asian origins and the experience of migration to a new and sometimes hostile country (as in Broadwater, Pleck and Stonebridge); from Republican or Protestant loyalties (as in the Ulster projects); or from religious conviction which may be a Protestant one (as in Caribbean groups) or a Catholic one (alive in parts of Scotland as well as Ireland, north and south – sometimes with the support of priests and ministers, sometimes despite their opposition). The education provided by social movements is profoundly important, and capable of transfer from one generation to the next. These movements teach more than the techniques of collective action; they teach generous loyalties, capacities for self-sacrifice, scepticism about established authority, and the ability to handle conflict. But they are not only based on social class.[11]

(3)   Charismatic leadership is not enough by itself. Some *paid staff* are needed. Even one person can make a big difference. The mobilized community, confronting an assault upon its interests, can be very effective. Stopping things is easy, compared with the long haul required to make things happen. As the drive for more positive action begins, there will be delays, complications and long periods of boredom when nothing seems to happen (while raising funds, applying for planning permission, negotiating with politicians and public service unions . . .). The impetus will be lost unless someone

is paid to remember what is happening, to keep the files, to answer the telephone, and work patiently for action.

(4) If paid workers are to have sufficient security to stick at the job for a while, there must be *a flow of funds* to pay them. The temptation at this point is to rely on urban programme or MSC funding – both of which tend to be snatched away just as the project begins to take off. So some more reliable flow of cash must be found.

(5) That usually calls for a *building* of some sort, or several buildings – an asset which can be rented out over the longer term or just for meetings and other activities. A building can also be used as collateral for the loans required to start up new enterprises, and the conversion of it may bring further grants, jobs and training opportunities to the community. If it achieves what its creators hope for, the Stonebridge Bus Garage will be the most dramatic example of this kind.

(6) To acquire staff and convert buildings means negotiating loans, grants and contracts, and securing permissions and approvals of many kinds. All that calls for skill, tact and staying power – and friends at court. Every successful community action project owes a good deal to one or two *friendly politicians or officials* who in their early days explained the bureaucracy to them (its annual financial cycle, how to fill in application forms . . .) and helped them gain access to the corridors of power (explaining how to approach charitable trusts for funds, how to get a meeting with a minister or the convener of a key committee, and what to say when they got there). In the Republic of Ireland the crucial contact may be within a Church bureaucracy, but the role is the same.

(7) But in politics friends, however powerful, are not enough. The leaders of a successful community action project have to establish a *workable balance of power with local politicians*, both to gain their support when it is needed, and to fight off take-over bids – for the politicians always attempt to gain some credit for themselves from successful projects of this kind. The activists must then retain their independence; and that will only be achieved if they earn it by putting down roots within the community, doing good welfare rights work which enables them to give the world an accurate

picture of the lives of local people and the operations of public services, and gaining the ear of local newspapers and radio stations. They become a political force in their own right. A group which has achieved those things can establish sound relations with the politicians, based on recognition that each needs, but neither can exploit, the other. Without that basis in reality, the goodwill of politicians will prove far too flimsy an influence to rely on.

(8) Their backers in the public authorities and the charitable foundations often press the leaders of community action projects to claim that they represent the communities they serve. They feel more comfortable giving funds to a group which can be described as 'representative'. The claim is easily made, for in terms of race, class and gender the group are usually more representative of their community (in the sense of resembling them more closely) than the local council or the trustees of a charity; and their activities are usually conducted in a more public fashion. So some groups do claim to speak not only for their project but for their 'community'. Later, however, when things go wrong – as, to some degree, they always will – their backers will be among the first to say that the group is 'not really representative'.

Shrewder groups refuse to claim that they represent anyone but those involved in their project. They try instead to *operate in an accountable fashion* – accountable to their members and neighbours, the people whom they serve, and to those who give them money. Different forms and procedures of accountability have to be developed for these different purposes. Meanwhile it is the job of democratically elected assemblies to represent people.

(9) *Financial accountability* is particularly important. It is predictable that when money is given to impoverished groups their leaders will before long be accused of fraud – often by their own neighbours first of all. It is not enough to say that the accusation is usually false. Thus, besides developing a fairly thick skin, the group must devise regular procedures for demonstrating to themselves and to outsiders how their money is being spent, month by month as well as year by year. In Ulster, where it is often alleged that public funds find their way to paramilitaries, people have devised particularly effective accounting procedures of this sort.

(10) Success often brings disillusionment; a falling off in public support and growing criticism from local people whose expectations have in some way been disappointed. The projects which surmount these hazards best are those which *welcome newcomers and encourage them to launch new projects*.

These are perhaps the ten most important lessons for community activists which we learnt from the experience of some of the most successful of them. But how they and their enterprises fare will depend heavily on the support they get from officials, politicians and charitable foundations. What lessons have we for them?

Lessons for administrators

In the field of community action the single purpose projects will be the most widespread and stable enterprises, and within their fairly clearly defined territory they can do very useful work. The more ambitious community-action projects will be fewer, and more precarious – but with greater potential, when they do well, for changing people and the wider society.

To succeed, both types of project need a delicate combination of official support and political independence. To tie them too closely to the state destroys their capacity to do new things in new ways, and makes it likely that they will be destroyed if the parties controlling the state change (as Liverpool voluntary organizations know to their cost).[12] But it will be easier to give community-based projects the elbow room they need if public authorities and foundations sort out with them a number of problems which are bound to arise before contracts are signed.

The need for financial accountability has already been mentioned, but that may not be best assured by bringing in a qualified, white male manager or accountant. It may be that the qualified people willing to work in what their own professional colleagues would regard as rather eccentric, underpaid jobs are not the ablest or most honest members of their professions. For whatever reasons, some of the more serious disasters we encountered arose from such appointments. So teaching the activists to do their own accounting and management may be a wiser strategy. But that will not happen unless it is properly planned in advance.

There are many other problems which can be foreseen and

clarified. When projects recruit staff and appoint contractors, are the selection of people with local knowledge and credibility, and the development of skills and entrepreneurial capacity within the local community, to be among the main aims? Or would the appointment of the project leaders' friends and neighbours be regarded as scandalous nepotism? If the group is to allocate scarce resources – houses, for example – are they expected to do that in ways which stabilize and strengthen the local community, or in ways which meet the more urgent needs to be found throughout the city? Are the trade unions which represent staff within the public services to continue to represent people doing similar jobs when a community-based project takes over these functions? Any of these answers could be the right ones; the questions, however, will be more constructively handled if discussed in advance and not left like unexploded mines to be stepped on later.

Fresh thought will be needed about many other questions, too. Established institutions, statutory and voluntary, are accustomed to sending their staff on training courses and to professional conferences. But to give local activists similar opportunities – as they must – will call for different arrangements, that is, different kinds of training, and conferences which meet at different times of the day and the week, and provision will have to be made for the care of young children while their parents are engaged in these activities.

In future, professional staff will more frequently move in the course of their careers between established statutory or voluntary organizations, the private sector, and community based projects. A whole career spent in one service and one type of local government department will become much less common than it used to be. To make those transitions easier will call for fresh thought about pension schemes, promotion procedures and trade union rights.

Conclusions

The broader conclusions of this paper may seem depressing to radicals with high hopes of community action. Community-based enterprises are not going to supplant the state and private enterprise. Even in Northern Ireland, where they had the best chance of doing so, all three sources of initiative are needed, and work best when the state gives a generous and consistent lead. Successful community-based action calls for continuing, patient advice and support from within the bureaucracy – preferably with some help from the charitable foundations. (In Northern Ireland, which lacks such foundations, the state was wise enough to set one up – the Northern Ireland Voluntary Trust.) Even with that kind of support, community action will not develop everywhere. The capacity for it is nurtured by social movements of various kinds – movements not confined to the revolutionary working class. (Indeed, organizations of the Left have sometimes been the enemies of radical, independent community-based action.) But, while every society and generation seems to find its own ways of keeping the flame alight, we cannot assume it will be burning in every neighbourhood. So community action will always be patchy.

Things will go best – the inevitable conflicts involved in this work will be handled most constructively – if all concerned share some common convictions about the fundamental purpose of community-based action. That purpose, I suggest, is to ensure that those who suffer injustice, pain or humiliation, gain a voice within the wider society, and thus find ways of conveying their own experience to that society and making more effective demands on the groups which dominate it.

The dominant groups always tend to interpret social problems in ways which suggest that they can be solved if only other people would change their behaviour – in ways, that is, which blame the victims. Those patterns cannot be changed by research and education alone. Unless the victims themselves gain a hearing, the comfortable and powerful will never get an authentic, honest picture of the underside of their own world or concede that it must be changed. That means that the victims – they may be people disabled by some disease, or residents of a poverty–stricken estate, or women exploited by their families – must take collective action which gains for them some control over the world in which they live. That may mean some control over their family situation, or over the services and resources they need. They may want medical or legal advice, or housing, or simply an opportunity to escape from squalor and have fun for an evening. Whatever it may be, if it is provided at the behest and under the control of others – the professionals, the politicians, the philanthropists – we may be sure that it will work in ways which ultimately reinforce the victims' exclusion, humiliation and sense of powerlessness. The purpose of community action should be to change that.

Once that objective is understood, other dilemmas will be more readily resolved. It will be recognized, for example, that we should not evaluate community projects only in the ways in which we would evaluate conventional, bureaucratic organizations – by asking about their turnover, their stability and their prospects of staying in business. Achievements of that kind are not to be derided, but if that is all that happens it may only institutionalize the projects and lead more quickly to their recapture by the state.

We should instead expect that people whose suffering and anger have for years been 'managed' by destroying their capacity for collective action are bound to express rage when that capacity is given back to them. Thus community-based action will frequently be contentious. Moreover, a sense of collective paranoia about the outside world is often deliberately fostered as a means of holding a potentially explosive group together. Established civic leaders and their officials should be patient about these negative things and look for more positive aspects of the projects concerned.

Have exploited and poverty stricken people gained confidence, got together, made demands of their own and developed new capacities to get things done? Did they enjoy themselves and have a good time? Have the mass media discovered places they previously neglected and found articulate people there to whom they will in future turn for well informed and authentic accounts of social issues and the city's problems? Have some of the people involved in these events gone on to do other good things which they would not previously have thought possible? Have professional staff and administrators in established institutions learnt new responses to their patients, tenants, clients, pupils ... responses which offer greater dignity and self respect, and which will not be forgotten when these officials move on to other jobs in future? If most of the answers to these questions are positive, the project may have been well worth supporting, even if it foundered after a few years.

Acknowledgement

I am grateful to Chris Elphick who collaborated with me in the study of community action groups reported in this chapter, and to the Rowntree Charitable Trust and the Barrow and Geraldine S. Cadbury Trust for supporting this work.

Notes

1 See F. Kitson, *Low Intensity Operations* (London: Faber & Faber, 1971).
2 See Lord Scarman, *The Brixton Disorders, 10–12 April 1981: Report of an Inquiry*, Cmnd 8427 (London: HMSO, 1981).
3 World Health Organization, *Targets for Health for All* (Copenhagen: WHO, 1985).
4 The mechanisms which in stable societies tend to give trade unions and other special interest groups growing power at the expense of the ordinary consumer are analysed in M. Olson, *The Rise and Decline of Nations* (New Haven, Conn.: Yale University Press, 1982).
5 See, for example, D. Blunkett and C. Green, *Building from the Bottom: the Sheffield Experience* (London: Fabian Society, pamphlet no. 491, 1983).
6 For a discussion of the privatization alternative, see J. Le Grand and R. Robinson (eds), *Privatisation and the Welfare State* (London: Allen & Unwin, 1984).
7 The story is briefly told in J. Birchall, *Building Communities the Co-operative Way* (London: Routledge & Kegan Paul, 1988). A fuller account can be found in L. Whitefield, 'Housing Co-operatives in Glasgow: the Community Ownership Programme'. M. Phil. thesis in Town and Regional Planning, University of Glasgow, 1985.
8 See S. Lock 'Self-help groups: the Fourth Estate in medicine?', *British Medical Journal*, 293, 20–27 December, 1986, pp. 1596–1600.
9 This dilemma is discussed in R. R. Reuther, *Women-Church* (New York: Harper & Row, 1985) pp. 23 and 36.
10 For a good recent example of the evidence on this point, see J. Henderson and V. Karn, *Race, Class and State Housing* (Aldershot: Gower, 1987).
11 The varied origins and character of social movements which have brought about major changes are discussed in M. Castells, *The City and the Grassroots* (London: Edward Arnold, 1983).
12 For some insights into this story, see M. Parkinson, *Liverpool on the Brink: One City's Struggle against Government Cuts*, Policy Journals, 1955.

13 Community development and the underclass

S. M. MILLER

I have been asked to comment in brief on two sets of issues; first on political participation and community empowerment; secondly on the concept of the underclass. The juxtaposition of the two topics has led me to see the two as joined in an underlying theme. The underclass thesis springs from the recognition that current economic and social policies are not reducing, and cannot reduce, poverty in at least one subsection of the poor. The move toward community empowerment derives similarly from the feeling in many low-income and/or economically decaying communities that national policies are inadequate for dealing with their problems. Indeed, national policies may undermine some local economies, even if neoclassical economic analysis views these policies as promoting Schumpeter's gale of capitalist 'creative destruction'.

Community action

At the local level in Britain and the United States, we seem to be re-inventing and reshaping the community action movements of the 1960s and 1970s. A major shift is that current community developments are not initiated by national government and may not be receiving much if any funding from that source. Current community action starts from the ground up rather than from the outside in as it did in its earlier incarnation, it is also more oriented to developing economic bases for the neighbourhood or region than were its predecessors. The criticisms of the earlier Community Development programme of the Home Office may have had some impact.

The current manifestation of the current drive towards local action has many other positive elements. The variety of on-going programmes suggests the strengths and human resources of many communities that are regarded as dying, incompetent, immobilized. The myth of apathy is hardy and ignores the enormous pressures against action that exist in most communities, especially those hit by poverty and economic dislocation. While, as David Donnison (Chapter 12) points out, we should not romanticize these communities and their efforts at self-direction neither should we easily accept notions that nothing can be done because of the outlook or quality of their inhabitants.

Current community action, unlike its 1960s forerunners in the UK and USA, repudiates the scientific, rational or professional model of social reform built around demonstration or pilot projects, evaluation, and cost-effectiveness calculations. This model assumed that everything could be measured or confidently estimated, that an effective programme on a small scale could be equally easily (and usually more cheaply) conducted on a national scale, and that (most significantly and wrongly) a pilot project that did well would automatically lead to a corresponding national programme. This de-politicization of social reform proved a flop.

Contemporary community development seeks to do what it can for its locality; it does not entertain itself with the hope that it will be the forerunner of national efforts; it has very simple notions of what is a useful programme, including non-monetary effects on the spirit of a neighbourhood or region as well as the more calculable elements of how many jobs may be produced. This approach has its problems, as David Donnison clearly notes, but at least it has the advantage of learning from the illusions of the past. Some useful lessons have been drawn.

Community action is a generally positive, if limited, response to the decay or disorientation of political party organizations in many low-income communities or regions. These organizations have lost appeal; often, they cling to old ways of thinking and actions that are unresponsive to new and disturbing conditions. In a number of countries, the loss of confidence in political parties has spurred the creation and strength of social movements. Community action is one form of social movement which is struggling to find out what can be done in their locations. Unlike some of its compatriots in political life, it is proactive, attempting to promote economic possibilities, rather than responding as a reactive veto group trying to prevent bad outside initiatives from taking root.

David Donnison's (Chapter 12) analysis without illusions points to some negative effects of community development efforts today. I would highlight several. One is the contrast between the increasing global nature of the world economy and localized community development efforts. It is one thing to recognize that national economic policies might not benefit or might even harm localities and decide that some initiatives by localities are absolutely necessary. It is quite another thing to abandon concern with national policies as though localities can go it alone and disregard the national and international economic scene. Tip O'Neill, former speaker of the US House of Representatives, is mostly right when he says that 'all politics is local'; but economies are not exclusively local. Community development may miss the importance of national economic policies and strategies.

Both community successes and failures can exact high prices. Factionalism as well as cynicism and naivety are high in low-income communities, so that community development efforts may be enveloped in conflicts about who controls and who benefits. Failures can leave a community more desolate than it was before. The grand gesture, over-blown hopes, and extravagant rhetoric can deepen the destructiveness of a failed effort. On the other hand, short-lived projects can led to positive legacies of strengthening myths, the necessary optimism of possibilities, and tested leaders who may reappear at an important time.

Empowerment is expected to be the outcome of community development efforts. Frequently, there is ambiguity about whether this empowerment will be of individuals or communities. While both individual and collective or community empowerment are desirable, the two may not always converge. How to make one lead to the other is one of the great problems facing community development.

A major problem of many community development efforts is that they concentrate on some activities which may produce worthwhile results for the locality, but they are likely to leave untouched major sources of funds and major institutions of the area. For example, we can construct some better school programmes in some schools in our area without improving the general nature of schooling in our neighbourhood. Or we can improve job prospects for some by developing an arts programme that attracts outsiders to spend money in our community. But we are not improving the well-being of those dependent on governmental transfer funds or those hurt by macro- or microeconomic policies of governments.

The hope is that there will be a spread effect from community development efforts and that the people of the area will become more politically involved and effective. Certainly this expansion of outlook does occur, but not as frequently as many community development supporters believe. Excessive localism can often result in the hope of insulating our community from what is happening outside it. Localism, frequently offered as an alternative political and social ideology, can encapsulate the spread of involvements and the widening of empowerments.

Nonetheless, community development has become for some an important part of a rethinking of the desirable character of economy and society. The dislike in many quarters of centralized, bureaucratic, alienating forms of socialism and capitalism has led to the beginnings of an alternative to both of the older systems, based on a local economic outlook, highly decentralized and democratic political forms, concern for feelings of empowerment, anti-bureaucratic and anti-elitist, more reliant on self-help and mutual aid, a widening of citizenship rights. In Europe, this outlook is being shaped by those of a Green mentality while in the United States the rallying cry is 'populism', a 'return' of power to ordinary people. In both version localism is very important and a mixed economy and society combining traditional market and socialist practices are (often implicitly) accepted. A mixed economy and society may not have the appeals of the purity of the 'free market' or the classic virtues of 'socialism' but the political, media and personal attractiveness of current community development efforts suggests that new ways of thinking about how to deal with current issues are entering into political and popular consciousness.

Community development is at a new stage; it will suffer if treated as a panacea or a free-standing form; it needs a political philosophy and a political voice. Meanwhile, it is helping some low-income communities overcome economic difficulties and some low-income people gain or regain a sense of competence and efficacy.

The underclass

The significance of the murky underclass term is that it is a recognition of the insufficiencies of current economic and social policies to bring a subsection of the poor out of poverty conditions. This statement does not imply that current policies are sufficient to pull other sections of the poor out of poverty; rather, that in the case of those thought of as in the underclass, there is explicit or implicit acceptance of the proposition that present policies do not and will not effectively deal with their poverty. At issue are the questions of who is in the underclass and what would help them.

In the United States and probably elsewhere, the term underclass is used loosely and broadly. For some in the United States, anyone who is characterized as 'persistent welfare' (that is, on public assistance, the Aid to Families and Dependent Children program) would be part of the underclass. Here the concern is with 'dependence' or financial costs. Others are equally or more concerned with unmarried, young mothers on welfare. They are seen as imposing social costs, for they are not only likely to become persistently on welfare but their children are predicted to become addicted to welfare and to become social charges as they age, drop out of school, reproduce, and perhaps engage in crime because of their early upbringing. The financial and social cost concerns concentrate on women as family heads. The third group who often come to mind when the term underclass is employed are young people, out of the regular labour force, and usually black men. Unemployed, underemployed, out of the labour force and/or engaged in illegal activities, they are seen as dangerous, involved in violent crimes and threatening. They are a disturbing underclass. Recently, the term underclass has been extended by some to include the homeless, de-institutionalized or un-institutionalized mentally ill.

These various subsets could add up to a sizable number in the underclass category. But for many, if not most, citizens of the USA the term mainly refers to minorities living in the centre of cities, not to the white and minority rural, small town and suburban poor. Consequently, the size of the underclass varies enormously; it appears large when all who have been persistently poor are used as the indicator. But if the centre-city minority poor who have been persistently on welfare are the standard, then the number is much lower and excludes the older minority, unemployed or those males out of the regular labour force, who are ineligible for public assistance but frequently at the centre of thinking about the underclass.

This muddled conceptualization strongly suggests that the designation underclass is not a bounded category as much as an expression of feeling – of dismay, fear or burden. Nonetheless, it is pointing to the inadequacies of current policies. Although it is not a candidate for analytical purity and clear boundaries, we are probably stuck with it because of its resonance in media and political circles.

What is seen as producing the underclass(es)? As is frequently the case in poverty issues, personal inadequacy and structural explanations compete. The personal inadequacy approach sees the members of the underclass as the authors of their fate. In the most simple and extreme of these formulations, this approach combines the worst features of culture of poverty and blaming the victim explanations. In more refined versions, inadequate coping with difficult circumstances is defined as the cause of falling into an underclass life of dependency and shiftlessness.

Structural approaches can now be of right as well as of left flavouring. Charles Murray (1985), in a book that was given enormous media play, argued that poverty was caused by welfare programmes, for the latter undermined the incentives for working. Despite the statistical undermining of Murray's thesis by a number of poverty experts, the book has had a good life because it accords well with many people's dislike of welfare systems and because refutations seldom catch up with well-orchestrated campaigns. In the social science world as well as in the world of celebrities, attention is all and frequently has little do do with quality.

The competing view of the structural sources of the underclass has been given some recent attention because of the advent of William J. Wilson's *The Truly Disadvantaged* (1987). This structural approach argues that the high level of unemployment of the post–1973 period, especially high for blacks, the elimination of good entry jobs that had been available to blacks, stagnating incomes and similar economic catastrophes produced an underclass that suffered chronic poverty, the lack of legitimate opportunities and unstable family situations. I find this explanation more convincing than the Murray thesis or the individual pathology stress.

What can be done about the underclass? Again, individualistic and structural approaches compete. The individualistic approach is oriented to 'escape who can', attempting to encourage the mobility of those who can with help improve their situation. An example is the widely publicized efforts of several millionaires to guarantee college education to young, presumably underclass teenagers who persevere in schooling and to provide some educational aid to them so that they can advance through the school system and be eligible for college. The theme is assisting selected individuals to be mobile, a pure case of sponsored mobility. This approach – helping those who will help themselves if given a hand – has a long pedigree, but it is not likely to affect many and is unlikely to change the outlook of low-income communities. It clearly does not embrace a community development approach to improving the situation of the inner-city concentrated poverty areas where the underclasses presumably live.

The standard structural approach emphasizes improved economic policies and structures, building approaches to decent jobs, overcoming the income stagnation and the 'quiet depression' (Levy, 1987) which has characterized the post–1973 period in the United States. Because of the social budget cutting of the Reagan years, the tendency is to call for the restoration of past programmes and for the enactment of long-sought legislation. But this is no easy agenda, either politically or economically.

The dangers in this approach are that it is assumed that underclass conditions pose no problems for the take-up of new opportunities and that old policies and proposals need only be defended, not changed. As with community development, we have to recognize that nations are in new stages requiring fresh thinking. That does not mean accepting the growing fashionable argument that we cannot afford to help low-income people but it does mean that we have to accept that to aid them requires new ways of dealing with the peculiar splitting world we face. Community development is one such approach, despite its problems and limitations.

References

Paul Levy, *Dollars and Dreams: The Changing American Income Distribution* (New York: Russell Sage Foundation, 1987).

Charles Murray, *Losing Ground: American Social Policy 1950–1980* (New York: Basic Books, 1984).

William Julius Wilson, *The Truly Disadvantaged: The Inner City, the Underclass, and Public Policy* (Chicago: University of Chicago Press, 1987).

14 *Social polarization, the inner city and community*

A. H. HALSEY

David Donnison has wise practicalities to offer us from his review of contemporary attempts to improve the quality of social services by basing them on local communities. I trust that they will be heeded by community activists. But above all it is imperative to underline his conclusion that the state has a continuing and central part to play in making the world a fairer place. There is no community-based alternative which will enable us to do without the state. But we must constantly find new ways of making its institutions more open and humane, more alert to the needs of the oppressed – and keeping it moving in the right directions.

Contemporary debate can be described as a struggle, which is ancient, over political definition of the state in relation to society. Economic liberalism and democratic socialism are the contenders. Economic transformation is the context. The advanced industrial countries are in the throes of transition to a new social order of high technology which involves a renegotiation of the division of labour between men and women, family and workplace, community and government. In consequence the conflicting claims of the individual and the social are such that we are thrown back to the arguments promulgated by the New Liberals a century ago where, as Charles Booth put it, the search is to find a new 'socialism in the arms of individualism'. This, we might remind ourselves, is a debate at the heart of the foundation of the London School of Economics. The School's Department of Social Science and Administration evolved out of competing definitions offered by the Charity Organisation Society version of individualism and the Webbs' version of statism, as José Harris elaborates in Chapter 2 of this book. L. T. Hobhouse, J. A. Hobson and the New Liberals discovered or rediscovered a benign role for the state in redistribution of unequal wealth and local creation of what we would now call the infrastructure of affluence.

They ushered in the era of progressive taxation, of state responsibilities for health, housing and education and of new encouragement to local authorities in pursuit of sound sewers, clean streets, 'gas and water socialism'. At that time economic liberalism was put on to the defensive by the reinvigorated community spirit in both the nation and the localities of Britain.

Today the position is reversed. There is a militant economic liberalism in command over Westminster and Whitehall which seeks to reconstruct the British social order. Mrs Thatcher affirms that there are no such things as societies, only individuals and families and that her mission is to drive socialism from the political agenda. The essential message underlying Donnison's comments is the need for a renewed social consciousness which is at the same time a realistic alternative to the central ideology of the Thatcher circle.

With my colleague Norman Dennis I have elsewhere[1] tried to detail the alternative tradition of ethical socialism which has had one channel of expression in the department we celebrate on this occasion. In the same context the report of the Archbishop's Commission on Urban Priority Areas, which appeared at the end of 1985, is a milestone in the long history of conflict and accommodation between individualism and collectivism in British culture. Against the background of the disarray of the political Left since the mid–1970s, the Church of England and its bishops in the House of Lords emerged in the 1980s, perhaps quaintly, as the voice of a socially responsible collectivism before the juggernaut of a triumphalist individualism. That *Faith in the City*[2] was immediately dismissed unread as Marxist theology could surprise no one. The use of such a self-contradictory phrase is not the point. The principal message was that the age-old search for koinonia, the fellowship of sharing, is at present diverted by the unsociological and, in a serious sense anti-political, doctrines of the currently dominant party. Both economic liberalism and democratic socialism claim to be effective political responses to the problems of advanced industrial society. Both are deeply rooted in British cultural history but economic liberalism represents a particular interpretation of economic transformation which has thrown the inner city into vulnerable precariousness. Urwick, Booth, Tawney, Hobhouse, Attlee and Titmuss

Table 14.1 *Distribution of original, disposable and final household income, 1976–1985*
United Kingdom   *Percentages*

	Quintile groups of households					
	Bottom fifth	Next fifth	Middle fifth	Next fifth	Top fifth	Total
Original income[1]						
1976	0.8	9.4	18.8	26.6	44.4	100.0
1981	0.6	8.1	18.0	26.9	46.4	100.0
1984	0.3	6.1	17.5	27.5	48.6	100.0
1985	0.3	6.0	17.2	27.3	49.2	100.0
Disposable income[2]						
1976	7.0	12.6	18.2	24.1	38.1	100.0
1981	6.7	12.1	17.7	24.1	39.4	100.0
1984	6.7	11.7	17.5	24.4	39.7	100.0
1985	6.5	11.3	17.3	24.3	40.6	100.0
Final income[3]						
1976	7.4	12.7	18.0	24.0	37.9	100.0
1981	7.1	12.4	17.9	24.0	38.6	100.0
1984	7.1	12.1	17.5	24.3	39.0	100.0
1985	6.7	11.8	17.4	24.0	40.2	100.0

1 Households ranked by original income
2 Households ranked by disposable income
3 Households ranked by final income
Source: Central Statistical Office, from Family Expenditure Survey.

are among the people associated with the LSE department who strove for an alternative 'right order' of urban civilization.

The inner city problem over the past century has manifested contradictory tendencies. Cities have been magnets for the rural poor with their offer of entry to industrial prosperity. Though the lowest rung of the ladder of affluence, houses and civic amenities, the inner city communities have played an historically liberating and mobility-promoting role. But since the post–war period ended in Western Europe with the oil crisis of the 1970s, social polarization rather than assimilation has been the more dominant feature. The ladder has turned in to a trap of urban squalor for the old, the sick, the unemployed and the unsuccessful ethnic minorities. The reasons are well known, the remedies reviewed by David Donnison are uncertain.

Yet the fact of social polarization cannot be denied. The evidence collected by the Archbishop's Commission on the Urban Areas continues to be reinforced and indeed has had a dramatic further affirmation in the British budget of 1988 with its spectacular revision of taxation in the direction of adding wealth to the wealthy, while the 1988 reform of social security arrangements threatens more punitive treatment to those dependent on state welfare support. Meanwhile the government, despite majority sentiment in the country, refuses to use state resources to meet growing needs of the National Health Service. In the context of these stark changes of social policy along the road towards a society of market individualism, the data in Table 14.1 are already an understatement of the increasing separation of two nations.

According to these official statistics the best-off one-fifth of households in 1985 took half of all market incomes while the poorest fifth took virtually nothing. Admittedly government still intervened to reduce the gap by taxation and benefits. Even before the 1988 budget signalled abandonment of the principle of fiscal transfer from the rich to the poor, however, the final incomes of the advantaged quintile improved from 37.9 per cent to 40.2 per cent between 1976 and 1985, while the poorest quintile worsened in their share of final income from 7.4 per cent to 6.7 per cent. The movement towards a divided nation continues to produce geographical pockets of arrogant wealth alongside blighted urban communities of high unemployment, physical squalor and social despair.

These trends have two notably ominous features from the point of view of those who, following the pioneers of the LSE department, seek social accord in a fair and generous society. First they remind us of the long and deep tendencies of markets to generate inequality. This tendency has been over-interpreted by Marx and indeed turned into an immutable law of social motion – the inevitable revolution of a poverty-stricken proletariat in desperate conflict with its capitalist exploiters. When the LSE department was founded seventy-five years ago it was believed that this theory had been destroyed by historical experience. But the alarming feature of contemporary polarization is that its public and political consequences can be neutralized in a democracy. For it is, unlike the Marxist thesis of the 1840s, a division of the affluent majority from the impoverished minority. Marxist polarization pointed to civil war. Economic liberal polarization points to social containment by minimal state welfare, police and burglar alarms with individualized failure, anomie and apathy made public only fitfully by occasional urban riot.

In class terms, the two polarizations are denoted differently. The urban workers of Europe in the nineteenth century could be portrayed as a militant working–class 'clad', as Kautsky once put it 'in the pride of its class'. Today manual workers are a declining minority of the work force and social attention is focused on what American writers call the underclass.

An underclass is essentially composed of those who are dispossessed or never achieve full citizenship. In our contemporary political economy this means principally an insecure attachment to the labour market but has associated with it a high probability of broken or weak membership of normal relations of kin. A punitive regime of social security for those dependent on the state completes the definition. The consequence is a disorganized category of people, mostly young, unqualified and unemployed who are alienated from the office culture and become, as Ralf Dahrendorf has described them, 'a cancer' in the social body. Their location is, usually if not exclusively, in the 'inner city' districts, whether in the central or the peripheral localities of industrial urban failure.

For such socially estranged people as well as for the conventionally prosperous the community impulse tends to be overwhelmed by appeal to egotistical individualism. During my many visits to the urban priority areas I was repeatedly reminded of Engels' description of the city of London in 1844:

> After roaming the streets of the capital a day or two, making headway with difficulty through the human turmoil and the endless lines of vehicles, after visiting the slums of the metropolis, one realises for the first time that these Londoners have been forced to sacrifice the best qualities of their human nature, to bring to pass all the marvels of civilisation which crowd their city; that a hundred powers which slumbered within them have remained inactive, have been suppressed in order that a few might be developed more fully and multiply through union with those of others. The very turmoil of the streets has something repulsive, something against which human nature rebels ... The brutal indifference, the unfeeling isolation of each in his private interest

becomes the more repellant and offensive, the more these individuals are crowded together, within a limited space. And, however much one may be aware that this isolation of the individual, this narrow self-seeking is the fundamental principle of our society everywhere, it is nowhere so shamelessly barefaced, so self-conscious as just here in the crowding of the great city.[3]

Descriptions like these, of human selfishness, loneliness, squalor and depravity, are the stock-in-trade of secular accounts of the British industrial city. The tragedy is that in inner city districts today the social services are pathetically inadequate. This was symbolized for me after midnight one Saturday when I witnessed a celibate priest trying to deal on his rectory doorstep with the distress of a homeless and battered wife. Yet behind it all one has to recognize that those who would reconstruct society in the image of the economic liberal are forced to destroy the intermediary organizations of power such as municipal authorities or trade unions which, in pure or distorted form, carry the communal as distinct from the individual impulse.

The challenge to replace atomistic anarchy, exploitation and inequality by a welfare society has presented itself in shifting guise in all the phases of industrial development. For the next generation of social scientists and social workers it is as morally urgent and intellectually difficult as it ever was to their predecessors.

Notes

1 N. Dennis and A. H. Halsey, *English Ethical Socialism: Thomas More to R. H. Tawney* (Oxford: Oxford University Press, 1988).
2 Archbishop of Canterbury's Commission on Urban Priority Areas, *Faith in the City: a call for action by church and nation* (London: Church House Publishing, 1985).
3 Engels, F., *The Condition of the Working Class in England in 1844* (Oxford: Basil Blackwell, 1958).

15 *Only disconnect: law and order, social policy and the community*

DAVID DOWNES

Long marginal to the field of social policy and administration, the study of 'law and order' is showing every sign of greater integration into its concerns. The reasons for the traditional separation are various: two interdisciplinary fields sought their own identity and only occasionally overlapped; criminology, with its students lodged in departments of law, sociology, social policy and psychology, clung for far too long to a focus on the 'causes' of crime; and 'mainstream' social policy and administration tended to leave the study of crime and delinquency to its social work wing, while criminal justice processes were left to the lawyers. But whatever the reasons, the two fields are now converging in a series of respects, not least because events have encouraged the logic of such developments. The inner-city riots of the 1980s led to proposals for new forms of 'multi-agency' response (Scarman, 1981; Gifford, 1986) as well as to a furious debate over police accountability (Lea and Young, 1984; Reiner, 1985). Newman's work on 'defensible space' (1973) has in the 1980s entered into British work on housing and social planning with the need to take acount of crime and the 'fear of crime' in community development. (Coleman, 1985; Hope and Shaw, 1987: Power, 1988). With the crime rate up by over 50 per cent since the first Thatcher administration assumed office, and the prisons bulging at the seams, it is hardly premature to ask how well current trends in research match the urgency of the problems.

Much current work matches up to the problems very well. A number of instances are provided by a recent collection of papers on

Communities and Crime (Reiss and Tonry, 1986), mainly composed of American studies, but containing an excellent chapter by Bottoms and Wiles on 'community crime careers' in Britain. Bringing an original slant to the tradition of area studies of crime, and using data gathered for the extensive Sheffield study (see also Baldwin and Bottoms, 1976), they focus on the ways in which some areas seem able to shift from high to low crime rates, whilst others experience the reverse. Building on the work of Morris (1957), they locate a causal sequence of some significance in the operation of the housing market, and of housing allocation policies in council estates. Clumping the most 'at risk' families together appears to have momentous consequences, as their children enter adolescence, as the more 'respectable' families move on, and as the estate 'tips' into the realm of social undesirability. (Damer (1974) and Gill (1977) have shown contrary and confirming developments in Glasgow and Liverpool respectively.) Modifying these trends should in principle follow from the more dispersed settlement of such families, and/or from other means to the revitalization of estates, by changes in estate management, greater tenant autonomy, and a more responsive policy to complaints and suggested improvements from residents. (Power, forthcoming) Whether such initiatives merely displace crime elsewhere, or can be sustained, has yet to be seen. And it is important to guard against the scapegoating of a small minority of families for the state to which some estates have been reduced by poor management and underinvestment.

McGahey (1986) shows how central the local labour market is to an understanding of the economy of crime in Brooklyn. White lower class youths have access to a primary job market through family members, while hispanic and black youths lack family contacts with these networks. The delinquency of the white youths is consequently shorter-lived and less predatory, while the non-whites resort to robbery and drug-dealing to provide income. Particularly interesting is McGahey's account of the relatively small gains, high costs and disproportionate risks of arrest and victimization to be made from such illegal sources. Similarly, the work of Ditton (1977) and Pahl (1984) in Britain stresses the extent to which the best 'fiddles' and forms of 'moonlighting' are mainly available to those already in work. The unemployed, triply deprived of all three sources of in-work income, then show up as more criminal – and as disproportionately likely to face custodial sentences (Box, 1987) –

due to their greater resort to street crime. Community cohesion suffers in the process and formal social control can make few inroads into the situation (Clarke and Hough, 1984).

Such studies show how law and order issues relate to the staple features of social policy analysis, such as housing, schools and labour markets, and their interrelationships. Whether or not these interrelationships are sufficiently close to justify talk of an emergent 'underclass' is another matter of crucial significance for policy analysis. For the main cleavage in society now seems increasingly to be between the fortunate majority who are, whether manual or non-manual workers, employed in primary labour market jobs, well-housed, and able to command decent schooling and health care; and those who are increasingly denied full citizenship in these terms – the rump of the old 'rough' working class, workers confined to secondary labour markets, the new long-term unemployed, especially the young who have never known what it is like to hold a job, the growing numbers of elderly poor, single-parent families, and the most discriminated against ethnic minorities. These groups combine the greatest dependence on welfare with the greatest vulnerability to welfare disservices and welfare sanctions (Garland, 1981). If social science and administration is defined as the study of the production, distribution and exchange of welfare services and resources, then the emergence of an underclass is of momentous significance.

The case for the emergence of an underclass in the USA has been made for decades (see the discussion in Giddens, 1973, pp. 216–22). It is now increasingly claimed that the conditions for its emergence have been created in Europe and, in particular, in Britain, in the 1980s. (See, for example, Dahrendorf, 1987). It can be argued that, when poverty is found to be increasing more rapidly in Britain than elsewhere in the European Economic Community (EEC Council of Ministers, 1987), when the junior Minister of Health tells the rich they have no business using the National Health Service, when the right of schools to opt out of local authority control is about to be enacted, threatening the basis of even such precarious forms of comprehensive schooling as now exist, when public housing seems set to become a thing of the past – except perhaps for the most deprived, when levels of income maintenance for pensioners and the unemployed, already among the lowest in Europe, are whittled down even further, whilst levels of taxation for the most prosperous are greatly reduced, the prospects for the emergence of an underclass in both economic and welfare terms are substantially increased.

The very concept of an 'underclass' can nevertheless be contested as a notion that falls apart upon close analysis. In a caustic examination of the history of the idea, MacNicol (1987) brilliantly disinters its roots in social Darwinism and the eugenics movement, and transcribes its decline in the 1930s as owing to its damaging association with Nazism and – above all – its adherents' failure to contrive an empirical basis for its validity. In certain respects, however, he argues it has been reborn in the guise of 'culture of poverty' and latterly theories of the 'underclass'. When Sir Keith Joseph, then Minister of Health and Social Security, made his ill-fated speech in 1974 on 'cycles of deprivation', he came close to reviving eugenist notions, by locating the sources of poverty in inter-generationally transmitted patterns of fertility and child-rearing among the most disadvantaged.

MacNicol is possibly misled by this recrudescence of the 'underclass' idea by Joseph, as well as by its long and undistinguished history, to state that 'it tends to be supported by those who wish to constrain the redistributive potential of state welfare and it has thus always been part of a broader conservative view of the aetiology of social problems and their correct solutions' (MacNicol, 1987, p. 316). There is little evidence, however, that the New Right, at least in Britain, *currently* embrace such a view. Rather, the main proponents of the 'underclass' idea may now be found on the Left, especially the liberal Left. There is, of course, a kind of Noddyland criminology of the far right, typified by the resolutions at annual Tory Party Conferences, in which – in Norman Tebbit's phrase – crime is to be attributed to 'human wickedness', and the answer lies in more 'bobbies on the beat', tougher sentencing, the restoration of the death penalty and so forth.[1] But those Conservative ministers most directly concerned with crime, successive Home Secretaries such as Leon Brittan and Douglas Hurd, have been keen to distance themselves from the idea that it has any necessary connection with inner-city decay, social deprivation or an 'underclass'. Indeed, they have greeted outbreaks of youthful disorder in Aylesbury, High Wycombe and the like as a sign that crime is not confined to the inner cities! There is considerable irony about the attention paid in recent speeches by the Home Secretary and his deputy to these upsurges of delinquency in Tory strongholds, since they cannot be

laid at the door of Labour councils encouraging crime by attacking
the police and therefore undermining 'law and order'. As Bernard
Shaw might have said, in Hertford, Hereford and Hampshire,
socialism hardly happens. The only explanation for this seeming
paradox is that the New Right are very keen to scotch the idea that
an 'underclass', with both economic and cultural incentives to resort
to street crime, may be the consequence of Conservative policies.

In this one respect, therefore, MacNicol's argument could be
upended. It is now the Left rather than the Right who have begun a
serious engagement with the 'underclass' concept. They do so,
however, from a basis which emphasizes the *positional* rather than
the *dispositional* foundations for its alleged emergence. On a recent
discussion on television (Channel 4, 1988), chaired by Michael
Ignatieff, three leading intellectuals of the liberal-to-Left spectrum,
Ralf Dahrendorf, Stuart Hall and Ray Pahl, were prepared to
countenance the possibility of an emergent underclass as the
product, not only of recent Tory policies in Britain – though they
were seen as intensifying and hastening its institutionalization – but
as general throughout industrial Europe, the consequence in the
main of a social polarization of secondary labour markets and
structural unemployment (Pahl, 1988). Connections have been
made between this phenomenon and rising levels of urban unrest
and street crime (Dahrendorf, 1987). The fourth member of the
group discussion, who alone rejected the whole basis of this
analysis, was Ralph Harris, founder of the Institute for Economic
Affairs, and a major source of New Right policies.

One project of the Left more generally is to re-connect the issues
of 'law and order' with the modes of impoverization analytically
linked by the notion of the 'underclass', but shorn of any biological
or eugenist remainder. That of the New Right is to disconnect these
phenomena, to treat each as a problem in its own right. The
problems facing those who argue for the reality of underclass are, as
MacNicol rightly points out, daunting and so far unresolved: there
is an inherent danger of circular argument (the old tautology
whereby problems such as 'soccer hooliganism' are both explained
by its emergence and serve as an indicator of its existence); the
plethora of research into 'cycles of deprivation' (Rutter and Madge,
1976) established the reality of the deprivation, but not – to any
significant extent – its inter-generational transmission; and if a term
of the potency of 'under*class*' is to be justified, then some substantial

degree of inter-generational impact is called for. By contrast, the task of the New Right is far easier: it is to regret the impoverization of certain groups, muddy the statistical waters by changes to key indicators of need, deny any long-term detriment is being caused, and claim that remedial action is being taken. One might note in passing that assertions about the near-perfect mobility of the second-generation poor out of poverty strain credulity, and that evidence to the effect that 'only' 6.5 per cent of the American population have received welfare for six or more years, and that 'only' 19 per cent of a sample of children of heavily welfare dependent homes were themselves heavily welfare-dependent – another 39 per cent received up to a quarter of their incomes from welfare – (cited in MacNicol, 1987, p. 315) are, as he notes, 'hazardous' as a basis for assertions either way. As the United States is a natural laboratory for the production of an underclass, American data assume prominence in this debate. But coming off welfare cannot be regarded as coming out of poverty, either in Britain or the USA.

All of which suggests a formidable research agenda for the field, and one which regrettably implies yet another phase of inquiry into the coping strategies of the poor when what, in terms of elementary balance, has long been needed is greater attention to be paid to the income aggrandizement practices of the rich. First, despite MacNicol's derision for yet more research on the issue, the claim that increases in poverty and polarization in income and wealth have no implications for the *creation* of an underclass – somewhat different from the claim that one has always existed – is so fundamental a challenge to the belief that poverty has structural causes and consequences, and therefore needs structural solutions, that it demands close and preferably longitudinal research attention. The implication that underclass divisions have now superseded those of social class in more traditional terms has obvious relevance here. One form such research might take is that suggested by McGahey: 'future research should concentrate on how some individuals succeed non-criminally in the difficult circumstances found in high-crime neighbourhoods' (1986, p. 262). As we now know from victim surveys, to the long list of regressive taxes to which the most deprived are subject, we must now add crime and its control. For those living in the worst housing estates and privately rented sectors are both under-protected and over-controlled by the authorities

(Downes and Ward, 1986). The means whereby some individuals and groups succeed in climbing out of such situations, or mounting resistance to unwanted changes, or effecting positive changes themselves, remain little understood. But the canvas could usefully be enlarged to include other forms of social process which work 'against the grain': multi-racial friendships which can flourish even in front-line areas, for example, or social experiments which take root even in the most hostile environments. A good example of the latter would be the work of the Barlinnie Special Unit (see Boyle, 1984; and Cooke, forthcoming): both in this volume and elsewhere, David Donnison (1977) has done much to explore this vein.

Secondly, communities vary not only in their capacity to move from high to low crime rates or the reverse but also in their capacity to accommodate forms of deviance that others would seek to expunge. Comparative work seems especially useful on this front: the Netherlands faces much the same crime problem as Britain, but responds to it with a much more sparing use of imprisonment, and far more humane prisons (Downes, 1988). Some police forces spurn 'community policing', others readily accept it (Foster, forthcoming). Such topics relate also to broader philosophical issues which our field has been too reluctant to explore. With the exception of Tawney, Marshall and Titmuss, taken for granted assumptions, such as altruism, citizenship, tolerance and public spirit have remained largely unargued. What passes for the 'high moral ground' has thus been ceded to the New Right.

Thirdly, there is a tendency in the field to focus on systems rather than processes, on – say – variations in standards of care and performance rather than on how they are accomplished. As a result, we know far too little about the working practices of bureaucrats and so-called controllers. With the exception of the police, there are few British ethnographies of teachers, social workers and civil servants. This makes it curiously easy to stereotype such groups, in ways we would criticize if the subjects were clients or patients. Political charges of ideologically biased teaching, inefficient social workers and passive bureaucrats would, one suspects and hopes, wither somewhat in the light of such studies. This tendency is in part the product of the 'social book-keeping' history of the subject (Rex, 1961) which is in fact one of the great strengths of the discipline. However, it has made for certain methodological inhibitions, in particular a neglect of the kind of approach favoured by interactionists and phenomenologists, who would direct attention to the study of how things are done, how people work together, what recurrent dilemmas they face, how they manage their competing priorities, and the like. If the greatest discoveries are at times to be made in the realm of the taken for granted, then we should direct more of our energies to the study of working practices. This limitation of the field is in my view more salient than the theoretical deficiencies argued by Ramesh Mishra (Chapter 3), though the two are obviously related. It leads, as Howard Glennerster (Chapter 5) points out, to the neglect of the actual business of *administration*.

Fourthly, the field of criminology has expanded to embrace deviance and control, socio-legal studies and criminal justice policy, in ways that have real bearing on social policy and administration. Three themes that have much to offer are:

(1)   *Social divisions in criminal justice*: Titmuss wrote thirty years ago on the 'social divisions of welfare', and those of criminal justice are equally pronounced. Durkheim's forms of restitutive and repressive justice, far from being planted millenia apart on some evolutionary tree, are alive and well and co-existing in the same contemporary legal systems. A perfect instance of restitutive justice is the way tax evasion is dealt with: only the *most* heinous cases are prosecuted, and only a handful imprisoned. Social security fraud is strikingly different in the response it elicts from the authorities. Though less repressively dealt with than a decade ago, it remains the norm for all but the *least* heinous cases to be prosecuted, and several hundred offenders are imprisoned annually (NACRO, 1986). Research into compliance strategies currently reserved for not only the advantaged but also for more administrative offences might show how far they could be extended to offences more characteristic of the least advantaged.

(2)   *'Hidden' forms of crime*: chiefly corporate crime; the informal or hidden economy; domestic violence; and occupational crime. These have begun to be explored, but so far only scantily. In combination, they are far more costly in terms of property loss and damage, and far more lethal, in terms of injury and deaths, than street crime (Box, 1983). A thorough inventory of their character and distribution would produce very different images of deviance from those that currently prevail. They would also produce much of policy

relevance regarding industrial and occupational safety; consumer protection; and the protection of women and children. It would also upset cherished myths, such as the view that the informal economy is chiefly peopled by 'scroungers' on the dole. Pahl (1984, 1988) has done much to establish that 'the distributional consequences of the pattern of informal work in industrial societies is to reinforce, rather than to reduce or to reflect contemporary patterns of inequality' (Pahl, 1988).

(3) *'Hidden' forms of control*: these range from what Mathiesen (1983) called the 'monitoring of whole groups and categories of people', for example, by electronic surveillance in shopping precincts, sports arenas and the like, to welfare sanctions (Garland, 1981) which bear most heavily on the poor. The processes which Cohen termed 'net-widening', 'mesh-thinning', blurring and penetration (1985) in connection with criminal justice should be examined in relation to the field of social welfare more generally.

If so daunting a research agenda has any justifiction, it is at least in part to be found in the present government's radical un-coupling of the ideas of structural change, social policy, poverty and 'law and order'. The new Enlightenment propounds a Thatcherite version of 'false consciousness' in which it is entirely a matter for the individual whether or not he or she chooses to remain in poverty, unemployment, commit crimes etc. If only they would show more enterprise, accept a lower wage which the market can bear, 'get on their bikes' to look for work, and obey the law, all would be well. In the meantime, tougher policing, harsher penalties, more prisons, and a more authoritarian and centralized state must hold the line. It is a suburban mirror-image of Stalinism, in which crime is due to human wickedness (nothing to do with society), pre-revolutionary residues (the fecklessness born of the 'permissive' society of the 1960s and 1970s), or socialist encirclement (bad Labour authorities undermining the police). Against this strategy of disconnection between present policies and social discontents, the task of social science and administration remains that proposed by C. Wright Mills (1959) for sociology some three decades ago: to seek the links between 'private troubles' and 'public issues'. That does not mean automatic acceptance for such notions as that of an emergent underclass, but it does imply their evaluation by means other than guilt by association.

Notes

1 The role of Enid Blyton in shaping modern conservative ideology deserves rescue from neglect. For a seminal essay by Colin Welsh, who later became 'Peter Simple' of the *Daily Telegraph*, see 'Dear Little Noddy', *Encounter*, January 1958.

References

J. Baldwin and A. Bottoms, *The Urban Criminal* (London: Tavistock, 1976).
A. Bottoms, P. Wiles 'Housing tenure and residential community crime careers in Britain', in A. Reiss and M. Tonry (eds) *Communities and Crime* (Chicago: University of Chicago Press, 1986), pp. 101–62.
S. Box, *Power, Crime and Mystification* (London: Tavistock, 1983).
S. Box, *Recession, Crime and Punishment* (London: Macmillan, 1987).
J. Boyle, *The Pains of Confinement: Prison Diaries* (Edinbrugh: Canongate, 1984).
Channel 4, 'Thinking Aloud', 1988.
R. Clarke and M. Hough, *Crime and Police Effectiveness*, Home Office Research Study 79 (London: HMSO, 1984).
S. Cohen, *Visions of Social Control* (Cambridge: Polity Press, 1985).
A. Coleman, *Utopia on Trial* (London: Shipman, 1985).
D. Cooke, 'Containing violent prisoners: an analysis of the Barlinnie special unit', *British Journal of Criminology* (forthcoming).
R. Dahrendorf, 'The underclass and the future of Britain', Windsor: St George's House (Tenth Annual Lecture) 1987.
S. Damer, 'Wine alley: the sociology of a dreadful enclosure', *Sociological Review*, 1974, no. 22, pp. 221–48.
J. Ditton, *Part-time Crime* (London: Macmillan, 1977).
D. Donnison, 'Special unit', *New Society*, 1977.
D. Downes, *Contrasts in Tolerance; Post-war Penal Policy in the Netherlands and England and Wales* (Oxford: Oxford University Press, 1988)
D. Downes and T. Ward, *Democratic Policing* (London: Labour Campaign for Criminal Justice, 1986).
EEC Council of Ministers, *Interim Report on the Second Poverty Programme*, Draft V, Strasbourg, 1987.
J. Foster, 'Two Stations', in D. Downes (ed.) *Crime and the City: Essays in Honour of John Mays* (London: Macmillan, in press).
D. Garland, 'The birth of the welfare sanction', *British Journal of Law and Society*, no. 8, pp. 29–45.
D. Garland and P. Young (eds), *The Power to Punish* (London: Heinemann, 1983).
A. Giddens, *The Class Structure of the Advanced Societies* (London: Hutchinson, 1973).
Lord Gifford, *The Broadwater Farm Inquiry Report* (London: Borough of Haringey, 1986).

O. Gill, *Luke Street: Housing Policy, Conflict and the Making of a Delinquency Area* (London: Macmillan, 1977).

T. Hope and M. Shaw (eds), *Communities and Crime Reduction* (London: HMSO, 1987).

J. Lea and J. Young, *What Is To Be Done About Law and Order?* (Harmondsworth: Penguin, 1984).

R. McGahey, 'Economic conditions, neighbourhood organization, and Urban Crime' in A. Reiss and M. Tonry (eds) *Communities and Crime* (Chicago: Chicago University Press, 1986), pp. 231–70.

J. MacNicol, 'In pursuit of the underclass', *Journal of Social Policy*, 16, pp. 293–318.

T. Mathiesen, 'The future of control systems – the case of Norway', in D. Garland and P. Young (eds), *The Power to Punish* (London: Heinemann, 1983), pp. 130–45.

T. Morris, *The Criminal Area* (London: Routledge & Kegan Paul, 1957).

National Association for the Care and Resettlement of offenders (NACRO) *Enforcement of the Law Relating to Social Security* (London: NACRO, 1986).

O. Newman, *Defensible Space* (London: Architectural Press, 1973).

R. Pahl, *Divisions of Labour* (Oxford: Blackwell, 1984).

R. Pahl, 'Some remarks on informal work, social polarisation and the social structure', *International Journal of Urban and Regional Research*, no. 12, 1988, pp. 247–67.

A. Power, 'Housing, poverty and crime', in D. Downes (ed.) *Crime and the City* (London: Macmillan, in press).

R. Reiner, *The Politics of the Police* (Brighton: Wheatsheaf, 1985).

A. Reiss Jr. and M. Tonry (eds) *Communities and Crime* (Chicago: University of Chicago Press, 1986).

J. Rex, *Key Problems in Sociological Theory* (London: Routledge & Kegan Paul, 1961).

M. Rutter and M. Madge, *Cycles of Deprivation* (London: Heinemann, 1976).

Lord Scarman, *Report of an Inquiry into the Brixton Disorders*, 10–12 April 1981 (London: HMSO, 1981).

C. Welsh, 'Dear Little Noddy', *Encounter*, January 1958, pp. 18–22.

C. Wright Mills, *The Sociological Imagination* (New York: Oxford University Press, 1959).

16 *The underclass, empowerment and public policy*

MARTIN BULMER

The issues raised in the preceding papers pose a number of challenges for social policy, centred around issues of local social structure on the one hand and local political power on the other. How can these issues best be addressed? The discussion period at the conference showed that there was far from universal agreement about the directions in which research should go, and some quite strong dissent was expressed about the terms of the debate. Some of the objections were from an explicit value standpoint, in effect arguing that it was not possible to be value-neutral in relation to social deprivation and powerlessness. It was also objected that there was an undesirable tendency to objectify particular social groups and their problems. Undoubtedly the diversity of response also reflected the heterogeneous character of issues covered under 'social policy and the community'.

It is incontrovertible that life chances are markedly unequal and are affected both by social circumstances and by where people live. There is much argument about what causes this state of affairs and sharp differences between analysts of the subject, though a measure of agreement about the facts of the matter. What scholars interested in these issues have in common is an increasing policy focus both in the explanation of such differences and in forms of intervention designed to mitigate some of the more severe social consequences. Such policy debates require theoretical clarity.

The need for such theoretical clarification was apparent in the conference discussion of the concept of the 'underclass'. While there might be quite general agreement that social polarization was increasing in industrial societies such as Britain and the United States, several participants were hostile to the concept of the underclass. One suggested this should be acknowledged more explicitly by reintroducing the Victorian concept of 'the dangerous classes'. Criticisms ranged from the role of the 'underclass' concept in political obfuscation (lumping 'the poor' together in an undifferentiated mass), its linking together of urban blight, crime and poverty when the three were not always associated, and the tendency to look from the top down, focusing on deviance and deprivation among the lower classes rather than in other strata of society.

There may be a danger here, however, of ignoring a phenomenon because it is unpalatable. This danger is particularly strong in Britain, where the study of social policy has had such strong normative overtones. William Wilson has suggested that this happened among American liberal scholars in relation to the black family in the wake of the controversial Moynihan report of 1965.[1] As a result of the controversy, liberals for a decade shied away from studying behaviour deemed unflattering or stigmatizing to racial minorities. When they returned to studying the phenomenon in the early 1980s, they were staggered by the deterioration in the already disadvantaged position of black families which they discovered.[2] Is there a possibility today in relation to urban poverty, social deprivation and crime in Britain that the seriousness of the problems will be underplayed by an insistence upon setting them within conventional categories?

Students of social policy need to reformulate the issue more sharply in theoretical terms. Free market critiques of the underclass, arguing that state provision tends to increase welfare dependency, have relied upon individualist explanations of social behaviour with infusions of 'person blame'. What is urgently needed is a *structural* theory of the underclass which locates the phenomenon in its social context. An adequate structural theory can be framed, which accords centrality to the employment and labour force experience of members of disadvantaged minorities, in relation to their demographic characteristics.

The central importance of employment and unemployment in inner city degeneration is shown in Figure 16.1. Its major hypothesis is close to that of William Wilson, that the condition of the underclass

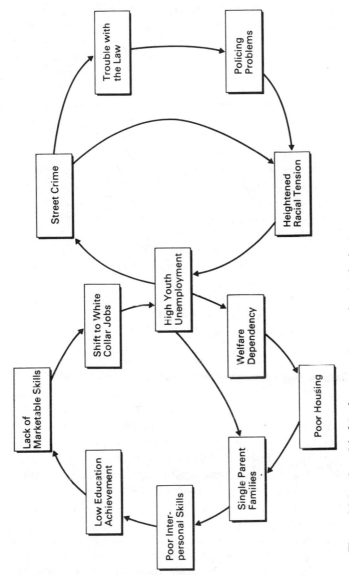

Figure 16.1   *A model of the factors creating an urban 'underclass'*

Source: Audit Commission, *The Management of London's Authorities: preventing the breakdown of services* (Occasional Paper no. 2) (London: The Audit Commission, 1987), p. 2. Reproduced by permission of the Audit Commission

is explained primarily in terms of joblessness and the social consequences which flow from this. It is useful, too, in connecting two themes of this section of the conference, the disadvantaged condition of inner city dwellers and the high incidence of crime, discussed by David Downes. The model suggests a common link through employment opportunites, setting off consequences for each circle which are then gradually worked out. Arguably the model is over-simplified, since the cause-effect chain which it purports to identify is a linear one, placing emphasis upon one variable at a time.

This is the case in relation to single parenthood and family structure, an increasingly important aspect of urban deprivation to which insufficient attention has been given in Britain. It is moreover an issue where the interconnections between this section and the preceding and following ones are very apparent. The proportion of female-headed families in the United States has been increasing, nearly doubling for the black population between 1965 and 1984. In 1984, one in eight of white families, one in four of Hispanic families and nearly nine out of twenty black families were female-headed. In 1983, nearly half of the American black children under the age of 18 lived in families with incomes below the poverty line, and three-quarters of those poor families were headed by women.[3]

Individualist analyses of the American underclass argue that there has been a causal connection between the increase in female-headed families and increased reliance upon welfare, and the Audit Commission model suggests that this may be a partial explanation, mediated by poor housing. Other evidence, however, suggests that the association is not so straightforward. During the 1970s only about one-quarter of the poor became poor because of changes in family structure. Most poverty occurred because of changes in jobs or incomes (including unemployment). Among white families there was some evidence of poverty due to family breakdown, but among black families, despite the increase in female-headed families, such families were likely to have been poor both before and after the change in their family situation.[4]

William Wilson's research in Chicago finds strong evidence of accelerating family breakdown and observes that 'economic hardship has become almost synonymous with black female-headed families'. The rise in female-headed black households closely corresponds with the rise of out of wedlock births, which have increased from 15 per cent of all black births in 1959 to 57 per cent in 1982. Among teenagers the rise has also been sharp, from 42 per cent of all black teenage births in 1960 to 89 per cent in 1983. In Chicago in 1983, nearly three-quarters of all black births were out of wedlock, compared to half in 1970. There is, moreover, a marked spatial distribution. The concentration of these problems is most acute in ghetto neighbourhoods. In the most impoverished areas of the city, predominantly black, with rates of household poverty exceeding 40 per cent in 1980, the proportion of female-headed households ranged from 61 per cent to 78 per cent in that year, and showed increases of between 50 per cent and 100 per cent over 1970.

Whether these patterns can be explained simply by welfare dependency, however, seems improbable. Wilson has disaggregated age structure, marital status and fertility rates and suggests that the decline in marital fertility and the proportion of women married and living with their husbands explains a good deal of the increase in fatherless families. Increased divorce and separation, and more women choosing not to marry, explains the decline in the proportion of women living with their husbands. There are also racial differences in the timing of first marriage and the rate of remarriage. Welfare receipt does appear to have a modest effect on separation and divorce for white families – one of the serendipitous findings of the negative income tax experiments – but black male joblessness is a much more important determinant of black family structure. This, indeed, is recognized explicitly in Figure 16.1.

Economic situation is indeed a critical dimension, both in relation to family structure and to education and to crime. The lines along which social polarization are occurring – socially, regionally and locally – are pre-eminently those of full participation or lack of participation in the employment market. They are reinforced by social processes which interact with the economic. One significant factor in the deteriorating social conditions of the American ghetto underclass has been the removal of a social buffer, the presence in black areas of a substantial middle-class and employed working-class element, which could absorb some of the effects of uneven economic growth and recession in inner-city areas. These strata of the population have progressively moved out over the last quarter of a century, leaving fewer social supports in the community.

It is more difficult in their absence to maintain the basic institutions of the locality – churches, schools, shops, recreational facilities

– as unemployment rises. There are also concentration effects of living in areas in which most of the population are socially disadvantaged, for the locality provides ecological niches in terms of access to jobs, availability of marriage partners and exposure to conventional role models. The two processes are connected. One consequence of the decline of basic institutions in a locality is likely to be a decline in positive identification with one's neighbourhood and the weakening of explicit norms and sanctions against deviant behaviour.[5]

A class is being created who do not share in the prosperity of the majority, and suffer disadvantage in work, housing, education, socialization and environment. The disadvantages are experienced particularly sharply by certain groups, such as children in single-parent families and the young unemployed who have never had paid work. Not all of these disadvantages are overlapping, neither do they necessarily endure for long periods of time, although with the disappearance of full employment one can be less confident that this will be the case in the long run.

There is strong evidence of such developments in the United States, and a good deal of evidence along the same lines in Britain. Conditions are as yet less extreme in Britain, but arguably American cities are a portent for the future, particularly given the convergence of the two countries in terms of free market philosophy. The Audit Commission puts the matter bluntly:

> The Commission foresees very considerable problems in inner London. The South Side of Chicago and Harlem and the Bronx in New York provide a foretaste of the future that is in store unless action is taken to redress the underlying problems: high welfare dependency and generation intervals of 15 years or less; youth unemployment of 70 per cent or more; extremely high crime rates, much of it drug-related; uneasy relations between the police and a disaffected and largely unemployable urban 'underclass' with no stake in the development of the society in which they live. This future cannot be allowed to happen.[6]

Moreover recognition of the existence of such social polarization in Britain is spread across the political spectrum from left to right, although the terminology used varies. Thus the Conservative MP Mr Michael Heseltine has recently written of the creation of an unemployment subculture or class where youth generations are growing up in the pincer grip of their own deprivation and other people's relative prosperity.[7] There is more disagreement about the policy measures to remedy the situation – Mr Heseltine favours a form of 'workfare', which is anathema to many on the left – but the underlying analysis has much in common with that put forward by the Audit Commission.

The debate about the underclass is just beginning in Britain and will surely lead to substantial empirical research to test some of the hypotheses derived from the American experience. Some of the formulations, for example, those of Ralf Dahrendorf, are so imprecise as to appear to identify as members of the 'underclass' members of any deprived group in society. Critics, of course, argue that we have been here before with the concepts of the 'culture of poverty'[8] and 'transmitted deprivation',[9] and further back with ideas about the deteriorating quality of the population.[10] There have been few recent attempts to relate the concept to mainstream stratification theory.[11] The idea implicit in the concept that disadvantage is transmitted for members of such a class between one generation and another was shown by the SSRC research programme on transmitted deprivation a decade ago to be at best a partial truth.

The value of the concept, however, lies in making a global statement about social processes and social structure underlying current social deprivation, and setting that deprivation in some sort of theoretical context. The difference from notions such as the culture of poverty is that the theoretical basis for the underclass concept is sounder, when the term is defined in terms of life chances in employment, housing, locality, health, education and family stability. In particular, the centrality of *present* economic circumstances in explaining social disadvantage avoids implications of 'person blame'. In these terms, different sections of the population *do* have significantly different life chances which form the backdrop to social policy measures, including state intervention, to try to moderate disadvantage.

David Donnison's Chapter 12, however, is a reminder that there are other issues to consider, particularly questions of political power and mobilization. He takes a very stimulating cut at the issue, from one angle, and in passing raises a number of others. He touches on, but does not fully develop, the way in which for disadvantaged minorities the state 'looks more like a stage for their oppressors' than an ally. In many countries an uncomfortably large share of the huge increases in resources devoted to public services seem to have been engrossed by the people who staff the services without finding its way through to the customer.[12] Relations between the public and large bureaucracies are an issue which have been intensively studied in some areas – policing is a good example – and relatively neglected in others – such as social workers and their clients.

Howard Glennerster has suggested that there has been a relative failure to study how welfare bureaucracies actually work. A key issue, raised by David Donnison, is how bureaucratic officials at more junior levels, in day-to-day contact with the public, actually operate. Pioneering work on 'street level bureaucracy' and 'people processing' has not been followed up in the way that it might. Some areas such as housing and supplementary benefits administration have been studied, but apart from some rather jejeune marxist theorizing, the issue has not received the theoretical attention that it deserves. This is all the more striking given the experiments currently under way to decentralize local authority services and try to bring them closer to the people for whom they are intended.[13]

Another issue which deserves to be developed is the capacity of the 'third sector' of voluntary and community-based action, located between state activities on the one hand and the private market on the other, to make social provision. David Donnison, by focusing on community action, does not say very much about the voluntary sector as a whole, and the long history of organized voluntary activity in Britain. Institutions such as the WRVS are little studied, yet they are both major service providers and meshed into elite networks. The significance of different forms of neighbourhood action – such as 'good neighbour' schemes for care delivery or 'neighbourhood watch' schemes for crime control – is increasing as government seeks to foster various forms of self-help. Action-oriented interest groups are another form to which more attention should be paid. Welfare pressure groups such as the Patients Association and MENCAP, self-help groups for members of particular minorities such as Gingerbread, advice and support groups such as Samaritans and Alcoholics Anonymous, and attempts to organize hitherto totally disorganized but numerically significant minorities such as the Association of Carers, are all examples of new forms of political action in the social policy field. As yet, little attempt has been made to theorize their place in social provision and look at their role in the political process. Yet this is crucial if responsibilities continue to be devolved from the state on to intermediary institutions. Durkheim put his finger on the essence of the general issue:

> A nation can be maintained only if, between the state and the individual, there is intercalated a whole series of secondary groups near enough to the individuals to attract them strongly in their sphere of action, and drag them in this way, into the general torrent of social life. [14]

More recently, Peter Berger has identified the importance of structures mediating between the megastructures of society – remote, impersonal and hard to understand – and private life carried on within a circle of intimates. [15] Albert Hunter and Gerald Suttles have observed that 'the question of how residential solidarities are keyed into other social arrangements bears on almost all the problems of societal integration'. [16] As the sources of social provision diversify in the mixed economy of welfare, a better understanding and more adequate theorization of these intermediary structures is a high priority.

One element in the public debate about welfare and locality is the observation that the two are connected through some types of area being more crime-prone than others. David Downes discusses this issue in detail, but the connection with issues of public order and disorder is clear. The tendency to view crime in individual terms – offences perpetrated by law-breaking individuals upon other individuals (their victims) – fits in conveniently with the market-oriented individualist approach to social problems, but is contradicted by a long tradition of research in sociological criminology, referred to by David Downes. This is also recognized in the considerable amount of recent official interest in ways of intervening at the community level to try to reduce crime. [17]

Moreover, various collective forms of social disturbance and disorder – notably football hooliganism and urban racial disturbances – cannot be explained purely in individualist terms and point to a direct connection between social conditions and unrest. Popular analyses sometimes grasp this. Michael Heseltine, in the discussion of an unemployment subculture quoted earlier, observes that contemporary youth 'live just a stone's throw away from a more affluent society whose benefits and attractions are brought daily by the television before their eyes, but yet there is no legitimate way in which they perceive their ability to share in it'. The result is political protest, urban unrest and crime.[18] The challenge to academic social policy, which is some way toward being met, is to provide more refined analyses of the genesis of such phenomena locating them in their social context. Some examples of such work are available.[19]

One lacuna in the conference, which has been only partially rectified in this short discussion, was sustained attention to issues concerning race and social policy. Issues of gender comprise a whole section of the book, and all the contributors are women. This reflects the salience of these issues in British social policy and the number of scholars working on them. Relative to gender, race in social policy is a neglected area. Though the sociology of race relations is flourishing, many of its concerns are more abstract and removed from the policy arena.[20] Race has also received attention in education, employment and to a lesser extent in housing and health. But there are lacking many in-depth studies of black people living in inner-city areas with a policy focus, exploring the effects on racial minorities of the social polarization discussed earlier. One of the most widely quoted studies, carried out in Bristol over a decade ago by Ken Pryce, developed a typology of black responses to mainstream British society which lacks validation and has been criticized as inadequate.[21] The sources of urban social unrest are also contentious.[22]

Much more public attention has focused on equal opportunities policies and their implementation, but here again studies are sporadic and those that have been carried out cast doubt on the efficacy of various forms of positive discrimination. The extent of, and trends in, racial segregation also deserve study. British cities are not residentially segregated by race in the way that Chicago or Detroit or New York are segregated, except in the sense that there are some areas (including not just owner-occupied housing but more attractive council estates) with very few black or brown residents. But at the micro-level there are trends apparent toward segregation, as particular council estates and particular inner-city schools become predominantly non-white in their ethnic composition. This, in turn, links to the question of whether among the most disadvantaged groups in society race or class is the most salient characteristic. It is very doubtful if one can yet speak of a *black* underclass in Britain, but among the inner-city underclass black people are disproportionately represented.

A better understanding is needed of the interconnectedness of the various aspects of social policy in the community. An example from Tower Hamlets may serve to make the point. A study of equal opportunities in the Tower Hamlets housing department in the mid–1980s showed that the unit responsible for promoting equal opportunity in housing was marginalized within the department and that (white) officers making housing allocations used various racial criteria in matching tenants and properties.[23] One consequence of this in the borough was the concentration of black tenants on certain estates. This raises issues about the concentration of disadvantage discussed earlier, but was of more immediate concern as black tenants in the area also became the object of racial attacks. A racial element in football hooliganism has also been observed, as an extreme manifestation of antagonism between sections of the white working class and the black working class. Tower Hamlets has also been the site of controversies about the housing of homeless Bangladeshi immigrants and about the implementation of the immigration laws, which bear on members of black minorities with relatives overseas very harshly. Disadvantage can be mutually reinforcing.

The issues are many-faceted, and suggest that an approach to social policy in the community which starts either from a particular location – the inner city – or a particular aspect of social structure such as the underclass – needs to be complemented by focusing upon particular disadvantaged minorities within the urban system – as in the above example of Asian minorities in east London. It is then necessary to examine the intersection of location, social structure and situation of the minority, including its political representation. One striking difference between black minorities in the United States and in Britain is that the former have achieved much more effective political representation at the city government level. To a considerable extent this can be explained in historical terms and in terms of their size as minority groups. It is also a reminder that there is nothing automatic about a disadvantaged minority achieving voice.

Notes

1   cf. L. Rainwater and W. L. Yancey (eds) *The Moynihan Report and the Politics of Controversy* (Cambridge, Mass.: M.I.T. Press, 1967).

2   W. J. Wilson, *The Truly Disadvantaged: the inner city, the underclass and public policy* (Chicago: University of Chicago Press, 1987), pp. 6–7.

3   ibid., Chapter 3.

4   M. J. Bane 'Household composition and poverty', in S. Danzinger and D. Weinberg (eds), *Fighting Poverty: what works and what doesn't* (Cambridge, Mass.: Harvard University Press, 1986) pp. 209–31.

4   W. J. Wilson, op. cit.

6   Audit Commission, *The Management of London's Authorities: preventing the breakdown of services* (London: Audit Commission Occasional Paper no. 2, January 1987) p. 16.

7   M. Heseltine, *Unemployment: no time for ostriches* (London: The Employment Institute, 1988).

8   cf. C. A. Valentine, *Culture and Poverty* (Chicago: University of Chicago Press, 1968) and E. B. Leacock (ed.), *The Culture of Poverty: a critique* (New York: Simon and Schuster, 1971). For a recent discussion see D. Piachaud, 'Poverty and inequality: analysis and action', Inaugural lecture, London School of Economics, 5 May 1988.

9   cf. M. Rutter and N. Madge, *Cycles of Disadvantage* (London: Heinemann, 1976) and M. Brown and N. Madge, *Despite the Welfare State* (London: Heinemann, 1982).

10   cf. J. MacNicol, 'In pursuit of the underclass', *Journal of Social Policy*, 16 (3), July 1987, pp. 293–318.

11   For one brief attempt see R. E. Pahl, 'Some remarks on informal work, social polarisation and the social structure', *International Journal of Urban and Regional Research*, 12 (2), 1988, pp. 257–61.

12   The evidence on this is reviewed in Stein Ringen, *The Possibility of Politics* (Oxford: Oxford University Press, 1987).

13   cf. H. Glennerster, 'A requiem for the social administration association', *Journal of Social Policy* 17 (1), 1988, pp. 83–4. On interaction between lower-level officials and clients, see M. Lipsky, *Street level Bureaucracy: Dilemmas of the Individual in Public Services* (New York: Russell Sage Foundation, 1980) and M. Prottas, *People Processing: the Street Level Bureaucrat in Public Service Bureaucracies* (Lexington: D. C. Heath, 1979). An unusual if controversial study of social security officials is S. Cooper, *Observations in Supplementary Benefits Offices*, The Reform of Supplementary Benefit Working Paper C, (London: Policy Studies Institute Research Paper 85/2, 1985). C. Cockburn, *The Local State: Management of Cities and People* (London, Pluto, 1977) remains a comparatively rare example of a theoretical study of local administration.

14   E. Durkheim, *The Division of Labour in Society* (New York: Free Press, 1933; first published in French in 1893).

15   P. L. Berger, 'In praise of particularity: the concept of mediating structures', in P. L. Berger, *Facing Up to Modernity: excursions in society, politics and religion* (New York: Basic Books, 1980), pp. 130–41.

16 A. Hunter and G. D. Suttles, 'The expanding community of limited liability', in G. D. Suttles, *The Social Construction of Community* (Chicago: University of Chicago Press, 1972), pp. 44–81.
17 cf. T. Hope and M. Shaw (eds), *Communities and Crime Reduction* (London: HMSO for Home Office Research and Planning Unit, 1988).
18 M. Heseltine, op. cit. note 7.
19 cf. E. Dunning, P. Murphy and J. Williams, *The Roots of Football Hooliganism* (London: Routledge & Kegan Paul, 1988); J. Benyon and J. Solomos (eds), *The Roots of Urban Unrest* (Oxford: Pergamon, 1988).
20 cf. works like R. Miles, *Racism and Migrant Labour* (London: Routledge & Kegan Paul, 1982); F. Reeves, *British Racial Discourse* (Cambridge: Cambridge University Press, 1983), P. Rich, *Race and Empire in British Politics, 1890–1962* (Cambridge: Cambridge University Press, 1986).
21 K. Pryce, *Endless Pressure: a study of West Indian life-styles in Bristol* (Harmondsworth: Penguin, 1979).
22 cf. some of the exchanges in Benyon and Solomos, *The Roots of Urban Unrest*. See also, J. Rex *The Ghetto and the Underclass: essays on race and social policy* (Aldershot: Avebury, 1988).
23 D. Phillips, *What Price Equality? A report on the allocation of GLC Housing in Tower Hamlets* (GLC Housing Research and Policy Report no. 9) (London: Greater London Council, 1986).

PART V

Social Policy and the Economy

17 *Introduction*

DAVID PIACHAUD

The original LSE social administration department was much concerned with the relief of poverty through charity and social work. By contrast, George Bernard Shaw, who spent much time with his future wife in her flat above the original London School of Economics, took the view that the poor were 'useless, dangerous and ought to be abolished'; his perspective was that of a political economist, albeit an idiosyncratic one.

In the 1950s and 1960s it is said that the guru of social policy, Richard Titmuss, and the guru of the economics department, Lionel Robbins, rarely spoke to each other. Economics was concerned with firms and finance, with production and efficiency. Social administration was concerned with distributing services according to needs and with those outside 'the economy'. Thus there was little to talk about, even if the inclination had been there.

Now a large number of economists are concerned with issues once the preserve of social administrators – poverty, public housing, health care, inequalities in access and allocation of social services, and many other areas. Most students of social policy have, however reluctantly, to take an interest in economics; this may be solely out of concern for levels of public expenditure which depend on levels of economic activity and economic policy decisions, but it may reflect a deeper concern with the impact of economic change on society.

In terms of practical policy, the link between social and economic thinking has never been more apparent. Market solutions are being pursued by the British government, among others, in order to promote competition and efficiency and reduce the tax burden. Cost-effectiveness is being pursued and the output of social services is being brought into question.

Yet it would be wrong to imply that all economists have simply

descended upon social policy bringing with them a baggage of
prejudice for market solutions and against the poor. The reasons
economists have become increasingly concerned with social policy
over the past twenty-five years are very different from the reasons
for the recent concern of some politicians. Academic economists
have been concerned with human capital and causes of inequality
and poverty, with understanding not merely industry and finance
but also the household economy, and with the pursuit of goals that
cannot always or easily be measured in terms of monetary values.
Right-wing politicians have approached social policy with an *a priori*
belief in markets and a concern to limit costs. Both the academic
economists and the politicians have been less concerned with the
history and organization of social services than with the question of
what they produce – with the outputs rather than the inputs.

Why did the change in the relationship between economic and
social policy come about? To answer this question it is worth trying
to understand why the separation existed and what were the
consequences of this separation.

For most of this century, indeed still to some extent today, social
policy was treated like a deserving charity. It was a 'good thing' to
improve hospitals and schools but this could only be done as and
when resources were available from the 'real world' of industrial
production. Social policy was, in economic terms, secondary and
separate. The secondary nature made its resources subject to the
vagaries of the economy. But its separateness meant it was largely
free to develop in its own way, usually according to the priorities of
the professional providers. One consequence may have been an
excessive concern with social service provision *for* people and a
neglect of people as producers in their own right. Social policy often
acted as the willing hand-maiden of the economy, ever ready to pick
up the human pieces that fell as a result of changes in the economy.
More attention has been devoted in social policy to picking up the
pieces than to preventing problems in the first place.

A second reason for separation of social policy and economic
policy was that the former was once almost exclusively concerned
with 'social welfare'. Titmuss pointed to the need to expand the
study of welfare and income distribution to include not merely
public services but also fiscal and occupational welfare. Others have
extended the boundaries of welfare to include voluntary activities
and unpaid work within the home and family. Now the public

provision of social services can be seen to be only one part of the total system of finance, subsidy and ultimately work-effort that contributes towards social welfare.

A third reason for separation was that social policies for the most part treated the distribution of productive opportunities as given and unchangeable. This was not surprising when, compared to the 1920s and 1930s, the economy appeared to be so much more successful in delivering full employment, at least for men. But with mass unemployment in many countries starting in the 1970s and showing no sign of ending, concern with the distribution of employment opportunities has increased among social policy analysts.

Increasingly the nature of the economy to which social policy is, in many respects, the handmaiden is being called into question by those concerned with social policy. In all countries the monetized economy is characterized by a high degree of inequality in aspects of direct relevance to social policy: inequality within the labour market and between those in and outside employment; inequality in housing, pensions and capital ownership of all forms; inequalities of class, gender and race. Social policy must, it was once implied, accept most of these inequalities and rely on the unpaid work that is not counted as part of the economy. Social policy can then alter opportunities a little (what Zsuzsa Ferge in Chapter 18 describes as *ex-ante* social policy) and, more and more, it can pick up pieces (Ferge's *ex-post* social policy). In the United Kingdom, as in most countries, social policy ameliorates and legitimates. But it is, perhaps, a delusion to think in terms of elaborate models and theories of social policy. Fine phrases about citizenship and extending democracy inspire a sense of self-importance and lead to self-congratulation but this may disguise the true role of social policy. Thus far social policy has come second to economic policy, by a large margin.

A clear distinction and separation between social and economic policy now appears impossible to sustain. The papers that follow in this section reflect the interrelation of the two.

Ferge's paper lies in the tradition of political economy and examines the role of the state generally, and social policy in particular, in different stages of the economic history of industrialized countries. Stewart extends this analysis to developing countries and assesses the role of government in influencing the primary and the secondary distributions of income. Both these papers examine the role – or 'action' – of social policy. Korpi discuss the impact of – or 'reaction' to – social policies: he does this in a manner that distinguishes passive (picking up the pieces) and active (tackling the causes) policies. He casts grave doubt on the jeremiads of what might be dubbed the 'reactionary school of social policy' who seem intent on showing that any attempt to alter, even improve, society is destined to end in failure, or worse.

Reflecting and intensifying the interrelationship of social and economic policy, the papers that follow do pose a problem: if the interrelationship is so strong, what is social policy as distinct from economic policy?

It is not enough for social policy to wrap itself in virtuous concern and assert that social policy 'professionals' care more about the poor. We need to say what we are about. Unless we define what we are trying to do we cannot know whether we have done it. The end result is that social policies end up getting blamed for all society's ills. Social scientists need to be hard-headed not soft-hearted in relation to social policy. Much published work is essentially pleading on behalf of the disadvantaged in the hope of marginal concessions (from politicians who are elsewhere roundly condemned). The failure in Britain to influence policy must be recognized. One reason for this failure is lack of bluntness: in order to win marginal concessions, unsustainable claims are sometimes made for the possible impact of social policies on the problems at which they are directed. Certain problems have *no* remedies within current terms of reference. This may be harder to say – indeed some may think it downright unconstructive – but it may be true. For instance, it may be that many problems of bad housing, drug addiction and child abuse cannot be more than marginally influenced with present mass unemployment.

What, then, is social policy?

Howard Glennerster in Chapter 5 saw it as a sprawling megalopolis, in contrast to a walled and dead city. But there are signs of inner-city decay and a lack of any plan or structure. He posed the question: is foreign exchange policy part of social policy? Since, in many countries, it is crucial in determining the level of poverty and the very survival of millions, it would seem to make little sense to separate it from social policy.

Ian Gough, in a contribution to the discussion at the Conference, saw economic policy as being state intervention in the sphere of *production* and social policy as being state intervention in the sphere of *reproduction* of the labour force, the household. Yet Caroline Moser in Chapter 10 had shown how, in the Third World, much production and reproduction occurred in the same place, making this distinction unclear. The provision of a midday meal for children illustrates the difficulty with Gough's distinction: it may be provided at school as part of the welfare state, or at home as part of the domestic economy, or in a fast-food emporium as part of the 'productive economy'. Each of these provides a child with a midday meal but each has very different consequences for production, particularly for the paid and home work of women, as well as for nutrition.

One central distinctive feature of social policy is that identified by Brian Abel-Smith in his essay 'Whose Welfare State?' (1958). Social policy, he argued, is concerned with inequality and divisions in society. It is concerned with inequality of life expectancy, of educational opportunity, of resources of money and of time. Social policy must, inescapably, be concerned with the entire range of policies and behaviour that affect such inequalities.

This definition of what is distinctive about social policy might usefully be extended to a concern with inequality and divisions in the global society. The central concern has been with inequalities of outcomes but some of this concern might be more productively directed to inequalities of opportunities. It is surely time social policy stopped being all about symptoms and relieving victims and started talking about causes. This requires social policy analysts to be better social scientists and concentrate less on prescribing policies and more on understanding their effects. Only then will social policy analysis carry the weight it could but no longer does.

Yet perhaps the search for the distinction between social policy and economic policy is, in the last resort, an academic indulgence, an unending quest for identity that should be left to academic Woody Allens. Rather than starting as economist or social policy analyst, it is perhaps more useful to address issues as social scientists, with the multidisciplinary perspective espoused in the Introduction to this book. Social policies in education, health, and housing are central to the study of the distribution of incomes or the dynamics of work, income and family formation. On the other hand, the interaction of work and income and the distribution of work – both paid and unpaid – are crucial to the nature of society and to social policy. Social policy lies at the foundation of economic policy just as economic policy is fundamental to social policy.

18 Social policy and the economy

ZSUZSA FERGE

Configurations of social policy in a historical perspective

The separation of the different spheres of the reproduction of social life has occurred and has become institutionalized in the last two or three centuries. With this process the economy – as well as the other spheres – has become 'disembedded' (Polányi). The relative autonomy of the various fields is a potential source of tensions and lack of adjustment between them.

The period in question coincides with the advent of capitalism and the creation of a fully fledged market economy. The turn taken by economic development leading to the prevalence of market and profit interests has certainly harmed many other interests. For example, many elementary human, communal and societal needs were squeezed out from being legitimately acceptable on the grounds that the necessary purchasing power was lacking. The coverage of the needs rejected by the market necessitated new forms of social organization. This was in line with the separation off, and relative autonomy, of the sphere of social reproduction. Thus the field of social policy or social welfare emerged, and has gradually become institutionalized.

The social welfare sphere has evolved in constant interaction with the political and economic spheres. Because of profound, far-reaching changes in all spheres the whole character of society has considerably altered. In consequence, besides an almost continuous expansion of the welfare sphere, there emerged different historical social policy configurations.

Some of the basic processes which affected social policy are worth mentioning. With *economic growth* more resources could be used for

Figure 18.1 Configurations of social policy in mixed societies

	Period or Stages	Whose needs	Main agent/s/	Needs covered	Main instruments	Access on what right	Relation to the economy	Appellation of the configuration
1.	from the 16th to the last third of 19th century	'paupers' and 'deserving poor'	state /+church, +feudal lord/	minimal survival	assistance, institutions of indoor relief	no right /discretion/ poor law/	marginal /problems look independent!/	politics of poverty
2.	up to Second World War	mostly working class /Exceptions: Scandinavia, New Zealand/	– state – trade unions and workers' movement in general	minimal support in case of risks caused by industrialization, urbanization	social insurance, beginning of public health, educational, housing services	– rights based on social insurance /'purchased' rights or based on tax payment/	dominated by the economic logic – in rights – in resources etc. /residual social policy/	state social policy, or era of social insurance
3.	from world war up to the present	citizens increasingly as individuals	state, social movements	minimal acceptable and acquired security, new needs accepted, beginnings of job security /need for a job/ for individuals	social security; enlarged and completed system of above services, some Keynesian economics politics completing the market	/individual/ citizen's right to life	almost equal partner	welfare state

3.(a)	end of 1980s /in some countries, especially Finland/	citizens as individuals and communities	state decreasing, citizens and their communities increasing, control, initiative, participation	as in /3./ taking into account also communities, enabling strategies to cope	as in /3./ but more initiative and participation from 'below'	as in welfare state	as in welfare state, plus formations of 'social economy /as in France/, when economic activity is not dominated by the market	welfare society
3.(b)	'Crisis of WS'	citizens handled as individuals, increasing differentiation between 'insiders' and 'marginals'/3+1/	state and capitalist interest groups on the increase, social movements /divided and weakening	as in 3. job security given up, some needs curtailed	return to instruments of periods 1 and 2	as in 3. but everything curtailed /moves back to 2. and 1./	1.+2. strengthening, especially purchased rights weakening	neo-liberal, social policy
4.	blueprint of social progression /social democracy/	members of society, their communities	as above and the institutions of 'industrial' and 'economic' democracy	all conditions of full social life /including production, consumption, politics, etc./	as in 3.a, but Keynesian economic policy replaced by institutions of 'industrial' and 'economic' democracy	membership in society	organic /economic and social interests merge/	societal politics, 'economic democracy', democratic socialism

objectives that were not immediately 'productive'; that is, the scope of non-market activities could expand. It also became clear that the majority of the activities having no immediate economic purpose after all served the economy: increasingly complex industrial technologies required workers with more culture, more education and more autonomy. Sheer waste of human resources had also to be stopped because of decreasing fertility – again, partly also in the interest of the economy. With many other *social and political* changes, the working class has changed from a class 'in itself' to a class 'for itself', and became a strong political factor. The system of political institutions has to accommodate these and other movements of political emancipation. In a relatively short time these movements started to request not only more resources but also a different system of access and delivery more in line with human dignity. Thus the character of the *rights* giving access to the non-market sphere had also altered. Arbitrary and discretionary concessions in the Poor Laws were first replaced by 'purchased rights', close to the market logic. They were in their turn partly superseded by 'existential' or 'citizens' ' rights.

Alongside the above changes, the contents of state social policy and the objectives of social movements have changed considerably. In the earliest phase of state social policy, the main objective was to handle mounting poverty by helping and policing measures. Social movements were too weak to have influence. Also, capitalist social relationships had not yet become transparent enough. It could not be easily recognized that there was a causal link between the new social ills and the new economic order (Hobsbawm). State social policy constituted itself as marginal to the economic order, without any direct confrontation with it (see Figure 18.1, the first configuration). The direct, causal links between the operation of the market economy and new human and social problems have become gradually clear and acknowledged from the mid-nineteenth century onwards. The pressure of the dominated classes could put pressure on state social policy to handle some of the consequences, but could not yet push it to interfere with the causes (see Figure 18.1, the second configuration). More profound social economic and political changes were needed for the formation of such political will.

At this point, history takes different roads. A number of countries adopted Keynesian methods in order to influence the economy. The purpose of state intervention in this case was not so much to check capital or the market as to complete or facilitate their operation. This policy, influenced by the ideas of Beveridge, has led to the creation of welfare states after the Second World War (see Figure 18.1, the third configuration).

Social democrats and other 'reform' parties having connections with the labour movement started on a different path. Instead of, or alongside, Keynesian methods they endeavoured also to control and to limit the operation of the market and capital. They intended to use the instruments offered by parliamentary democracy and relied on the strength of the labour movement to give the desired orientation to constitutional politics. In this approach the deep conflict between capital and labour is clearly recognized. The objective of politics was not to abolish the conflict, but to handle it by means of the political confrontation of the various interests. Various policy instruments were adopted in the different countries. It is probably true that Sweden has been the most successful in working out and in implementing a complex set of policy instruments which could simultaneously check the market forces and promote both economic and social interests (see Figure 18.2). This policy has an intellectually innovative character which makes it worthwhile to probe into some of the details later on. The ultimate purpose of this policy is described as configuration 4 in Figure 18.1.

The Communist party of Russia in 1917, and the parties of Eastern European countries after 1945, opted for a revolutionary solution rather than reforms. They endeavoured to change the operation of the economy by abolishing both capital *and* the market. The assumption was that under the altered conditions the owner of the means of production would also become its operator: decision-making and execution would merge; producers and consumers would fully overlap. On this basis the former clash between economic and welfare interests would automatically disappear. Hence – the assumption was – there would be no need for separate institutions to represent the economic and the social interests. Social policy as a separate institutionalized sphere could be abolished, because the social interests would already be built into the operation of the economy. The final outcome would be practically identical with that already described as configuration 4 in Figure 18.1. The extent to which this grandiose social project materialized is by now the subject of many probing analyses. Later in this chapter, some of the results, in terms of successes and failures in the social sphere, will be considered (see also Figure 18.3).

The developments in market economies are, then, subsumed in configurations 1 to 4 of Figure 18.1 and in Figure 18.2. Of course the schemes simplify the course of history. It has to be emphasized, for example, that the configurations are simplified ideal types. We do not mention many hybrid forms, and even some special configurations; for instance the social policy of fascist regimes are entirely left out. Also, there is no pre-ordained 'historical necessity' underlying the sequence of configurations; various economic, political and other processes happened to produce these results.

A word is needed about continuity and change, too. The emergence of a new configuration does not imply a clean break with the past: there are many continuities. Many former instruments may survive, albeit in a somewhat modified form. Social assistance, for instance, outlived the era of the politics of poverty but its arbitrary and humiliating nature was altered in order to fit it into the later systems. Configurations 1 to 4 in Figure 18.1 suggest that historical development is following a straight line, that growth is continuous in the social sphere. Obviously, this too is a convenient generalization. History can make turns – even U-turns. One of them is described as configuration 3b in Figure 18.1 which is, in truth, hardly a new configuration. It is rather a new combination of old elements.

From the mid-1970s onwards, the economic crisis has bred the ideology of the crisis of the welfare state. In many countries the ideology has found credence and has spread rapidly. It was supported not only by the ruling, capitalist, upper middle or middle classes whose interests have been harmed or threatened by the welfare state. The genuine shortcomings of the welfare state played an important role, too. The welfare state did not fulfil all its promises. More to the point, it did not adjust well to the changing aspirations for more individualization, more flexibility and more participation and control. It remained over-centralized and paternalistic.

The reaction of different countries has varied. Some have made only small adjustments, slight cuts or institutional alterations. Some, most unequivocally, Finland, have tried to 'fly forward'. They want to transform the welfare state into a more participatory, more decentralized, more democratic 'welfare society' (Wiman,

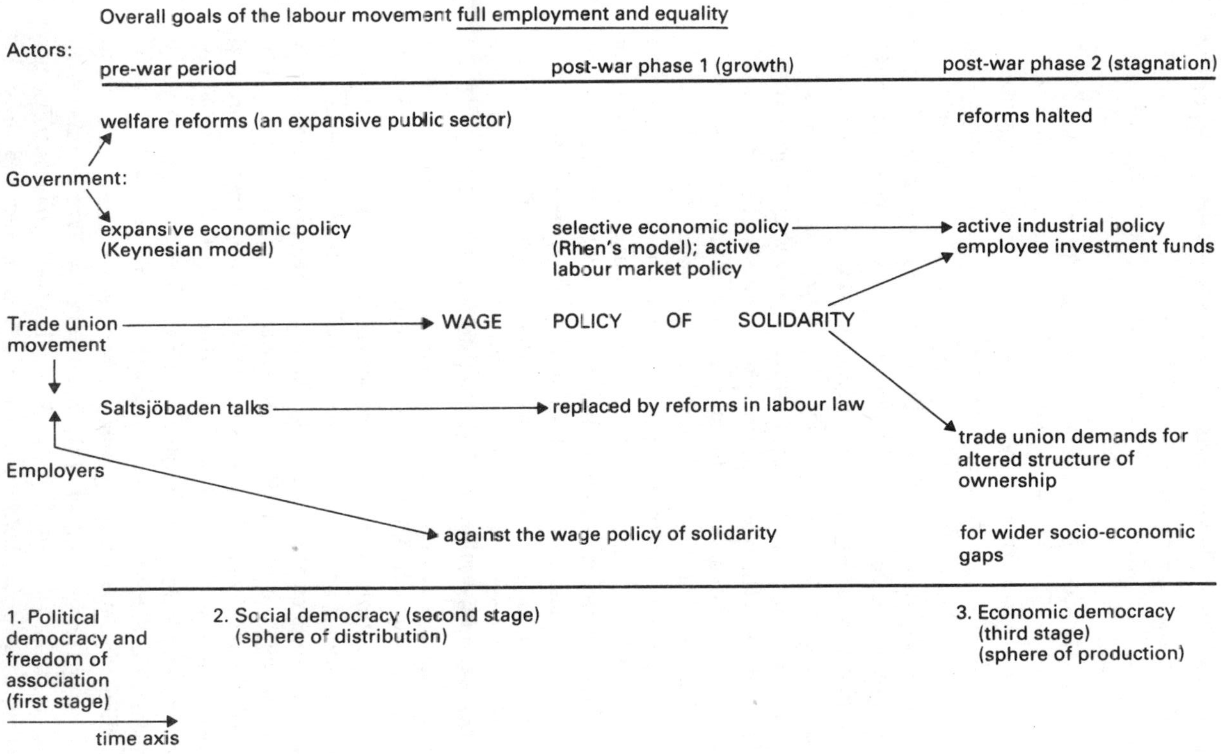

Overall goals of the labour movement <u>full employment and equality</u>

Actors:	pre-war period	post-war phase 1 (growth)	post-war phase 2 (stagnation)

welfare reforms (an expansive public sector) → reforms halted

Government:
expansive economic policy (Keynesian model)

selective economic policy (Rhen's model); active labour market policy → active industrial policy employee investment funds

Trade union movement → WAGE POLICY OF SOLIDARITY

Saltsjöbaden talks → replaced by reforms in labour law → trade union demands for altered structure of ownership

Employers → against the wage policy of solidarity → for wider socio-economic gaps

1. Political democracy and freedom of association (first stage)

2. Social democracy (second stage) (sphere of distribution)

3. Economic democracy (third stage) (sphere of production)

time axis →

Figure 18.2 *The Swedish people's home model*

Source: Anna Hedborg, Rudolf Meidner: *The People's Home Model*, 1984

1987). The goals and characteristics of this policy are described in the configuration 3a in Figure 18.1. Finally, there are some which withdrew from the welfare state to positions characteristic of the first and second configurations, many of which were shaped by classical liberalism. In this sense these moves are consistent with neo-liberalism.

If neo-liberal social policy is pursued in terms of its own logic, many former social problems will reappear in a slightly altered form. Many signs point already in this direction in some countries, the UK among them. One may expect, for instance further, perhaps radical, cuts in the resources of social welfare. Global resources as measured by Gross Domestic Product are obviously much higher than they used to be sixty or eighty years ago, and – despite the crisis – they are scarcely reduced from the heyday of the welfare state, and in some countries are greater. The implication is that the distribution of resources may be significantly altered when compared to these periods. On the one hand, incomes created in the market will become more unequal partly because of milder taxation and partly because both state action and social movements, especially trade unions, imposing constraints on these income inequalities will weaken. One may also expect an increased inequality between average market and non-market incomes. On the whole the absolute and relative share of market incomes is likely to increase.

On the other hand, the total number of clients of the welfare state is not likely to decrease significantly in the years to come. The process of aging has slowed down, but the number of the aged and the very aged is still on the increase. Self-insurance, whether voluntary or not, which is currently encouraged will give a sizeable return only in some years time, or, rather, after some decades. The number of non-employed housewives will probably grow, partly because the impact of conservative values is reinforced, and partly because of the contraction of the labour market. Since it is hard to assume a fall in the divorce rate, single parents will remain potential welfare clients. As for unemployment, liberal economic policy does not necessarily entail any change in either direction, but in some countries its *high* rate has been remarkably stable in recent years.

If, then, former clients remain beneficiaries, and the overall resources are shrinking, a fall in the average welfare income is an almost unavoidable consequence. The fall in the welfare income per capita may be slowed down if selectivity increases and only the 'truly needy' are assured access to welfare incomes. If this comes about, the gap between average market and welfare incomes is even more likely to grow. (Means-tested assistance has always been prone to use the less eligibility principle.) The contraction of the clientele will simply entail an even more considerable fall in the resources for social welfare than would be the case otherwise (Jenkins and Miller, 1987).

Increased income inequalities are likely to be transformed into more significant social inequalities. One of the factors underpinning this trend is the new form of unemployment. With economic expansion the rate of unemployment may decrease. However, a relatively high – 6 or 8 per cent, or even higher than 10 per cent – rate of long-term, structural unemployment has a strong likelihood to persist. Powerful interests operate in this direction. In the liberal ideological climate, many unemployed may easily be classified as undeserving, that is, unemployed through their own fault. This helps not only in reducing their benefits. It also represents a threat to those in employment, forcing them into acquiescence and to give up solidarity with the unemployed. The material poverty of the long-term unemployed may then be coupled with their social and political marginalization, depriving them of the least hope of upward moves. This trend may lead to the enlarged reproduction of deprivation – and also to strengthened racism. In most countries ethnic minorities are over-represented among the unemployed. Therefore prejudices against the unemployed are, by the same token, racial prejudices. One may even assume that latent racism played some part in shaping and institutionalizing the new patterns of unemployment.

A further factor aggravating the impact of growing income differentiation is the probable 'marketization' of large chunks of collective consumption. Traditional 'public services' may be split in two, into paying and means-tested free services. They may also be dismantled via individualized insurance systems entailing a finer gradation. In both ways unequal money will buy unequal services. Since many of those services, especially health and education, were instrumental in reducing to some extent unequal social and physical life chances, these latter inequalities are prone to increase too.

In short, neo-liberal social policy is reviving many of the 'poor law' traditions, with consequences reminiscent of this era. Only a century ago resources were so scarce and social movements so weak

Figure 18.3   Periods of social policy development in Hungary after 1945

Period or stages	Whose needs	Main agent/s	Needs covered	Main instruments	Access on what right	Relation to the economy	Appellation of the configuration
A 1945–1948 blueprint of democratic socialism /as in 4/	members of society /as in 4/	state, parties, citizens and their communities /as in 3 and 3a/	needs defined as in 4, but on a very low economic level	as in 4, in spontaneously evolving, often embryonic forms	right to life, not law but norm	almost organic, as in 4	democracy for popular welfare
B 1949–1956 Stalinist dictatorship	workers and part of employees, others discriminated against	central power, especially the party	as in 2, plus need for jobs	as in 2, but no independent social policy, only a politically organized economy /politics of poverty abolished/	rights based on work in state sector /2, slightly modified/	formally organic, substantively the social interest dominated by economic and political interests	'dictatorship of the proletariat'

C 1957–1980 pragmatic search for building socialism	all working members of society /as in 2, with a move towards 3 in health/	central power, i.e. party and state, some attention to popular wishes	as in B but levels higher; some poor relief	elements of configuration 2 expanding, elements politics of poverty revived; constraints on economy released, but still no independent social policy	rights 'purchased' by work and social insurance contributions, plus citizen's right in health care, plus discretionary right to assistance /a mix of 1., 2., and 3./	as in B but more scope for social considerations	'existing socialism', some 'societal policy'
D since the 1980s adjustment to the economic crisis	all working members of society, plus the 'deserving' poor /some new rights for handicapped, for elderly without pensions/, for unemployed through 'no fault of their own'	as in C, social movements slowly emerging	as in C, but job security given up	as in C but economy sheding its social obligations. Possibly emergence of an independent social policy	as in C, but more emphasis on purchased rights, more scope for assistance	increasingly dominated by the economic logic /as in 2/	defensive social policy

Note: Numbers refer to configurations in Figure 18.1

that the 'politics of poverty' approach had some excuses and even some 'rationality'. Nowadays those excuses lack any foundation – thus the situation is more contradictory and also more tragic.

One may hope that neo-liberalism will not be able fully to carry out its social policy projects. This depends, in my view, mainly on the strength and ability of progressive social forces and movements. Alternative movements – which have an increasing appeal – represent a challenge and threat to market and profit interests; however, up to now it is not clear whether they will be able to formulate a coherent programme in which the creation of adequate resources and the universal coverage of a wide range of needs form a part. In other words, it is not evident that alternative movements will be forced to touch upon the general problems of the relation between economic and social interests, instead of some ramifications or components of this issue. The same holds true for the 'anti-utilitarian' movement with its strong anti-economic and anti-work tendencies (Mauss, 1987). It seems to me, though, that popular support will be hard to gain without such a programme. That is why the Swedish experience is important.

Social policy in Eastern European socialist countries, with a focus on Hungary

Before 1945, Hungarian social policy followed the Western trends with some time lag because of its relative backwardness in social, political and economic matters. The elements of configuration 2 of Figure 18.1 were mostly present, albeit the role of the 'politics of poverty' was relatively much bigger, and that of social insurance smaller than elsewhere.

In 1945 Hungary, like other countries of Eastern Europe, followed the original revolutionary model of the Soviet Union. In terms of social policy this meant that the country proposed to implement directly the socialist ideal with full societal citizenship, a democratic multi-party system and the organic unity of social and economic interests. In the first three years successful attempts were made to assure progress in this direction. (See period 'A' in Figure 18.3.) This innovative and buoyant period finished, however, with the onset of Stalinism in 1949.

The original revolutionary project was fundamentally distorted by Stalinist dictatorship. The project, as already mentioned, assumed that with the expropriation of capital the 'owner' and the 'producer' would merge, thereby abolishing the conflict between the economic and social interest. This assumption did not come true. The former structural inequalities were replaced by an unequal, or even monopolistic, distribution of power and knowledge; the former gap between manual and non-manual labour has remained. The abolition of the institutions of parliamentary democracy strengthened the power monopoly. Thus, while the place of private owners was taken over by non-owners, the former functions of the owner remained with one group, with many of the well-known consequences.

Dictatorial leadership, however, completely ignored this reality. It declared that the objectives of socialism had been reached or were at least close, including the organic fusion of the economic and the social interest. Social policy was declared to be superfluous. The existence of various old and new tensions and conflicts – those between the social and the economic among them – were not acknowledged by the central power and therefore could not be adequately handled.

The policy of carrying out *social* objectives through the operation of the *economy* was in many respects successful. A wage policy was forced upon the economy by which the low wage fund was distributed relatively equally. The politically enforced 'anti-rich' price system, to use an expression of Peter Wiles, made possible access to basic needs such as food, housing, light and heat and transportation even for the poorest, despite the dire scarcity of these goods. The biggest social advantages were produced by the policy of full employment. This goal was reached around the late 1960s.

Those three economic policies, especially rapidly increasing job opportunities, were the main instruments in reducing massive pre-war poverty. (Ferge, 1986) The latter strongly promoted the emancipation of women and the integration of marginal groups, especially gypsies, or at least it helped to prevent their further marginalization.

However, the relation between the two spheres was neither genuinely organic nor harmonious. In the blueprint of socialist progression, the link between the social and the economic interest is based on democratic movements, and on building up the conditions of full social citizenship. In Hungary those ingredients were almost absent. Secondly, in the blueprint the two interests are supposed to strengthen and not to throttle each other, as was the case with Hungary. The *social* element was forced upon the economy by politics in a controversial way. The constraint of assuring full employment and job security operated in such a way as to conserve jobs with low productivity and to prevent industrial restructuring. At the same time, it also conserved the worst jobs, and thereby the reproduction of the least qualified, least demanding, worst paid labour force. The social harm caused in this way was aggravated by the economic damage, through the long-term conservation of economic backwardness. Price policy also triggered irrational production and consumption and, in the long run, produced general scarcity (Kornai, 1980).

The politically defined *economic* interest, in its turn, dominated and distorted the social interest. It turned out, maybe paradoxically, or at least contrary to a widely accepted view on the Left, that the operation of the economy might adversely affect, even destroy, many social values and interests, even if it were not a market economy. Former tensions might persist, or even new ones might be created simply by a 'disembedded' economy separated from the other spheres of social reproduction – even if this economy deliberately rejected market and profit interests, as did the Hungarian economy. The Hungarian non-market economy followed 'market' practice in evaluating human beings, namely in attaching a much higher value to those currently at work than to the past or future labour power – the elderly and children – let alone those unwilling or unable to work. These latter categories had practically no right to resources. The same clash of interest explains the underfinancing of so-called 'non-productive' sectors such as, for instance, health or educational services. Or, to take a final example, the non-market economy has proved as detrimental to the environment as any capitalist economy, even though the explanation is different. The destruction of local and global solidarities and the strengthening of egoistic individualism had political rather than economic reasons, but some economic mechanisms – such as the differentiated wage-system – strengthened these processes.

Because of the very different socio-political structure, the social policy prevailing from 1950 on cannot be described in the framework of Figure 18.1. There were different periods – from 1950 to 1956; from 1957 until the end of the 1970s; and the last few years.

None of them coincides, however, with any of the configurations already described (see Figure 18.3). The elements of the configurations were dismantled and re-united according to the specific arbitrary logic of power. Several examples of this can be cited:

1 The 'politics of poverty', together with social work, were abolished from 1950 until 1960. Social assistance was revived in the 1960s and social work in the 1970s both on a small scale. In the last years they have been gaining ground. Social assistance is increasingly seen as a necessity in mending the shortcomings of other social policy arrangements. Many of these early connotations, including its highly discretionary character, did not change, however.

2 The social insurance system has developed at a very rapid rate from the 1960s onwards. It broke away in many respects from the Bismarckian model by incorporating solidaristic elements such as the introduction of ceilings and minima, and the waiving of waiting periods and former contributions. All this happened pragmatically, without ever explicitly endorsing a solidaristic course or the goals of overall 'social security', and without accepting the 'right to existence'. The principle of *equivalence* between total contributions and total benefits did not apply in monetary terms, but all provisions have remained thoroughly related to paid work.

3 The Western welfare states have been either ignored or criticized on ideological grounds. Some of their components do exist, such as a public health service based on citizen's rights. These achievements are, however, due to the early struggles and claims of the workers' movements rather than any influence of the West.

4 Finally, as has already been shown, the supposedly organic relation between the social and the economic sphere did not materialize. On the contrary, the clash has been strong, and to some extent destructive, for the social interests.

Thus, all the periods were rather eclectic, without a coherent system or framework. The lack of coherence and the lack, or at least the weakness, of social legitimation make the achievements rather vulnerable. In fact, since the advent of the economic crisis, a number of processes have started which are reversing former tendencies.

These developments – the strengthening of the 'politics of poverty', of purchased rights, the acceptance of unemployment, the doubts about universalism, etc. – are reminders of neo-liberal tendencies. There are similarities in some of the consequences, too, such as increasing existential insecurity, impoverishment of the weakest strata, and partial marketization of collective consumption. These are disturbing facts, even if the social context is different.

In short, the original communist ideology assuming that, with the abolition of private property, the clash between the economic and the social interest would automatically disappear, did not come true. Politics succeeded in forcing some important social functions on to the economy. But the economy could not operate in a rational and efficient way because of too much political intervention (not only in the case of some social issues). And social policy could only incompletely fulfil its social functions partly because it was very strongly dominated by the politically defined, but relatively autonomous, economic interest, and partly because the popular forces which should have fuelled and legitimated it were not allowed to function.

The original assumptions have therefore to be modified. It is becoming clear that, at least under the present national and international conditions, a relatively autonomous economy complete with market forces is needed. This view is forcefully presented by so-called reform economists (see 'Change and Reform', 1987) and partly accepted by government. But it also had to be recognized that a relatively autonomous and strong social policy is the necessary counterpart of the above economy – if one wants not only to cure but also to prevent social harms such as poverty or unemployment. *Ex post* social policy – the healing of social ills – can operate separately from the economy, without trying to influence it.

The social policy position would remain relatively weak and precarious, though, in this case – as in the case of configurations 2 and even 3 in Figure 18.1. *Ex ante* social policy presupposes a well-developed co-operation between the two spheres, in which both interests are represented strongly enough in order to obtain compromises not too detrimental for any of the parties. In this bargaining, the strength of economy is assured in practice by the relatively free play of market interests. Social policy may match this strength only if *social* forces can also freely organize. Hence both reforms need important modifications in the *political* system; the economy needs legal guarantees for safe contracts and against arbitrary, central interventions, and social policy needs constitutional institutions allowing the confrontations of interests and freedom of organization for social interests. The necessity of combining the three reforms – economic, social and political – is by now publicly recognized. Whether this project will be realized is a matter for the future.

A number of details should be clarified in order to carry through the complex reform in question. In what follows, only one aspect of this maze is dealt with, namely the possibility of new ways of co-operation between the social and economic spheres.

Sweden as a possible model

Sweden has been the most successful nation in working out the instruments of co-operation of the two spheres in question. The term 'model' refers here to these set of instruments, not – as is usual – to the Swedish welfare state as a whole. The model in question is of the utmost interest because it is based on a logically sound construct which is not, however, the result of 'armchair thinking'. It was gradually built up over the last fifty years or more, with a constant interaction between strong social movements, especially of workers, parliamentary politics strongly influenced by social democrats, theoretical work carried out by left-wing, especially labour organization, economists, and experience, including the operation of the economy, economic and political bargaining, and so forth. It is not pure pragmatism, and maybe it is even more than 'principled pragmatism', to use Heclo's expression (Heclo and Madsden, 1987). It seems to be motivated by some clearly defined values and some, maybe less clearly spelt out, theoretical assumptions. The central values are defined as full employment, equality and solidarity. The theoretical assumptions are connected with the 'social democratic way' of overcoming capitalism, assuming a long co-existence with capital.

It is not suggested that these politics have always been successful, that they are not in jeopardy right now, or that they are sure winners in the long run. Up to now, however, they have proved their worth. After all, the Swedish economy was thoroughly restructured in the last decade or so, without high unemployment – the

highest rate did not exceed 4 per cent – and without too strong a
tension in any field.

The socio-economic policy has separate, but interconnected,
elements. They are widely known separately, so here only their
most interesting aspect is highlighted, namely their interconnectedness. Full employment is promoted by an 'active labour market
policy', implying 'programs which promote either job creation
(demand-oriented programs) or the readjustment of labour to the
intersectoral or inter-area differences and variances in the structure
of demand (supply-oriented programs). Efforts to promote the
matching of supply and demand through information and an
effective Employment Service also fit the concept.' (Rehn, 1985,
p. 62). Unemployment benefits have a minor role in this policy.
They used to be less than 10 per cent of all expenditures on labour
market policy, which in total add up to 2 or 3 per cent of the GDP
(Rehn, 1985).

The limitation of wage inequalities is achieved by the 'solidaristic wage policy' aiming at limiting excessive wage differentials,
and claiming equal pay for equal work – regardless of the profita-
bility of the company. In this way low productivity firms are not
'subsidized' by low wages. If this leads to unemployment, workers
are protected by the active labour market policy. On the other
hand, the excess profit gained in this way by successful companies
caused concern for the labour organization. Hence the elaboration
of the third element of this policy, the wage earner fund, channell-
ing an agreed part of the extra profit into funds controlled by the
employees. This complement to the solidaristic wage policy aims
'to counteract the concentration of wealth which stems from
industrial self-financing', and also 'to increase the influence which
employees have over the economic process' (Meidner, 1978,
p. 15). Employee funds are intended 'as a new step on the long
road towards our continuing goal of equality and economic
democracy' (p. 124).

Swedish economic policy comprises many other elements, from
the meticulously worked out bargaining strategies to tax policy,
from the concern with the links between the bodies responsible for
education, training and labour policy to the concern with inflation-
ary pressures, quite apart from a 'principled' welfare policy.
However, the three elements referred to above appear of para-
mount importance in showing that economic policy can *incorporate*

non-market, or, rather, anti-market mechanisms which serve the social interest *without being detrimental to the economy*.

The possible use of the Swedish experience

Obviously, no country can import the Swedish model or any part of it in a crude form, since its long history and the social forces behind it cannot be borrowed. The message is clear, though. It proves the theoretical assumption of S. M. Miller that 'economic policy is the best social policy'. The Hungarian experience does not fully contradict this assumption. It only shows that political will alone is insufficient for the implementation of long-term objectives. Without participation and control it fatally goes astray, and without adequate policy instruments it cannot be effective.

Under the Hungarian conditions the aim of limiting the power of the market might require less elaborate policies than in Sweden. Large private ownership is absent from the scene – and this is one of the legitimated, practically unquestioned, achievements of the system. This is not true of small private ownership. In Hungary, similarly to Czechoslovakia, and unlike East Germany, only about 4 per cent of the labour force remained in the private sector (outside agriculture). Dogmatic and rigid nationalization, together with the 'big is beautiful' ideology, has disturbed smooth economic reproduction in many ways. The importance of having productive units of different size and variety of ownership forms is by now acknowledged. The main problem in this respect is how to define by legal means a ceiling to private ownership, and how to assure the transition from the private form to some kind of collective ownership, without undue pressure or compulsion. (Alec Nove, 1983, tries to cope with this problem.) The gradual building up of a collective fund within a private firm may offer a possible solution, to mention just one use of this instrument. It may have other functions, too, especially in the case of big state monopolies.

Many of the elements of an active and selective labour policy, as well as those of a solidaristic wage policy, could be put to use. Pricing and tax policies could probably be more easily influenced by mass interests than under the Swedish conditions. Theoretically this is true, even if some of the current tendencies – for instance the recent adoption of a system of personal taxation very similar to that of Western countries – contradict this assumption. (The tax system was adopted by Parliament despite very widespread popular misgivings and apprehensions.)

The doctrinaire approach claiming that there is just 'one road' to socialism has been undermined in the last decades. There are different ways, and Hungary had to find its own. The failures, mistakes and crimes of the Stalinist rule render a new start very difficult. This would be difficult even without the impact of the economic crisis and the influential neo-liberal tide following in its wake. There are strong groups interested in maintaining intact the role of central power, and others interested in increasing the role and the power of a new technocracy or managerial elite. Thus, the future of the country, and within it the future of an emancipated economy and an emancipated and co-operative social policy, depend on the future of the political system. Participatory democracy – well-informed citizens having the right to organize, to intervene and to control all social processes – are necessary to pave the way to an economic democracy 'not opposed to social and socialist interests and values.'

Conclusion

Under different socio-economic conditions, social policy arrangements show different systemic patterns or configurations, such as the early 'politics of poverty', the welfare state and the socialist projects, namely the social democratic and the communist one. The patterns of Eastern European countries, especially Hungary, are less systemic than those in the West, because of the special role of 'voluntaristic' policies. The configurations show various characteristics, out of which special attention is paid to the relation between the economy and social policy. Social policy may coexist with the economy without directly affecting its operation, following the market model; it may co-operate with the economy and modify to some extent its course, in line with the Swedish experience; and it may be built into the economy, as in Hungary. In the first case social policy is easily defeated. The last solution has positive, but also other very negative, consequences for both sides. The Swedish model offers important lessons. Hungary, for example, could profit from them only if both the economy and social policy would be reformed together with the political system, so that the economy could be freed from arbitrary state interventions and social policy could be based on mass movements and citizens' participation.

References

'Change and Reform' *Acta Oeconomica*, 38, (3–4), 1987.

Gösta Esping-Anderson, *Politics Against the Market* (Princeton: Princeton University Press, 1985).

Adalbert Evers, *Social Policy in Transition*. European Centre for Social Welfare Training and Research, Vienna 1987.

Zsuzsa Ferge, Chapters from the history of politics of poverty in Hungary, Magveī, 1986, in Hungarian, and a shortened unpublished version in English.

Hugh Heclo and Henrik Madsden, *Policy and Politics in Sweden*. Principled Pragmatism (Temple University Press, 1987).

Anna Hedborg, and Rudolf Meidner, 'The Concept of the Swedish Model'. In *Folkhems-modellen*, 1984, Raben Sjögren, Stockholm.

Margaret Jenkins and S. M. Miller, 'Upward redistribution in the United States', in Zs Ferge and S. M. Miller (eds) *Dynamic of Deprivation* (Aldershot: Gower, 1987).

János Kornai, *A hiány (Scarcity)*. Közgazdasági és Jogi Könyvkiadó, 1980.

Mauss, Bulletin du Mouvement Anti-Utilitariste dans les Sciences Sociales. L'allocation universelle. No. 23, 1987.

Rudolf Meidner, *Employee Investment Funds. An Approach to Collective Capital Formation* (London: George Allen & Unwin, 1978).

Alec Nove, *The Economics of Feasible Socialism* (George Allen & Unwin, 1983).

Karl Polanyi, *The Great Transformation*. (London: Beacon Press, 1944).

Gösta Rehn, Swedish Active Labour Market Policy, Retrospect and Prospect. *Industrial Relations*, vol. 24, 1985.

Ronald Wiman, *From the Welfare State to a Welfare Society*. National Board of Social Welfare, Helsinki, 1987.

19 *Inequality in developing countries: a comment on Ferge*

FRANCES STEWART

In Chapter 18 Zsuzsa Ferge presents a wide ranging and stimulating review of the interactions between economic developments and social policy in the course of the history of Western economies over the past two hundred years, and of Eastern Europe in recent decades. In this chapter, I shall consider how far the models presented in the previous chapter also apply to today's developing countries. To do so I present an alternative terminology to help analyse these developments.

Basically Professor Ferge puts forward two models of historical development: that of the 'mixed' but predominantly capitalist economies, and that of social economies.

The 'mixed' economy has evolved, according to Ferge, in the following stages:

1 Feudal system of production, and feudal traditions of protection for the weak.
2 Capitalist stage, where feudal economic and social systems are dismantled and replaced by virtually unbridled capitalism. This stage leads to the worst deprivation, for the weak are protected by neither the economic nor the social system.
3 Keynesian economic policy and social interventions (the welfare state) improve the position of the more deprived.
4 Reinforcement of the market, reduced state intervention and modifications to the welfare state which have occurred in Western Europe in recent years. The position of the deprived

(the unemployed and those on low-incomes) is weakened as a result both of economic forces and reduced social support.

The socialist economies of Eastern Europe followed similar developments initially (that is, the feudal and early capitalist stages described above), but these economies underwent a socialist revolution rather than following the Keynesian path. The socialist revolution was egalitarian both in economic system and social policies; in the 1980s, however, it has also begun to be dismantled, although it is not clear how far this will go.

In considering the application of such models to developing countries, it is helpful to start by making a distinction between *primary* and *secondary* income distribution.[1]

Primary incomes are all incomes (in cash or kind) that arise from the working of the economic system. They include incomes from employment, from self-employment and from assets. *Secondary* incomes are the incomes people have to spend, or their disposable incomes. They consist of primary incomes after tax plus any transfers people receive from the state in the form of social security payments, subsidies and public goods, and also transfers received from other members of society. It is secondary incomes which determine the extent to which people are able to meet their basic needs for food, shelter, etc. In terms of the terminology of Ferge, the primary distribution can be viewed as the distribution arising out of the *economic* system, while the state interventions which affect secondary distribution are the elements of *social policy*

The distribution of goods in society depends on secondary distribution. This means that any target distribution can be achieved by a variety of combinations of primary distribution and state interventions. In other words, how a given primary distribution translates into secondary distribution and therefore into the distribution of goods depends on state interventions towards taxes, subsidies, social security, etc. In theory, then, an egalitarian secondary distribution could be achieved by an egalitarian primary distribution with little state intervention, or by an inegalitarian primary distribution accompanied by a strongly egalitarian state intervention at the secondary stage. In practice, however, this is a misleading proposition – because as will be discussed below – there are political economy interconnections between primary distribution and secondary interventions which make it very difficult, if not impossible, to achieve some combinations. Some of the combinations of primary and secondary distribution turn out to be empty boxes, that is, not feasible combinations.

Reviewing the Ferge models of historical developments, using this terminology, we can describe the same stages of development in different terms.

For the mixed economy, the feudal system involves a fairly high degree of inequality of primary income distribution, but the conventions of the system clearly delineate and limit the extent of this inequality, while there is some state and intra-family transfers which improve secondary distribution compared with primary, and limit the extent of absolute deprivation. Early capitalism breaks down limits on inequality both with respect to primary distribution and secondary transfers, and at this stage very substantial deprivation emerges, with primary distribution moving in an inegalitarian direction and offsetting secondary interventions being reduced. In contrast, at the Keynesian stage full employment tends to reduce primary inequality, while welfare state interventions further improve secondary. The recent monetarist reaction has increased primary inequality, while the dismantling of the welfare state has accentuated the inegalitarian effects on secondary distribution.

Socialist systems typically involve highly egalitarian primary distribution, partly because of the near abolition of private asset ownership, partly because of the full employment that normally occurs, and partly because of some limits on differentials among workers. Secondary interventions usually further increase equality, with universal provision of high priority public goods, controlled prices for basic commodities, and generous pension schemes. Recent modifications of the socialist system towards a more market orientation are likely to increase primary inequality, and a similar modification is taking place with respect to secondary interventions.

There are, of course, huge differences between different countries, so that generalizations about developing countries are inevitably over-simplistic. However, it does seem that many developing countries are undergoing similar stages of development to those experienced by the industrialized countries in the past, as described above, with some differences.

In the pre-industrialization pre-colonial phase, countries' economic systems were generally characterized by conventions determining production and distribution, as was the European feudal system, but with many differences in detail. While there can be considerable poverty in such societies, its extent tends to be limited by conventions which ensure that each person has access to some assets (usually land), while the distribution of the product is often determined by conventions (for example, sharing within the family or community along traditional lines), and not according to wage rates arising from supply and demand. Favourable land-labour ratios – and the existence in many countries of a land frontier – also limits inequality. Destitution is constrained by customs and institutions such that families and communities support their needy. In such a system – where the state plays only a minor role – the line between primary and secondary distribution is blurred, since the conventions which determine primary distribution already incorporate elements of transfer. While there can be considerable inequality in such societies, absolute destitution tends to be limited.

The capitalist phase of development – often ushered in by colonial powers – tended to increase primary inequality, and to break down the ties within and among families and communities that had previously prevented destitution. The wage-labour system, associated with capitalism, involves very low wages so long as the marginal product of workers is low, which is the case where the population is large in relation to assets (land and physical capital), where technology is primitive in much of the economy, and where employment opportunities in the modern sector are small in relation to the size of the workforce. This is the typical situation for developing countries during the labour-surplus phase of development. With the development of a capitalist system of production, traditional support systems weaken and sometimes disintegrate. For the most part, the state has not yet taken on the obligation of supporting the destitute, public goods are limited in quantity and concentrated geographically, and consequently neither informal (family, community), nor formal mechanisms of redistribution exist on any significant scale, so that very severe inequality and poverty emerges. Primary and secondary distribution then work in the same inegalitarian direction, as they did in the early stages of capitalism in most of the industrialized countries.

When and if countries move out of the labour-surplus stage and a labour-constraint emerges – which has happened in those few countries that have experienced rapid growth in labour-intensive industries – real household incomes of the lower income groups

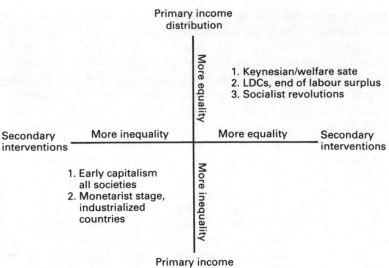

Figure 19.1   *The relationship between primary income distribution, secondary interventions and equality and inequality*

start to improve and primary distribution then also gets less unequal. Secondary interventions have also become more extensive and egalitarian in these cases.

The overall picture then is similar for the historical evolution of both the now industrialized countries and developing countries: inequality at primary and secondary stages rises in the initial stages of capitalist development, and may fall at later stages if growth in demand for labour outpaces population growth sufficiently to eliminate the labour surplus. Empirical support for this three-stage process was first put forward by Kuznets, in his famous 'inverse U' curve, which described the movement of primary income distribution over time.[2] However, less systematic data is available on secondary distribution over countries and over time.

A close relationship emerges between the primary distribution and state and other interventions which affect secondary distribution at each stage, in both the industrialized countries historic experience and in the experience of developing countries today. In those phases when primary inequality is increasing, secondary offsets tend to diminish, while in those phases where primary distribution is becoming more equal, secondary interventions also tend to act in an egalitarian or poverty-reducing direction. This is shown in Figure 19.1.

This close correlation between the two types of intervention are due to what can be termed political economy factors. Secondary interventions when conducted by the state are basically the result of political decisions. According to these findings these decisions seem to reflect what is happening at the primary level. One mechanism leading to the correlation shown is that those who acquire assets and incomes through the economic system also acquire power over the decision-making process, which is then reflected in secondary distribution. Another mechanism – to be observed in Britain in the 1980s, for example, or in socialist economies – is that whichever interest groups have political power, they use this power both to change the rules of the economic system and the nature of the secondary interventions in the same direction. Thus in Britain in the 1980s, the market orientation of the government shown in privatization and monetarism, resulting in high unemployment, have led to an increase in primary inequality. At the same time, changes in the tax and social security system and in the level and nature of public expenditure have also been inegalitarian. The opposite can be seen – with respect to both primary and secondary distribution – in the changes typical of an economy which has undergone a socialist revolution.

These political economy connections between primary and secondary distribution are very important because they limit the feasible combinations of primary and secondary distribution open to societies. The implication is that those who are concerned with secondary distribution – that is, the distribution of goods and services – cannot leave primary distribution to random forces, confident that their concerns will be taken care of by secondary interventions.

Most developing countries today are in the middle of the second stage – that is, the era of increasing inequality and a breakdown of traditional support systems. It is for this reason that we observe the large and frequently growing incidence of absolute poverty in so many countries. However, while this is the typical situation, there are exceptions in that there are countries which have managed to avoid the worst excesses of poverty while going through the second stage of development. It is therefore worth analysing these exceptions. In terms of their political economy, three types can be distinguished:[3]

1   Mainly capitalist economies, whose economic system moderates inequality and provides reasonable income-earning opportunities for most of the population. Taiwan, South Korea and Singapore are examples. They achieved this situation first by limited inequality in asset ownership. In the cases of Taiwan and (to a lesser extent) South Korea this was the result of an initial and effective land reform. (Singapore, lacking a significant agricultural sector, also lacked the inequality of land ownership which characterizes most societies.) The high rate of growth and the pattern of growth generated a fast spread of employment opportunities. In Taiwan, two features were responsible: first, the spread of rural non-agricultural opportunities; and secondly, the fast increase in labour-intensive manufactured exports. Together these factors meant that the lower 40 per cent of the population was able to earn above subsistence primary incomes, even before the exhaustion of the labour surplus, and the move towards the third stage of development.[4] But this pattern of capitalist development has proved unusual. The typical second stage exhibits high, and often increasing primary, inequality.

2   The second exception occurs among those economies which have bypassed the capitalist stage and moved to a socialist system. Cuba, North Korea, and China are examples. In these economies, employment, and therefore income from employment, is virtually guaranteed to everyone, and is not limited, as it is under capitalism, to workers whose marginal product exceeds their wage. Moreover, since most private asset ownership has been eliminated, primary income distribution is typically much more equal in these societies than in capitalist economies.[5] Secondary interventions also tend to be equalizing, with universal provision of basic health and education services and subsidies on basic foods.

3   The third exception consists of welfare state type economies. These are mixed economies which generally do not have the most severe inequality in primary incomes, often because the distribution of land is less unequal than in some countries, a consequence of the colonial experience and of the availability of land. But the main sources of support for the poor came from strong secondary

interventions to provide for basic needs through the provision of education and health services and of subsidized goods. Good examples of this type are Costa Rica, Sri Lanka and Kerala State in India. In each case, these secondary interventions, together with the not too unequal primary distribution, have cushioned the poor and have resulted in relatively low levels of absolute poverty and relatively good indicators of health and literacy. The examples of these countries indicate that in certain circumstances secondary interventions can modify primary distribution significantly, despite the connections noted above.

Of these three types, the last – the welfare state model – would seem to be the most accessible for most countries, because it does not require a political revolution, as in the socialist case, or an economic one, as in the rapid growth case. However, the model turns out to be very vulnerable to external and internal pressures. In Sri Lanka, much of it has come unravelled under pressure from the international financial community and as a result of internal political changes. In Costa Rica, the economic crisis of the 1980s and the need to fulfil IMF stabilization programmes has also much modified the social interventions.

A further problems with the model is that state expenditure on secondary interventions can be misused, with high levels of expenditure (for example, on food subsidies, education and health services), going to the middle classes and little to the poor. This arises because of the close political connections between primary and secondary distributions discussed above. There is a major political problem about securing poor-oriented secondary interventions to offset unequal primary distribution. This political problem may be reduced with enfranchisement of the deprived, which may be promoted through organization and education, but this is by no means easy to achieve. Democratic institutions facilitate the achievements of such enfranchisment and empowerment, but are not in themselves sufficient to ensure it.

In conclusion, it seems that social policy can rarely achieve very much in improving the position of the poor without more egalitarian economic systems. Consequently, it does not make sense to focus on social policy (secondary interventions), in isolation from an examination of developments in the economic system and in primary income distribution.

Notes

1 This distinction is developed in F. Stewart (ed.) *Work, Income and Inequality* (London: Macmillan, 1983).
2 S. Kuznets 'Economic growth and income inequality' *American Economic Review*, 45 (1), March 1955.
3 The methodology to identify these exceptions and the characteristics of the economies are developed in more depth in F. Stewart *Planning to Meet Basic Needs* (London: Macmillan, 1985), Chapter 4.
4 For in depth analysis of income distribution in Taiwan see J. Fei, G. Ranis and S. Kuo *Equity with Growth: the Taiwan Case* (Oxford: Oxford University Press, 1979).
5 See the evidence of M. S. Ahluwalia 'Inequality, poverty and development', *Journal of Development Economics*, 3, 1976.

20 Can we afford to work?

WALTER KORPI

The relationship between social policy and the economy is a dual one. On the one hand economic development obviously generates tasks and sets conditions and limits for social policy. On the other hand, however, social policy and the welfare state are also likely to have consequences for economic development. I will here briefly discuss both these issues.*

The reversible welfare state

Since 1973, the worldwide economic crisis has provided the Western welfare states with an economic environment hitherto unknown during the post–war period. In connection with the economic crises, the welfare state has been a target for political attacks as well as for a general questioning. Students of the welfare state, such as Göran Therborn and Claus Offe, have argued that the Western welfare states have withstood these attacks and that the welfare state is irreversible (Therborn and Rosebroek, 1984).

However, the conclusion about the irreversibility of the welfare state is probably too hasty. It appears to be based on the fact that during the period of economic crises, social expenditures have continued to grow in most Western nations, including Britain under Thatcher and the United States under Reagan. But this widely used indicator of welfare state development – social expenditure as a proportion of the GDP – is only a partial indicator of the condition of the welfare state, and an indicator which in addition can be a seriously misleading one. This is because social expenditures are only indirectly related to the development of social rights and thereby to social citizenship, which T. H. Marshall (1950) saw as the basis of the welfare state. The social expenditure indicator does not reflect the fact that, since 1973, in most Western countries, basic changes have taken place in the content of social citizenship. These changes refer to the possibilities which citizens have to earn their living through their own work.

Already Beveridge (1944) regarded full employment as the foundation of a welfare state. By the 1960s in many Western nations full employment – or at least the absence of mass unemployment – was taken more or less as granted. By this time we had become accustomed to view social rights in the welfare state not only as the right to claim a minimum standard of living during unemployment but also to regard the right to gainful employment as part of social citizenship. The possibility of finding gainful employment for all those capable and willing to work was seen as a basis for personal freedom and individual independence.

As we all know, however, since 1973 full employment has disappeared with 20 million unemployed persons in western Europe, 30 million unemployed in the OECD area, and unknown millions of 'discouraged workers' – the majority of them women – who would want to have a job if it appeared realistic for them to search for one.

The return of mass unemployment is a radical setback for the welfare state, indeed a reversal of the welfare state. Only a narrow focus on social expenditures can stop us from recognizing that, during the past fifteen years, the prime achievement of social citizenship and the foundation of the welfare state has been eroded. The social right to a measure of independence through the possibility of finding gainful employment has been devalued to handouts of often means-tested allowances.

Coming from Sweden, where unemployment levels approaching four per cent still cause national alarm, I am somewhat surprised to find that at the seventy-fifth anniversary celebration of what in the rest of Europe often has been regarded as the intellectual headquarters of the international social rights movement – the Social Administration Department of the London School of Economics and Political Science – the issue of the present mass unemployment is not given a central place in the discussions. But the fact is, of course, that since 1912 we have gone almost full circle as far as the unemployment issue is concerned. Perhaps you might think that this particular aspect of the journey is not all that much to celebrate. In any event the situation should remind us of just how fragile social rights actually are. It also illustrates the remarkable flexibility of academic minds, when what was taken as a self-evident right only fifteen years ago now appears to many as 'Swedish exceptionalism'.[1]

The present situation of mass unemployment poses two questions which are of significance for the future of social policy. The first concerns our treatment of the unemployed, the second the possibilities to return to a full or near-full employment situation. I will now take up these questions in turn.

Social rights in unemployment insurance

At least for the short-term unemployed, the economic conditions during unemployment are largely determined by available unemployment insurance. These conditions can be described by data from a comparative research project in which I am currently involved. This project focuses on welfare state development in eighteen OECD countries since 1930. In this project we have quantified the legislated or mandated social rights accorded citizens through the four main social insurance programmes – old age pensions, unemployment insurance, sickness cash benefits, and work accident insurance.[2] The countries included are Australia, Austria, Belgium, Canada, Denmark, Finland, France, Germany, Ireland, Italy, Japan, Netherlands, New Zealand, Norway, Sweden, Switzerland, United Kingdom and the United States.

In this research project the development of social rights in unemployment insurance is described in terms of different characteristics. One aspect is the net replacement level during short-term (one week) and medium-term (twenty-six weeks) unemployment. We relate the net unemployment benefits of a typical industrial worker to the average net wage (after taxes and social security contributions) of industrial workers.[3] Net replacement levels are determined for two traditional types of households, that is, a single person, as well as a four-person family with one wage-earner and two minor children. In addition, both the number of waiting-days before benefits are paid out, as well as the duration of benefits, are included. These data have been collected for the years 1930, 1933, 1939, 1947, 1950 and then every fifth year up to 1980. We are still in the process of assembling the data for 1985.

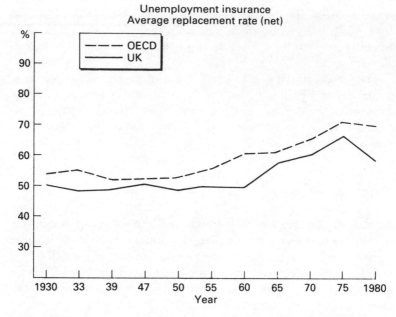

Figure 20.1   *Average net replacement levels in unemployment insurance in the United Kingdom and in eighteen OECD countries, 1930–1980.*

Let us here take a brief look at the development of average benefits levels (for the two types of households and for short- as well as medium-range unemployment) since 1930, and compare the developments in the United Kingdom with that of the average of all eighteen countries (OECD). As Figure 20.1 indicates there was some downward movement in the relative levels of unemployment compensation from 1933 up to about 1947, when an increasing trend sets in. During the period between 1975 and 1980, however, replacement levels have tended to decrease. In the United Kingdom, replacement levels have been somewhat below the OECD average throughout this period. Here the post–war increase started only in the mid–1960s and the decline after 1975 has been relatively strong.

We can also make a combined index of 'social rights' in unemployment insurance, which takes into account waiting days and the duration of benefits in addition to benefit levels.[4] Such an index of social rights during unemployment shows that, on the whole, the United Kingdom has followed the OECD average (see Figure 20.2).

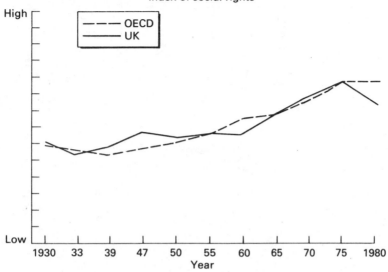

Figure 20.2   *Social rights in unemployment insurance in the United Kingdom and in eighteen OECD countries, 1930–1980.*

Since the 1960s the level of social rights in unemployment insurance has tended to diverge among the OECD countries. Thus in the early 1980s, in the countries with very high levels of unemployment, we find large differences in the economic conditions of the short- and medium-term unemployed. This development is exemplified in Figure 20.3.

What appears to have happened in some European countries was that a stalemate between the Left, which argued for measures to maintain a low level of unemployment, and the Right, which was more willing to accept increasing levels of unemployment, a political compromise was struck, resulting in relatively generous conditions of unemployment insurance. In the Netherlands, Belgium and Denmark the unemployed thus have relatively good economic conditions.

The United Kingdom, however, joins the United States, Canada and Australia in offering their numerous unemployed a rather meagre economic treatment. The five countries, Sweden, Norway, Austria, Switzerland and Japan, which – through very different

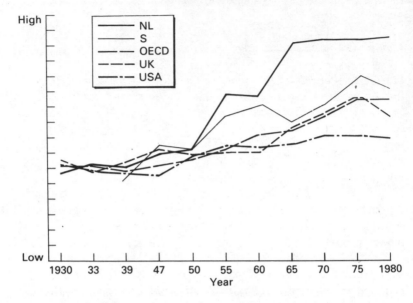

Figure 20.3 *Social rights in unemployment insurance in the Netherlands, Sweden, United Kingdom and the United States, 1930–1980.*

types of policies – have managed to maintain relatively low levels of unemployment, all have conditions in unemployment insurance close to the OECD average.

The decline in the average levels of generosity in unemployment insurance in these OECD countries between 1975 and 1980 indicates that, in many parts of the Western world, the treatment of the unemployed may grow increasingly niggardly as the economic crisis continues and unemployment levels remain high. Thus, for instance, in the United Kingdom the conditions of unemployment insurance have been made more severe since 1980.

The political background to this development appears to be that unemployment tends to be socially and politically divisive. Once unemployment levels have been allowed to remain high for a longer time period, the strength of the political coalitions in favour of a return to full employment policies are weakened. A minority, the unemployed, relatively soon come to be regarded as a group separate from the rest of the population and are gradually defined as

'the undeserving poor', who largely have themselves to blame for
their unfortunate situation.

Can we afford to work?

During the depression in Sweden in 1932, when what later became
known as the Keynesian programme of demand-management to
combat the high levels of unemployment was proposed and began
to be practised, those opposed to these policies argued that they
were too costly. The question that was then formulated was: Can
we afford to work? Such a question poses a rather intriguing
dilemma for those equipped with a protestant ethic.

During the present economic crisis, this question is raised anew.
Since the market does not provide employment, tax money has to
be used if we want to create employment opportunities. The natural
objection to such proposals is that we cannot afford them.

But how much would it actually cost to provide work or
occupational training for those now unemployed? Here we must
remember that public expenditure on income maintenance for the
unemployed (that is, expenditures for unemployment insurance as
well as means-tested supplementary benefits for those not covered
by unemployment insurance) is relatively high. Let us compare
these public expenditures for 'passive labour market policies' with
the alternative of using 'active labour market policies', primarily for
the creation of jobs or occupational training for those unemployed.

In Table 20.1 such figures referring to 1985 are given for five
countries: Sweden, United Kingdom, Germany, France, and the
United States.[5] In the four European countries, the total expenditures for passive as well as for active labour market policies were
relatively similar, ranging from 2.1 per cent of the GDP in Germany
to 2.9 per cent in Sweden and Britain, and 3.5 per cent in France. In
the United States, expenditures for these purposes were much
lower, only 1 per cent of the GDP.

But the uses and consequences of public expenditures for labour
market policies differed among the countries. Here Sweden stands
in a rather sharp contrast to the other countries. With precisely the
same proportion of the GDP going to labour market policies in
Sweden as in the United Kingdom, in Sweden almost three-quarters
of these expenditures were used for providing occupational training

Table 20.1 *Public expenditures on passive and active labour market policies, unemployment and labour force participation in France, Germany, Sweden, the United Kingdom and the United States*

	Total expenditure as % of GDP	Of which: active labour market policy (%)	Unemploy- ment 1983–85 (%)	Labour force participation 1983 (%)
Sweden	2.9	71	3.1	81
UK	2.9	28	11.3	73
Germany	2.1	34	8.2	65
France	3.5	34	9.4	66
USA	1.0	18	8.1	73

or for different types of job creation measures. In the United Kingdom, on the contrary, almost three-quarters of public expenditures were used for passive labour market policies, that is, unemployment insurance or supplementary benefits to the unemployed.

With roughly the same level of public expenditures on labour market policies as the United Kingdom, during the period 1983–1985 Sweden managed to keep its level of open unemployment to less than one-third of the British rate. In the same year, Germany and France, while accepting a level of unemployment two to three times higher than that in Sweden, were not successful in bringing their public expenditures on labour market policies very much below the Swedish level.

The above figures indicate that as a device for keeping public expenditures at a low level, passive labour market policies – at least at their present levels of generosity – are no more effective than the various measures involved in the active labour market policies. To provide those presently unemployed with jobs or occupational training would thus not necessarily require a long-term increase in tax levels. It should also be pointed out here that active labour market policies have consequences for the maintenance of human capital, as well as for the production of goods and services – something not taken into account in the above figures – which differ favourably from those of passive labour market policies.

The cost situation is somewhat different if we look also at the 'discouraged workers', most of them married women who in many countries are now often outside the labour force. In Sweden the record high level of labour force participation – 81 per cent in 1983 – has been made possible only by employing an increasing number of women in the public sector. This clearly has necessitated tax increases. An alternative strategy for increasing the level of female labour force participation would be to accept an increase of the low-wage private service sector. Such a development appears to partly explain the increasing female labour force participation rate in the United States.

Does the welfare state decrease efficiency?

A serious charge levelled increasingly often during the past decade is that the welfare state decreases economic efficiency. This charge has its basis in neo-classical economic theory. As is well known, standard economic theory maintains that political intrusions into the working of market mechanisms (such as progressive taxation and measures to effect the distribution of goods and services) will – in most cases – decrease economic efficiency and economic growth. The hypothesis is that such attempts to use political measures to change the outcome of the distributive processes of markets will distort the central and crucial signalling mechanism in the market, that is, relative prices and earnings.

These fears were captured in the title of a book – *Equality and Efficiency: The Big Trade-off* – by the late Arthur Okun (1975). To describe the inefficiency of the redistributive efforts of the welfare state, Okun used the image of the leaky bucket. 'The money must be carried from the rich to the poor in a leaky bucket', he wrote. 'Some of it will disappear in the transit, the poor will not receive all the money that is taken from the rich' (p. 91).

In recent years in all Western countries it has been argued that the negative economic effects of the welfare state are not only large but have become prohibitive. Thus, for instance, it has been maintained that in Sweden for each additional Swedish crown which the state claims in taxes, up to about seven crowns are lost in decreased economic efficiency (Hanson, 1984). Claims of negative effects of a similar order have also been made for the United States. If we are to believe these estimations, the welfare state bucket is thus no longer only leaking; the bucket has now lost its bottom.

It goes without saying that the issue of the consequences of the welfare state for economic efficiency and growth must be taken seriously. A day as a tourist in Moscow is enough to convince most of us about the blessings of a well-functioning market economy. Those who demand further evidence can find it, for instance, in Chapter 18 by Zsuzsa Ferge on the Hungarian experience with a planned economy, or can take a look at European agricultural policies.

But it must be remembered that the choice between the market and politics as strategies for mobilizing resources and distributing rewards is not only a question of economic efficiency. This choice is also crucial for the question of on whose terms the distribution of man's worldly goods is to take place. At issue here is thus also to what extent different interest groups in society are to affect the outcomes of the distributive process in Western societies. This is a question about what types of power resources different interest groups or collectivities have at their disposal and how these power resources can be applied on the markets and in politics (Korpi 1983, 1985).

The power resources that can be used on the markets – primarily different types of capital – are more or less unequally distributed. In the political arena, however, the central power resources – the right to vote and the right to organize – are, at least in principle, equally distributed. Because of their size, numerically large interest groups and collectivities which are relatively weak in terms of market resources can often be better off in terms of political resources. For such interest groups it is rational to attempt to use their political resources in efforts to effect the conditions for, and the outcomes of, distributive processes on the markets. Those who are rather advantageously positioned in terms of market resources can be expected to resist such attempts. In democratic societies a tension between markets and politics is thus created.

This tension between markets and politics is, in turn, likely to introduce what Gunnar Myrdal (1929, 1953) has called 'the political element' into economic theory on the relationship between markets and politics. The political element comes in because on issues of great societal relevance social science theorists are likely to allow their values – consciously or unconsciously – to affect their thinking. In this situation it is therefore necessary to rely not only on theories –

which in the last instance are articles of faith – but to examine the hard empirical evidence for or against different hypotheses.

Are efficiency costs forbiddingly high?

The issue which I would like to raise here is whether we have enough empirical evidence to support the claims now often made that the negative consequences of the welfare state and of social policy on economic efficiency and growth are of such an order that they prohibit efforts to maintain our present social policies and forbid us to intervene into market mechanisms to decrease unemployment. At issue here is thus not whether or not the welfare state can have some negative economic effects. I accept that political interventions into market mechanisms and social policies can be arranged in ways which decrease efficiency. Nor do I here want to raise the question about the possibility that social policy can make a positive contribution to economic efficiency. In the present situation, the most important question posed to empirical social science is, rather, whether the hypothesis that the welfare state now has prohibitive negative consequences on economic efficiency can be supported by hard empirical data.

In view of the claims often made that the negative consequences of welfare state policies are very large, it would appear easy to corroborate this hypothesis by empirical data. I am struck, however, by the cavalier ways in which the question of empirical evidence is often treated. Thus, for instance, Okun provides no empirical evidence – not as much as a footnote – in support for the existence of a big trade-off between equality and efficiency, the theme of his book.

Most of the empirical work in this area has been micro-level studies on the effects of taxation and social policies on labour supply and savings. Thus American income maintenance experiments indicate that social policy measures of the negative income tax type may have some negative consequences on the labour supply of the poor. Furthermore, old age pensions and sickness insurance tend to decrease the labour supply of the elderly and of the ill, while unemployment insurance may prolong spells of unemployment. And in the absence of old age pensions, private savings would probably be higher.[6]

But the above empirical results are, however, only of marginal relevance for the problem stated here. Savings can be achieved in many different ways, not only via individual savings for old age. Social policies can be arranged so as to avoid the poverty traps created by measures such as negative income taxes. And the explicit purpose of social insurance is partly to relieve the elderly, the sick, and the unemployed from pressures to participate on the labour market. Furthermore, in a situation of mass unemployment the crucial problem would not appear to be a too low labour supply. In my interpretation the micro-level empirical data thus far presented on the effects of social policy on labour supply and saving are not enough to support the claim that the negative consequences are prohibitive.

In view of the difficulties of determining the actual effects of macro-level policies on economic efficiency through non-experimental social science research, it seems that the comparative method has something to recommend it. In the Western nations, social policies and welfare states have been arranged in so many different ways as to constitute a very interesting series of 'natural experiments'. In spite of the methodological problems involved, it would appear that if the negative consequences of large welfare states and high levels of taxation indeed are as great as is often claimed, these negative effects can be expected to show up in differing growth rates among the OECD nations during the post–war period.

A preliminary effort which I have made to look into these data, however, does not show the expected large negative consequences (Korpi 1985b). Thus, during the period 1950–1982, neither cross-sectional nor time series analyses indicate any large negative effects of social security expenditures and the size of the public sector on economic growth rates. Of particular relevance appears to be that the severity with which different countries were hit by the economic crises after 1973 does not appear to be related to the size of their previous public sectors or welfare states. Thus indicators of public sector size and social security expenditures during the period 1968–1973 do not show the expected negative relationships between the development of rates of growth of GDP and productivity up to 1982.[7]

Free to choose?

In conclusion then, it appears clear that economic development sets tasks for social policy and affects the political climates around social policy development. My reading of the evidence, however, does not indicate that the claims for the very great negative effects of social policies on economic efficiency have been corroborated by empirical data. The claims for such large negative effects of welfare state measures on economic efficiency are instead based primarily on deductive theoretical arguments, and must therefore be regarded as hypotheses rather than as established facts.

To end on a positive note: Articles of theoretical faith notwithstanding, the hard empirical data presently at hand do not contradict the working hypothesis that, to a much greater extent than is often believed in the area of social policy development, we are still free to choose.

Notes

* This form of my comments on Professor Ferge's highly interesting paper reflects the fact that I agree with her main arguments. I have therefore chosen to complement her discussion with a few other 'outlandish' views. I wish to thank Joakim Palme for helpful comments on the paper. The research project discussed here has been supported by the Swedish Delegation for Social Research, the Bank of Sweden Tercentenary Foundation, and the German Marshall Fund of the United States.

1 In Britain, Professor Adrian Sinfield stands out as one who has maintained the commitment to full employment (cf. e.g. Sinfield, 1983).

2 The research project is based at the Swedish Institute for Social Research. Only legislated, mandated, or at least partially state supported insurance programmes are included. Details of the data collection and analyses will be reported in later publications from the project.

3 Unemployment insurance benefits are thus determined for a worker earning an average industrial workers's wage during each year in each country. Net replacement levels for medium-length unemployment spells are based on the taxed income from a combination of twenty-six weeks of earnings and twenty-six weeks of unemployment benefits.

4 In the additive index of social rights, average net replacement levels are given the same weight as the combination of waiting days and duration.

5 The data on expenditures on labour market policies are based on Schmid, Reissert, and Bruche (forthcoming).

6 Reviews of these empirical studies are given in Brown (1983); Danziger, Haveman, and Plotnic (1981); and Killingsworth (1983), among others.
7 As discussed in Korpi (1985b) Japan differs from the other seventeen countries analysed here by combining extremely high rates of growth during the post–war period with a small public sector and low social expenditures. Because of a rather highly interventionistic state working in close co-operation with private industry, however, the Japanese case does not support the *laissez-faire* implications of neo-classical economic theory.

References

W. Beveridge, *Full Employment in a Free Society* (London: Allen & Unwin, 1944).
C. V. Brown, *Taxation and the Incentive to Work* (Oxford: Oxford University Press, 1983).
S. Danziger, R. Haveman and R. Plotnic, 'How income transfer programs affect work, savings, and the income distribution – A critical review', *Journal of Economic Literature*, 19, 1981, pp. 975–1028.
I. Hansson, 'Marginal costs of public funds for different tax instruments and govenrment expenditures', *Scandinavian Journal of Economics*, 86, 1984, pp. 115–30.
M. R. Killingsworth, *Labour Supply* (Cambridge: Cambridge University Press, 1983).
W. Korpi, *The Democratic Class Struggle* (London: Routledge & Kegan Paul: 1983).
W. Korpi 'Power resources approach vs action and conflict – On causal and intentional explanation in the study of power,' *Sociological Theory* 3, 1985a, pp. 31–45.
W. Korpi 'Economic growth and the welfare state – Leaky bucket or irrigation system?' *European Sociological Review*, 1 (2), 1985b, pp. 97–118.
T. H. Marshall, *Citizenship and social class* (Cambridge: Cambridge University Press, 1950).
G. Myrdal, *The Political Element in the Development of Economic Theory* (London: Routledge & Kegan Paul, 1929, 1953).
A. Okun, *Equality and Efficiency: The Big Trade-Off* (Washington, DC: The Brookings Institution, 1975).
G. Schmid, B. Reissert and G. Bruche, *Arbeitslosenversicherung und aktive Arbeitsmarktspolitik*, (Berlin: Edition Sigma, forthcoming).
A. Sinfield, 'The need of full employment', in H. Glennerster (ed.), *The Future of the Welfare State – Remaking Social Policy*, (Hampshire: Gower, 1983).
Göran Therborn and J. Roebroek, 'The irreversible welfare state'. Paper presented at the conference on The Future of the Welfare State, Maastricht, 1984.

PART IV

Conclusions

21 Concluding thoughts: an inside view

BRIAN ABEL-SMITH

It would not be possible to present objective conclusions to a wide ranging discussion of this kind. Therefore let me start by making clear my own value premises – or perhaps prejudices. My perspective is that of an unrepentant Fabian. Incidentally, this modern term of abuse cannot be correctly directed at Richard Titmuss because he never joined the Society. Secondly, my perspective is that of a European – if by somewhat late conversion. The European Community does represent some protection from the near dictatorship which we are now learning our own political system can generate.

Thirdly I am not a believer in the 'crisis of the welfare state', in any of the sophisticated and theoretical senses in which some people have written about it. The current hiccup in the upward trend in social expenditure seems to me to have a very simple explanation. It is just the inevitable response to low rates of economic growth and the high costs of supporting the unemployed instead of enjoying their contributions to income tax and social security. If at some stage the Community countries were to reflate their economies at the same time, a considerable part of the underlying problems would melt away. Whether or when they will do this is difficult to predict.

Thus there are good grounds for optimism about the future. Those who deploy theory to explain 'the crisis' should notice that, with the possible exception of the Netherlands, there is no talk of dismantling the essential pillars of the welfare state in the other countries of the Community. Of course there are cuts, but cuts accompanied by apologies rather than dogmatic assertions. Talk of dismantling is almost entirely an Anglo-American fashion – part of the special relationship between President Reagan and Mrs Thatcher.

The concerns which were central to the discussion of social policy a decade ago are still very much in evidence both in the continental countries and in the European Parliament. Morover, it seems likely that pressure to harmonize social protection will grow within the Community over the next twenty years. In this respect the new Treaty may prove to be a powerful weapon to rope in laggard member states like ourselves. And harmonization, for obvious political reasons, can only mean harmonization upwards.

We often forget that we in Britain are laggards. While we have one of the best developed traditions of social research in Europe, in the actual delivery of social policies, we do everything on the cheap. When there were nine member states we alternated with Ireland in having the lowest expenditure on social protection as a proportion of GDP. Everything is done better somewhere else – children and child care in France, pensions in Germany, health services in Denmark and provision for the disabled in the Netherlands.

What, then, should be the goals of social policy? They may be grouped under four themes – one very old and three somewhat newer, at least in the breadth of their application. The oldest goal – still not achieved – is what the Webbs called 'a minimum of civilized life'. Even an effective income minimum is not achieved here or elsewhere. The Final Report of the First Poverty Programme counted 30 million poor in the Community of the Nine for 1975. The figure for the Community of Twelve is put at 45 million for 1985. The increase is not solely due to the expansion of the Community; poverty has been increasing in nearly every member state, with the largest increase in the United Kingdom.

The age group most affected by the increase here and elsewhere is children. Discussion on how to create an effective minimum is very active in both Belgium and France. It is also attracting considerable interest in Portugal and Spain. Even Germany has woken up to the problem of the substantial non-take up of local social assistance.

The second theme is prevention. The importance of preventive medicine was, of course, stressed in the 1909 minority Report on the Poor Law. But it has recently been stretched by the World Health Organization to have a much wider application. No longer do we talk about health promotion. The new 'in' phrase is 'health public policy'. Prevention has application throughout the whole field of social policy. We have recently re-learnt the need to try to prevent skill-lessness and diploma-lessness as well as preventing crime, institutionalization and unwanted children.

My third theme is to counter discrimination. One category discriminated against are women in access to skills and jobs, in being treated as dependants, and in being loaded with the caring role of children, the frail elderly and the disabled. A second category discriminated against are the disabled. A third category is discrimination by race. A fourth is discrimination by social class.

My fourth theme is what the Europeans call 'the humanization of services'. This is a reaction to the tarnished model of the altruistic professional or public servant. The aim is not just to make services user-friendly but responsible to individual wishes, which is very different from professionally determined needs. The suggestion is not that the answer is simply to give civil servants and professionals a course in British Airways video trained smiles.

These four themes open up a vast research agenda. How are other countries developing systems of minimum incomes within their main line social insurance systems? Do they work better than Britain's? In what political context are they made acceptable? What preventive actions are really worth pursuing and do they work? How does one develop non-discrimination policies, for example, for women and the disabled in social security, for blacks and social classes IV and V in health and education, and for all these groups in the job market?

Finally how does one humanize? There are a vast range of options. Does social housing run by co-operatives and non-governmental organizations (NGOs) on the Continent give a better service than Britain's council housing? How does it tackle the problem of access and how successfully? Do free, publicly financed hospitals run by NGOs work better in Canada than NHS hospitals in the UK? Or does the answer lie in the internal market for hospitals in the Netherlands where religious, NGOs and municipal hospitals compete for insurance paid patients? What really are the *full* effects of paying hospitals by diagnostic-related groups in the United States? How far can choice be taken in education without undermining fundamental aims? Is the answer to these questions to be found in *scale* (small is beautiful) in *participation* (but who will do the participating?) in *choice* (voice and exit) or in *profit* (but will vulnerable people be exploited?).

My claim is not that these questions are new but that like

examination questions they emerge again and again in new contexts often gilded to look new by dressing them up in more imposing terminology. What is sad in all this is that we are now faced over here with politicians who are convinced they know the answers and no longer think they need social research to help them find them. Let us hope that one day humility will come back into fashion. For without it no goals of social policy will ever be achieved.

22 Concluding thoughts: an outside view

ALBERT WEALE

The worlds of social administration and politics rarely intersect in academic circles. My background is that of a political theorist. From this different background, I should like to direct my remarks to three issues: the problem of defining the boundaries of social policy; the relationship between social theory and social policy; and the nature of the LSE Social Administration Department. I could have chosen a large number of themes, but I have identified these partly because they are obviously central to social policy and administration as a continuing academic enterprise, and partly because in several crucial respects the conference has shown that the LSE tradition is not nearly so homogeneous on these issues as might be supposed.

The boundaries of social policy

In essence there are two views that can be taken about how the boundaries of social policy are to be drawn, which I shall label the 'ascetic' and the 'indulgent'. The ascetic view is intolerant of including anything in the study of social policy that is not firmly part of the central core of the welfare state. This core will clearly include income maintenance, health policy, the personal social services and housing, and in one of its more liberal variants may include certain aspects of the study of education. It will almost certainly exclude from the field of study such topics as: the division of labour in society and its effects upon the relative benefits and burdens enjoyed or endured by different social groups; the determination of wages and of life chances more generally; the social and economic origins of health and illness; the processes of socialization that create and nurture the established patterns of caring in society; the study of social movements, such as consumerism or the women's movement, which seek to express new views about how responsibility for social welfare should be divided among various agents in society; and the analysis and interpretation of political and social values that shape and give meaning to welfare institutions. Ascetics do not deny that these topics are important. They merely insist that the study of social policy should not become, in David Piachaud's words, 'a shameful rag-bag' of concerns that have no intrinsic intellectual connection with one another. On this line of argument, unnecessary topics of investigation should not be multiplied. Dire warnings are uttered to the effect that once a topic has become rooted as a serious focus of investigation it is extremely difficult to control its growth.

The indulgent camp is not so worried by the prospect of luxuriant growth. Indeed, their ideal may be the thick wood rather than the well-tended garden. In this camp, for example, stands Hilary Land (Chapter 7) reminding us that if we are properly to understand the causes of dependence and independence in society, then we shall necessarily have to pay attention to traffic planning and the increasing use of the motor car in our society. Modes of transport, and the road engineering that responds to the demand for greater car use, have differential effects upon members of society, perhaps seriously exacerbating previous inequalities of advantage. According to this approach, therefore, if we are properly to understand patterns of risk, we shall find ourselves drawn to investigate matters that have little to do with the welfare state as conventionally understood. This analysis stands in the tradition of Richard Titmuss, who pointed out how social policy was concerned to interpret the 'dis-welfares' that arose from the processes of production and consumption. Clearly its logic is not to place any *a priori* restrictions on the fields of investigation. Indeed from the viewpoint of this approach it would be an intellectual mistake to place such restrictions on investigation, since society will be creating new sources of dis-welfare, and it is important to remain open-minded about the identification of their effects.

The argument between the indulgent and the ascetic is not likely to be resolved with ease. My own view is that the intellectual value of a discipline is measured more by the rigour with which it investigates a problem than by its correspondence to a particular conception of its scope. Sometimes, of course, the study of a particular social problem will lead the investigator to areas of inquiry that have already been successfully developed by other disciplines. In this case there is surely no alternative to taking a deep breath and making sure that we really do understand what the other discipline is saying (a great many people in social administration have been doing this in respect of economics in recent years; perhaps geography and the environmental sciences are the next challenge.) Equally as often, I suspect, when we have traced a social problem to its putative causes, we shall find that there is no established tradition of inquiry to guide us, and we shall have to fashion our own instruments of analysis.

To accept that the boundaries of social policy are open-textured is not, however, to assume that nothing of substance can be said about the likely topics of investigation outside the field of the conventional social services. One fertile field of investigation in recent years has involved examining what might be termed non-statutory welfare agencies including the family, patient and claimant groups and voluntary bodies. There is no single message that emerges from these studies, but there is perhaps a theme that keeps recurring, namely that, if the statutory services risk being unresponsive to the consumer by virtue of professional rigidity and power, the non-statutory sector, and in particular women as carers, risk being exploited as providers by the burdens that are assumed.

By comparison with the studies that have been conducted among informal and non-statutory welfare providers, there has been relatively little by way of investigation on the welfare aspects of non-welfare agencies. Richard Titmuss identified occupational welfare as a potent source of inequality, and this alone should have alerted subsequent researchers to its importance. There has, of course, been some work in the area of occupational pensions, but occupational health and safety has been virtually untouched. Perhaps the dominance of the National Health Service hitherto in the field of health provision has led to an underestimation of occupational provision, unlike the situation in pensions where public policy has been based on an official pluralism of provision. Yet if social policy is to avoid the frequently asserted charge that its habits of analysis are too removed from an understanding of the productive parts of the economy (a charge that can be heard from both left and right), then much greater attention to occupational welfare provision is called for.

Two other aspects of the boundary problem are worth mentioning. The first is to note the phenomenon of European integration. Throughout the conference I have noted this as a missing
element in the discussion, so much so that at the end I was reminded
of the famous newspaper headline: 'Fog in Channel. Europe cut off.'
The influence of European integration has in fact been experienced
directly in UK social policy, for example, in the ruling on equal
treatment for men and women in social security. I hope that the
influence of Europe would be felt also in the intellectual analysis of
social policy. For example, it is striking how often when considering
the organization and finance of health services comparison is made to
the United States, when comparison to other European countries is
more directly relevant. In the work of William Beveridge there was a
serious and systematic attempt to come to terms with the lessons that
could be learnt from the European experience. It is a pity that the
tradition of concern has receded so much in social policy.

A second omission that I have frequently noted in discussions of
the boundaries of social policy is any consideration of where the line
is to be drawn between social administration on the one hand and
public administration and public policy on the other. In the latter
fields there is interesting work both on decision-making and on
policy implementation, tailor-made for application to the world of
social policy. Here is another area where a few brave souls manage to
cross the boundary successfully, but too many remain inhibited from
doing so. Strong fences do not always make for good neighbours.

Theory and social policy

The traditional image of theory in the discipline of social administration is rather like the role of travellers' tales for the Victorian
bourgeoisie: some intrepid individuals explore the strange delights
that are on offer, but mass consumption only takes a second-hand
form. It is a great merit of José Harris's Chapter 2 that it shows how
distorted this traditional image is. In fact there is a sense in which the
displine of social administration has been talking theory all its life,
right from its earliest infancy. As Harris points out, the early work
of the LSE department was under-pinned by moral and political
philosophy. In a sense this is hardly surprising. It is difficult to have
a disciplinary focus on the sources and nature of human welfare

without taking into account the concerns of moral and social philosophy. What may have temporarily obscured this relationship is the eclipse within philosophy, under the influence of logical positivism, of normative philosophy, so there was little with which social policy as a discipline could connect. Since the late 1960s, predominantly under the influence of Rawls, this trend has been reversed, so that normative theory is now one of the major growth points in philosophy generally. Among the social sciences, social policy has absorbed the work of Rawls, Nozick and Dworkin as much as any discipline, and the nature of the discussions that take place are perhaps as close to those that occurred at the beginning of the twentieth century as any that have taken place in the intervening period.

There remains, however, the question raised by Ramesh Mishra, namely, should there be a unified theory of social policy? Two points are worth making in response to this question. First, it is easy to develop the impression that other branches of the social sciences are organized around a unified theory, and therefore that social policy is somehow deficient in not having its own equivalent. Yet, though it is easy to acquire this impression, it is somewhat misleading. Even in the case of economics, which has the greatest claim to a unified theory, there is dispute about the foundations of the subject. Certainly I should be the last to underestimate the power and the elegance of the neo-classical paradigm, but it is far from being the unchallenged champion among its rivals. Alongside the modern development of neo-classical theory there has co-existed the continuing tradition of institutional economics in the work of authors like Galbraith and Boulding, and in the last few years John Roemer has provided a sophisticated analytical base for Marxist economics. In my view this pluralism of analytic foundations is to be welcomed, and I see no reason for not extending the same indulgent attitude to the study of social policy.

The second point is more specific to the practice of social policy. There is a tendency to continue to worry about the question of whether social policy is a subject area or a discipline. If it is a discipline, then the implication is that it can have its own theory, whereas if it is a subject area it is potentially prey to any set of social scientific interests that happen to be around. From this point of view the drive towards a theory is rather like the need that some small countries have to develop an ideology of nationalism to prevent their being swallowed up by larger and more aggressive neighbours. But to seek to develop a theory in this way is not only a demanding task, it is likely to remain a fruitless one. For better or worse, social problems do not come neatly packaged with their character stamped upon them. They usually have an economic component, a sociological component, an administrative component and a political component. More often than not we can analyse one of these components without the need to take into account the effects of the others, as we might use economic theory to understand the labour supply responses of families to social security changes or sociological analysis to understand demographic changes. But at some point these various discrete pieces of analysis will have to come together if we are to make a sensible judgement, for example, as to whether social security should be organized on a contributory or a non-contributory basis. Indeed, if we are to answer this sort of question with any degree of sophistication, we shall need a great many disciplinary tools. So I am an unrepentent advocate of the view that social policy is best seen as a mulitdisciplinary approach to a set of questions that arise from a given subject area. The reason why departments of social policy ought to exist and flourish in an academic environment is not to do with the underlying logical structure of a particular discipline, but with a simple organizational fact about productive intellectual work, namely that people from different disciplines must work with one another on a regular and continuing basis if they are going to tackle successfully the demanding problems that confront society. In this respect the LSE department is surely something of a model to be emulated.

A particular feature about the study of social policy is remarked upon by Robert Pinker (Chapter 4) when he notes that the questions around which social policy is organized inevitably involve the consideration of values. The Fabian tradition within social policy can sometimes obscure this fact. The Fabian insistence, undoubtedly correct as far as it goes, that the collection of evidence and the discussion of technical details are necessary conditions for any successful social policy can be misread as the stronger proposition that they are sufficient. This they cannot be. No accumulation of evidence and no amassing of technical detail can substitute for the judgement and choice that are at the heart of policy-making. In this respect social policy should be able to benefit from what I personally regard as one of the most exciting contemporary intellectual developments, namely the growth of rigorous and analytic social and political philosophy with an applied interest. There has seldom been a better time to seek to marry the considerable technical understanding that social policy has produced with the consideration of values that modern political and social philosophy allows. Here is an example where future challenges spring out of past achievments.

The LSE department

What is the nature of the department with which those of us from elsewhere are associated, somewhat akin to country club members? The discussions at the conference led me to consider a number of ways of describing the department. One term that is frequently used is that of 'missionaries'. Certainly the department has contained a number of leading lights, and it has always sent forth its sons and its daughters for service in the emerging departments of social policy and administration up and down the country. Moreover, as Howard Glennerster (Chapter 5) has emphasized, hypotheses for testing in social policy have often arisen out of moral outrage, so that the image of missionary may not be so far from the truth. And yet, as he also emphasized, the testing of those theories is not a matter of faith but of logic and evidence, as is amply demonstrated in Chapter 12 by David Donnison, Chapter 18 by Zsuzsa Ferge and Chapter 20 by Walter Korpi. So the comparison to missionaries is not entirely accurate, since missionaires must keep the faith despite the evidence, whereas academics always run the risk of permanent scepticism.

Another image that occurred to me was that of a family. After all, the department is like a family in many respects. It comprises a set of individuals living together over a number of years, most of whom had little to do with the arrival of any of the others. No doubt also, like any family, the department contains a cross-section of personal affections and dislikes, with each person recognizing that the association is voluntary only in an attenuated sense. Moreover, one reference to a particular member throwing metaphorical hand grenades in the middle of department meetings reminded me that some problem families are candidates for systems therapy, and perhaps at times any department faces similar points of decision. Certainly if the department is a family, it is a large Victorian one, whose members pursue their own eccentricities while remaining conscious of the family line.

For my part, however, I prefer to think of the department not in terms of metaphors, but in the literal sense of what they are: a community of scholars united in the pursuit of learning. It is the sort of learning that having interpreted the world will sometimes change it, remoulding it that much closer to the heart's desire.

Index